This is a devotional commentary that engages the heart and inspires spiritual intimacy with God. Excellent as a daily allegorical meditation on the Song of Songs love story, thereby providing spiritual love language for interfacing with our bridegroom God.

—Dr. Wes Adams, PhD
International House of Prayer University
Kansas City, Missouri

As a pastor and Christian counselor for more than forty-five years, the single most damaging trend I have observed in the body of Christ is "intellectual" vs. "experiential" Christianity. As a reaction to emotional pain, many believers have erected defensive walls around their hearts that hinder them from feeling and experiencing God's love for them. Yet it is the ability to live from the whole heart that makes Christianity work, since it is through the heart that we experience the love of God (Rom. 5:5), believe or exercise faith (Rom. 10:10), and learn to fellowship with God's Spirit (2 Cor. 13:14), enabling the Lord to live His life through us. When understood as a spiritual allegory made living and active by the revelation of the Holy Spirit, I believe the Song of Solomon can be used powerfully by the Lord as a balm to bring healing to damaged hearts. As it is turned into an affectionate prayer-dialogue with the Lord, the Holy Spirit will open our spiritual eyes to see the beauty of our Bridegroom King and enlarge our hearts to believe on a deeper level His incredible love for us.

—John Smeltzer, ThM, LPC

THE LOVE SONG

OF THE AGES

STACIE SHIVELY

CREATION
HOUSE

THE LOVE SONG OF THE AGES by Stacie Shively
Published by Creation House
A Charisma Media Company
600 Rinehart Road
Lake Mary, Florida 32746
www.charismamedia.com

Unless otherwise noted, all Scripture quotations are from the New American Standard Bible. Copyright © 1960, 1962, 1963, 1968, 1971, 1972, 1973, 1975, 1977, 1995 by the Lockman Foundation. Used by permission. (www.Lockman.org)

Scripture quotations marked AMP are from the Amplified Bible. Old Testament copyright © 1965, 1987 by the Zondervan Corporation. The Amplified New Testament copyright © 1954, 1958, 1987 by the Lockman Foundation. Used by permission.

Scripture quotations marked ASV are from the American Standard Bible. Copyright © 1960, 1962, 1968, 1971, 1972, 1973, 1975, by the Lockman Foundation. Used by permission.

Scripture quotations marked KJV are from the King James Version of the Bible.

Scripture quotations marked NIV are taken from the Holy Bible, New International Version®, NIV®. Copyright © 1973, 1978, 1984, 2011 by Biblica, Inc.™ Used by permission of Zondervan. All rights reserved worldwide. www.zondervan.com The "NIV" and "New International Version" are trademarks registered in the United States Patent and Trademark Office by Biblica, Inc.™

Scripture quotations marked NKJV are from the New King James Version of the Bible. Copyright © 1979, 1980, 1982 by Thomas Nelson, Inc., publishers. Used by permission.

Design Director: Justin Evans
Cover design by Judith McKittrick Wright

Visit the author's website: stacieshively.com.

Library of Congress Cataloging-in-Publication Data: 2014956292
International Standard Book Number: 978-1-62998-416-2
E-book International Standard Book Number: 978-1-62998-417-9

While the author has made every effort to provide accurate telephone numbers and Internet addresses at the time of publication, neither the publisher nor the author assumes any responsibility for errors or for changes that occur after publication.

First edition

15 16 17 18 19 — 9 8 7 6 5 4 3 2 1
Printed in Canada

DEDICATION

This book is dedicated first to our magnificent
Bridegroom, without whose help it could not have
been written. My greatest desire is that it would
bring glory to Him. Second, to my husband Randy,
a man after God's own heart. And finally, to
Mike Bickle and Dr. Sam Storms, who believed
in me and made time for me on many occasions.

CONTENTS

FOREWORD

J ESUS SAID THE greatest commandment is to love God with your whole heart, mind, soul, and strength. So much in the kingdom of God flows from our response to this glorious commandment, including the second great commandment—loving others as ourselves. But as the apostle John taught, it is impossible to grow in our love for God and people without first growing in the knowledge of His love for us (1 John 4:16–19).

Many in the church today are trying to love God and serve others, but they are missing the critical foundation—the revelation of God's extravagant love for them. It is not enough to know with our intellect that God loves us. Mental assent alone will not result in the quality of worship that He desires nor will it produce lasting change in our lives. The apostle Paul taught that we are transformed in our hearts by renewing our minds (Rom. 12:2). Therefore as we renew our minds with the revelation of God's love, we will find our hearts transformed in the process. I have found the Song of Solomon to be a powerful portion of Scripture that the Holy Spirit uses to impart deeper understanding of Jesus's extravagant love for His people. When read as an allegorical story, the Song of Solomon gives us insight into how Jesus the Bridegroom King feels toward the body of Christ as His cherished bride (Eph. 5:27–32). However, we only read the Song of Solomon through the lens of who Jesus is and what He did as revealed in the New Testament Gospels, epistles, and the Book of Revelation.

I encourage you to turn this portion of God's holy Word into an affectionate prayer-dialogue with the Lord Himself. Those who engage in long and loving meditation on King Jesus using this Song, praying the very Word of God back to Him, will find their hearts exhilarated with the knowledge that Jesus's heart is ravished over them (Song 4:9). It is this understanding of the Lord's love for us that will enable us to love Jesus in the overflow of the love the Father has for Him (John 17:26), the very love that will bring the body of Christ to maturity as a prepared bride (Rev. 19:7).

King David wrote, "Your people will offer themselves willingly in the day of Your power, in the beauty of holiness…" (Ps. 110:3). I believe the Holy Spirit is raising up a generation of men and women, young and old, who will worship the Lord in the beauty of holiness because they have glimpsed the depths of His incredible love for them. This is a paradox in God's kingdom: the width, length, depth, and height of His love is beyond our ability to fully comprehend (Eph. 3:18–19), yet the Holy Spirit delights to escort our hearts into the vast ocean of His love (Rom. 5:5; 1 Cor. 2:9–12). Those who ask the Holy Spirit to do this, as they seek to know and to love Jesus with all their hearts in the beauty of holiness, will be the kind of people who will follow the Lamb wherever He goes (Rev. 14:4).

—MIKE BICKLE
DIRECTOR OF THE INTERNATIONAL HOUSE OF PRAYER
KANSAS CITY, MISSOURI

PREFACE

BEFORE ANYTHING ELSE, I would like to express my indebtedness to the man who first introduced me to the Song of Solomon as an allegory representing the believer's growth in passion for Jesus—Mike Bickle. As of this writing, he has not compiled his teaching into book form, but I pray it will be soon forthcoming. Mike was told in a rather amazing way by the Lord many years ago that Song of Solomon 8:6–7 was to be his life's message. As we will see, Song 8:6–7 encapsulates the bride's progressive journey as she grows in passion for Jesus and learns to "abide in Him"—or we could say, as she learns to walk out the first commandment in her life—loving God with her whole heart, mind, soul, and strength. As a result of this word from the Lord, Mike has spent many years both studying the Song and praying for revelation. His teachings and detailed notes are available free online at his website: www.mikebickle.org. I would highly recommend his material to those who want to go deep in the revelation of this incredible book.

I would also like to clarify that the prayers inserted after most of the verses in the Song have been included simply to jump-start you as you turn the Song into a prayer dialogue with the Lord. As Mike says, if we are to receive the full benefit and revelation of the Song, we must turn it into an ongoing affectionate prayer dialogue with Jesus. It is not enough to study the Song; the language must get into our prayer and thought life before it will transform our emotions. My hope is that the prayers I have written will simply be an aid in the introductory season of your study, until the language of the Song is engraved on your heart.

I pray that as you read this devotional commentary, your spiritual eyes will be opened to see Jesus the Bridegroom King more clearly, and your heart enlarged to believe His incredible love for you. I pray also that you will begin to see yourself as Jesus's inheritance from the Father—His bride and eternal companion who will be yoked to Him in love throughout eternity (Ps. 2:8; Eph. 1:18; Rev. 19:7).

INTRODUCTION

THE SONG OF Solomon, or Song of Songs in the original Hebrew, is without doubt the most controversial and misunderstood book of the Bible. Both Jews and Christians alike have often rejected its literal interpretation and allegorized it due to its sensual nature. However, much of the early Christian thought along these lines was influenced more by the Greek philosophy of the time, which sometimes promoted unbiblical marital asceticism, than by the Bible itself. It is my belief that God intended both the literal and allegorical interpretations of this book when He included it in the canon of Scripture. If the book is taken as the words of a couple anticipating an imminent wedding, it reveals that God intended married couples to honor and enjoy the beauty of love within marriage. We have only to look at the explosion of sexual sins and perversion in our culture to see how the enemy has twisted and defiled what God created to be beautiful and holy within the marriage relationship. As has been said, the presence of a counterfeit only proves that the genuine article exists. The literal interpretation of the Song of Songs reveals God's genuine article.

Without denying the validity of the literal interpretation, in this devotional commentary we will focus on the allegorical or symbolic interpretation of the Song. It is important to remember that an allegorical interpretation does not necessarily deny the literal interpretation of a text, it merely asserts there is another, deeper meaning which God intended.

Jesus often taught His disciples using parables, or short stories drawn from everyday life that revealed spiritual truth. In this devotional study of the Song, we will examine it as an allegory, or extended parable, illustrating the believer's progression in developing an intimate relationship with Jesus, or what the Scripture calls "abiding in Him."

For most of us, when we read, "For God so loved the world that He gave His only Son, so that everyone who believes in Him will not perish but have eternal life," the words lodge in our minds, but don't always connect with our hearts. Or, we may believe God loves *the world*, but find it hard to believe that He loves us personally and individually. The apostle Paul understood that believing facts in our minds (mental assent) does not produce faith in our hearts. He wrote, "I pray that the eyes of your *heart* may be enlightened..." and "...with the *heart* [man] believes..." (Eph. 1:18; Rom. 10:10, emphasis added).

Stories have the power to bypass our minds and speak to our hearts. When understood as an allegory, the Song of Songs is a powerful love story that will help us see with the eyes of our hearts. As we identify with the maiden, the Song will enable us to see ourselves, personally and individually, as Jesus's beloved—His precious bride. The great desire in the heart of God is that the love story of the Song would reveal to our hearts the breadth, length, height, and depth of His amazing love for us. To this I can only pray, Amen, Lord; let it be so!

I do feel the need to give a word of caution. In the vast majority of cases when we read God's Word, the historical-grammatical interpretation of Scripture should be used. This method seeks to understand the plain meaning of a passage by taking it at face value. It seeks to understand the historical context of the passage, examining how the author intended it to be understood, and relies on Scripture to interpret Scripture. Only on a limited number of occasions did the apostle Paul give an allegorical interpretation of an Old Testament passage of Scripture (1 Cor. 9:9–11, 10:4; Gal. 4:21–31; Eph. 5:31–32). However, with reference to the Song of Solomon, the majority of theologians throughout church history have interpreted the Song as an allegory portraying the relationship between Christ and the church. Paul alluded to this truth in Ephesians 5:31–32 when he spoke of marriage as a great mystery that pointed to the relationship between Christ and the church. Further, as Mike Bickle points out, the Song of Solomon is an "eternal" book. (Isa. 40:8; Matt. 24:35;

etc.) Although marriage does not exist in the age to come, we will still be edified by reading it a million years from now in the resurrection (Matt. 22:30; Mark 12:25; Luke 20:35). Therefore, although it has meaning when applied to natural marriage, the Song's fullest meaning is revealed in Jesus as our Bridegroom King.

Chapter 1

ESTABLISHING THE FOUNDATION OF INTIMACY

1:1 "The Song of Songs, which is Solomon's."

THIS SONG IS attributed to Solomon, who wrote 1,005 songs (1 Kings 4:32). "The Song of Songs" is a reference to the superlative sense of *the best* of songs.

Solomon wrote three books of the Bible: Proverbs, Ecclesiastes, and the Song of Songs. Ecclesiastes was written to show the futility of life "under the sun" or life lived in the natural arena, apart from obedience to God. Mike Bickle teaches that in many ways Ecclesiastes is a vital preparation for the Song of Songs because it is difficult to fervently seek fullness of life in Jesus without understanding how futile life is outside of Jesus. He explains that the Book of Ecclesiastes stresses how impossible it is to be truly satisfied with even the most desirable external circumstances. The Song of Songs reveals the true joy of life that can be attained without any regard to external circumstances. It highlights how meaningful and full life is when our one consuming passion is to know and love the Man, Christ Jesus. This is the only place of true satisfaction!

> Lord, I ask that You would reveal Your beauty to me through my meditation on the Song. Give me a spirit of wisdom and of revelation in the knowledge of You, and open my mind to understand the Scriptures. Help me begin to see myself as Your beloved, the one who has captured Your heart, and give me faith to believe how much You truly love me.

1:2 "May He kiss me with the kisses of His mouth! For Your love is better than wine" *[Bride speaking].*

Watchman Nee relates this "kiss" to a *personal expression of love* from the Lord. A kiss is an expression of a personal relationship. Unless we come to a real dissatisfaction with a general relationship, and desire a deeply personal relationship with our Lord, we cannot expect to know Him intimately. The wonderful truth is, the Lord desires an intimate relationship with us even more than we desire it with Him!

Jeanne Guyon wrote that this kiss is the union of God's Spirit to your spirit:

> When a person is first converted he is united to God but has not yet come to *experience Him deeply.* There is a deep and abiding *union with Christ* that you can come to know.... There are two kinds of union with God. One is to feel a sense of His Presence for a few moments or hours. Deep and lasting union, however, continues in the midst of any circumstance.... *There is a deeper union with God that can be thought of in terms of a spiritual marriage. Your spirit is fully united to Him. You are His without reservation.... This journey toward complete union is what is being described in the Song of Songs. It is a place where your spirit is completely possessed by God* (emphasis added).[1]

Madame Guyon wrote that this kiss is the final thing that the bride will receive, although she asks for it at the beginning of her spiritual walk with Him. *It represents intimacy in union with Him.*

Mike Bickle equates the "divine kiss" to God's hand touching his heart and expanding his capacity to give himself to God and to receive from Him. He also relates it to the "kiss of God's Word" speaking of the scriptures that tenderize and empower our hearts in the love of God by the Holy Spirit. It is noteworthy that the Jewish rabbis for the last three thousand years have interpreted this as the "kiss of God's Word" or the "kiss of the Torah."

Mike relates four ways the Lord communicates His kiss to us: meditation on the Word of God and then turning the Word into personal conversation with Jesus; the Word of God through others (sermons, songs, or testimonies); prophetic revelation from the Holy Spirit (dreams, visions, or revelation from the Holy Spirit as we read the Word); and the ministry of other people (prayers of others for us, acts of kindness, or in the context of genuine friendship). I would also add a fifth way the Lord communicates His kiss to us: through the touch of the Holy Spirit in true worship.

"...For Your love is better than wine."

Zechariah 10:7 says wine makes the heart glad. God's love revealed to the human heart is more intoxicating, more enjoyable, more "freeing" than wine, which represents the best the "world" has to offer. As we focus our hearts on Jesus and His incredible love for us, the things of the world lose their hold, and we begin to desire the far superior pleasures of His kingdom.

The maiden is asking the Lord for His divine kiss in this verse: for her spirit to be united to His in intimate fellowship as she learns to abide in Him. She declares that the revelation of His love for her is better than anything the world has to offer.

> Jesus, kiss me with the kisses of Your mouth: may Your Spirit touch my heart and enlarge my capacity to believe Your love for me. Lord, You said just as the Father loves You, to the same measure You love me (John 15:9)! Unite Your Word with faith in my heart to believe this amazing truth.

1:3 "Your oils have a pleasing fragrance, Your name is like purified oil; therefore the maidens love You" *[Bride speaking]*.

"Oils" is the Hebrew *shemen* and means oil or ointment, which was sometimes perfumed. Oil played an important part in the sacrifices and worship of ancient Israel, as it was used to anoint objects of worship (Exod. 30:22–29, 40:9) as well as priests and kings when they took office (cf. Exod. 29:4–7, 30:30; Lev. 8:12; 1 Sam. 10:1, 16:1, 13). The Hebrew word for "anoint" is *mashach* and means to smear with oil, to anoint—and by implication—to consecrate or devote to

God. The Hebrew title for our Lord, *Messiah*, as well as the Greek word, *Christ*, both derive from words meaning "anointed one." *Our anointed Bridegroom's "fragrance" is what ultimately draws us to Him—fragrance in this context implying the perfections of His character and personality that can be perceived by our spirit, but not by our natural senses.*

"…Your name is like purified oil…"

"Purified oil" in this verse literally reads, "oil which is emptied from one vessel to another." As the oil was poured from vessel to vessel, the sediment or impurities would be left behind in the previous vessel. Thus, the oil would become pure or untainted. The Hebrew word for "name" in this verse is *shem* and means a name that describes a person as a mark of individuality and by implication, character. Combining these two ideas, *this verse speaks of the character, or essence, of Jesus's personality as being pure—true, sincere, without guile or duplicity, "real."* The maiden knows He can be trusted because there is nothing false in His character. He is true, and His Word cannot fail, because He is true to His Word.

The Lord's names express the many facets of His character and personality which are fragrant or appealing to us as the Holy Spirit pours out revelation of His nature into our hearts. It is interesting to note that scholars have discovered over six hundred names for Jesus in the Bible. These names will enable us to progressively come to know Him in a deeper way as we devote time to study them, asking the Holy Spirit for revelation of this glorious Person—of His character and personality, and of His passionate emotions toward us.

> Lord, I ask that You would reveal Your names to me, and that You would open the eyes of my heart to see the many facets of Your character and personality. Increase my faith as I progressively come to know that You are true, and Your Word cannot fail, because You are true to Your Word.

1:4 "Draw me after You and let us run together! The King has brought me into His chambers. We will rejoice in You and be

glad; we will extol Your love more than wine. Rightly do they love You" *[Bride speaking].*

The maiden has had her spiritual eyes opened to see, in a measure, the beauty of the Lord. This produces a longing in her heart for both a deeper revelation of His personality ("draw me after you") and to be yoked with Him in service ("let us run together").

It is significant that she acknowledges Him as "King" in this verse, recognizing His claim upon her life. She understands that she is no longer the master of her own destiny; her life is now His to do with as He chooses. Watchman Nee wrote that before we know the Lord as our Beloved, we must first know Him as our King. A life of consecration must come before a life of love.

King Jesus leads her *first* to be alone with Him. J. Hudson Taylor wrote:

> Could we be satisfied to meet a beloved one only in public? No, we want to take him aside—to have him all to ourselves. So with our Master: He takes His now fully consecrated bride aside to taste and enjoy the sacred intimacies of His wondrous love. *The Bridegroom of His church longs for communion with His people more than His people long for fellowship with Him* (emphasis added).[2]

The "chambers" represent the inner rooms of a house, where casual acquaintances are not invited. Before the maiden can run with Him in service, King Jesus first takes her into the inner chambers to establish intimacy in their relationship. *He wants the foundation of everything that she will do to be intimacy with Him.* Put in biblical terms, He wants her to learn to "abide in Him." *Bringing her into His chambers speaks of the "secret place" of communion and intimacy with Him.* The Bridegroom said, "My sheep hear My voice..." (John 10:27). The maiden believes that His Word to her is true and that He will speak to her as she quiets her heart and waits in His presence.

This issue of learning to hear the Lord's voice is paramount to our progress in developing an intimate relationship with Him. For those wanting to grow in their ability to hear God's voice, I would recommend an excellent book, *Dialogue with God*, by Mark and Patti Virkler.[3] In this book, Mark describes his struggle to learn to hear God's voice and reveals how the Holy Spirit taught him specific principles from Habakkuk 2:1–2, "I will stand on my guard post...and I will keep watch to see what He will speak to me...Then the LORD answered me and said, 'Record the vision...'" He stresses four keys in learning to hear God's voice: learning what His voice spoken within sounds like, becoming still (quieting our thoughts and emotions), presenting the eyes of our hearts to God as we pray (asking Him to show us through visions or dreams what He is saying), and journaling (writing down our prayers and then listening to hear what the Lord would speak to us in response). His book is firmly grounded on Scripture and includes practical insight from his own journey in opening the door to two-way prayer with God.

> "...We will rejoice in You and be glad; we will extol Your love more than wine. Rightly do they love You."

The maiden now changes her focus from "I" to "we." Her heart is filled with joy and delight as she realizes the depth of the Lord's love for her and understands that He desires a personal relationship with her. However, she also realizes that He loves all of His children in this way and desires an intimate relationship with each one of them. Thus she determines to share this wonderful discovery of His love with others, desiring to bless them as she has been blessed.

As mentioned earlier, wine represents the best that the world has to offer. It makes the heart happy and produces a sense of contentment, even though it is a false contentment. *The Lord's love is far superior to the effects of wine, and instead of giving a false sense of contentment, actually produces in the heart of the maiden a sense of security and worth that cannot be shaken, even by the storms and trials of life. There is nothing that can make us as secure as knowing that He created us for fellowship with Himself and loves each of us passionately, even though He knows all our faults and sins.*

Jesus, draw me into Your chambers and commune with me by Your Spirit. You said Your sheep would hear Your voice. Open my spiritual ears to hear Your voice, Lord. Make me secure in the revelation of Your awesome and unconditional love for me, and help me to establish intimacy with You as the foundation for all that I do.

1:5 "I am black *[Bride speaking]* but lovely *[Bridegroom speaking]*, O daughters of Jerusalem, like the tents of Kedar *[Bride speaking]*, like the curtains of Solomon" *[Bridegroom speaking]*.

The tents of Kedar were made of black goat's hair. *The maiden compares her heart to these black tents as her spiritual eyes are opened to see the extent of her sin nature in the light of His holiness.* She does not yet realize that His love for her will be relentless in purifying her heart—that He loves her far too much to leave her in her present condition.

The Bridegroom interjects, "but lovely...like the curtains of Solomon." These curtains were made of fine linen, symbolic in Scripture of the righteous acts of the saints. "And it was given to her [Christ's bride, the church] to clothe herself in fine linen...for the fine linen is the righteous acts of the saints" (Rev. 19:8).

It is comforting to remember that the Lord sees not only our present condition, but what we will become as we are transformed by His love. In our immaturity, He calls those things that be not as though they were (Rom. 4:17). *Although He knows our every character flaw and sin, He loves us passionately still!* This knowledge gives us strength and encouragement to persevere through the trials and dry seasons when we feel we are regressing instead of progressing in the sanctification process. It is also something we can pray for the grace to do in our relationships with others. *If we looked at people the way the Lord does, and spoke words of blessing over them, calling forth the budding virtues that the Lord sees, just think of how our relationships would be transformed!*

It is fascinating to trace the Holy Spirit's use of types and symbols throughout the Word of God to depict spiritual truth. The curtains of Solomon's temple referenced in this verse are a perfect illustration. Alex Ness writes that they were magnificently crafted and very beautiful; made of fine twisted white linen, they were embroidered with blue, purple, and scarlet cherubim (2 Chron. 3:14). These colors and the four faces of the cherubim beautifully depict our Lord in each of the Gospels.

In Matthew, Jesus is revealed as the Lion of the tribe of Judah, corresponding to one of the faces of the cherubim, the face of a lion. The lion is perceived as the mightiest and most majestic of animals, often portrayed as the "king" of the jungle. Jesus is further revealed in Matthew's Gospel as the King of the long awaited kingdom of God, corresponding to the purple embroidery, which symbolized royalty.

The color scarlet speaks of blood. Another of the faces of the cherubim was the ox: a beast of burden, one who served. While other beasts of burden died of old age, the ox served and then was slaughtered. The Gospel of Mark records more cases of Jesus healing, casting out demons, and raising the dead than any other Gospel. Jesus is revealed in Mark's Gospel as the faithful Servant: faithful unto death, even death on a cross (Phil. 2:8).

The color white signifies the Lord's humanity and His Name Emmanuel, or "God with us." A third face of the cherubim was that of a man. Jesus was the spotless, sinless Son of God, but He was also a "Son of man," born of a virgin. He lived His earthly life as a perfect man dependent upon the Holy Spirit. All of the miracles that occurred during His earthly ministry were performed as a man, One who only did what He saw His Father doing. Philippians 2:6–7 tells us that Jesus did not consider equality with God something to cling to, but instead gave up His divine privileges, taking the form of a bond-servant. (The Greek word for "bond-servant" is *doulous*—one in a permanent relation of servitude to another whose will is altogether consumed in the will of the other.) The Gospel of Luke presents Jesus as the pure, spotless God-man.

The color blue symbolizes deity. This corresponds to the Gospel of John, which emphasizes the deity of Jesus. "In the beginning was the Word, and the Word was with God, and the Word was God...All things came into being by Him, and apart from Him nothing came into being that has come into being" (John 1:1, 3). "And now, O Father, glorify Me together with Yourself, with the glory which I had with You before the world was" (John 17:5, NKJV). The fourth face of the cherubim is that of an eagle, the majestic bird who dwells in the heavens.

In this verse, the maiden's focus is on her sin nature, symbolized by the tents of Kedar, which were made of black goat's hair. However, the Lord responds to her introspection by telling her what He sees when He looks at her. He sees her heart as lovely, comparing it to the curtains of Solomon. These curtains were not only beautiful, but crafted of fine linen, which is symbolic of the righteous acts of the saints. The Lord is calling forth the budding virtues in her heart!

> Lord, give me confidence that You see not only my present condition, but also what I will become as I am transformed by Your love. Give me revelation of the incredible truth that You love me passionately, even though You know all of my character flaws and sins. Thank You that You are continually calling forth the budding virtues in my heart. I ask You for grace to do this in my relationships with others!

1:6 "Do not stare at me because I am swarthy [black], for the sun has burned me. My mother's sons were angry with me; they made me caretaker of the vineyards, but I have not taken care of my own vineyard" *[Bride speaking].*

In verse 5 the maiden says she is black because she sees her sin nature in the light of the Lord's holiness. However, she is describing a different principle in this verse. The sun's burning rays have darkened her skin while she was taking care of the vineyards: "My mother's sons were angry with me; they made me caretaker of the vineyards, but I have not taken care of my own vineyard." "My mother's sons" symbolizes the church, our brothers and sisters in Christ; however, not to the church inclusively, but to those in it who have settled into "religion" instead of a living and intimate relationship with the Savior.

The ardent zeal of new believers tends to unsettle religious believers. They may be threatened by the depth of relationship that new believers sometimes find with the Lord. Or conviction may arise if the Holy Spirit reveals they have "left their first love" and settled for religion (works) instead of pursuing the more difficult path of learning to abide in Him—in other words, to maintain a living and continual communion with the Lord, doing the things He gives them to do (John 5:19), not good works to earn His love. Those who have settled into religion (instead of relationship with the Lord) often put new believers to work in the church, knowing that their love for the Lord causes them to want to serve, even as their Lord was a servant. Unfortunately, this preoccupation with serving often leads new believers to fall into the same trap as the religious: "...I have not taken care of my own vineyard" (i.e., my own heart, symbolizing my relationship with the Lord).

Our relationship with the Lord and growing friendship with Him must always be our priority but especially in the early days of our walk with Him when He is laying the foundation for our faith. The Lord desires this intimate relationship with Him to be the *foundation* for our service. When service becomes our priority over relationship with Him, we fall into the trap of religion. Jesus is the True Light which gives light to the world and the Sun of Righteousness (John 1:9, 1 John 2:8, Mal. 4:2). Therefore, the false or "damaging sun" in this verse speaks of the *false sun of religion*, which attempts to *earn* favor with God and produces good works based in wrong motives and wrong theology.

> Lord, help me avoid the snare of being distracted by what is good and missing what is best—an ever-deepening friendship with You. Help me establish intimacy with You as the foundation for my service. And engrave on my heart the truth that I can only produce fruit for Your kingdom as I abide in You, for apart from You I can do nothing.

1:7 "Tell me, O You whom my soul loves, where do You pasture Your flock, where do You make it lie down at noon? For why should I be like one who veils herself beside the flocks of Your companions?" ["Veils herself" can also be translated "wanders astray"; *Bride speaking.*]

In this verse the maiden reveals her desire to return to the intimacy of their betrothal—the season where she was resting in His presence, learning to hear His voice and establishing an intimate relationship with Him. She has been burned by the false sun of religion, and is seeking to reestablish relationship with Him as her priority. *She asks where He feeds His flock and where they lie down to rest. She acknowledges that she is one of His sheep and longs to hear His voice again in the intimate communion they shared at first.*

Jesus said in John 10:27, "My sheep hear My voice, and I know them, and they follow Me." He said in John 14:26, "But the Helper, *the Holy Spirit, whom the Father will send in My name, He will teach you all things*, and bring to your remembrance all that I said to you" (emphasis added); and in John 15:26, "When the Helper comes, whom I will send to you from the Father, that is the Spirit of truth…He will testify about Me." The Holy Spirit said through the prophet Isaiah, "…He awakens My ear to *listen as a disciple.* The Lord God has opened my ear; and I was not disobedient nor did I turn back" (Isa. 50:4–5, emphasis added).

The apostle John wrote, "As for you, the anointing which you received from Him abides in you, and you have no need for anyone to teach you; but as His anointing teaches you about all things, and is true and is not a lie, and just as it has taught you, you abide in Him" (1 John 2:27). The Greek word for "anointing" here is *chrisma*, and is only found in this verse, and in 1 John 2:20. It means a communication and reception of the Holy Spirit! Using this substitution, this verse would read, "And as for you, the Holy Spirit which you received from Him abides in you, and you have no need for anyone to teach you; but as the Holy Spirit teaches you about all things, and is true and is not a lie, and just as the Holy Spirit has taught you, you abide in Jesus."

Luke 24:13–32 gives the account of the two disciples traveling to Emmaus who are approached by Jesus. They are prevented from recognizing Him and He asks them what they are discussing. They explain that a prophet named Jesus has just been crucified after being delivered up to Pilate by the chief priests and rulers. They had hoped He was the Messiah. Then some of the women disciples went to His tomb and found it empty. They claimed to have seen angels who said He was alive. Jesus rebukes them for not believing the prophets and then explains to them all of the scriptures that were written about Him. After the two disciples convince Him to stay with them, they recline at the table together. "...He took the bread and blessed it, and breaking it, He began giving it to them. Then their eyes were opened and they recognized Him..." (Luke 24:30–31). Like many narratives in the Scripture, this account has a deeper spiritual meaning than is obvious at first glance. Jesus said He is the bread of life (John 6:48, 63). In other words, He (meaning relationship with Him) is the nourishment that our spirits need to thrive. The Holy Spirit is the third person of the Trinity who enables us to have a living relationship with Jesus and the Father, through our fellowship with Him. *As the Holy Spirit takes the Bread of Life, Jesus, and gives Him to us, testifying to us about Him, our spiritual eyes are opened and what has been mental assent becomes living faith in our hearts.*

"...For why should I be like one who wanders astray [alternate translation] beside the flocks of your companions?"

Here the maiden acknowledges the danger of following men instead of her Lord. She does not want to "wander astray" again, taking her eyes off Him and putting them on men, even men of God. Acts 17:11 tells us, "The people of Berea...listened eagerly to Paul's message. They searched the Scriptures day after day to see if Paul and Silas were teaching the truth" (NLT). *The Bereans did not even accept what the great apostle Paul taught them without confirming it for themselves in the Scriptures!* Regretfully, this could not be said about many in the church today. However, the maiden is "of more noble character" as the NIV describes the Bereans, having a teachable spirit but confirming what she is taught in the Word of God before accepting it as truth.

Lord, You are my Shepherd. Help me look to You to feed me from Your Word and not rely on men alone to teach me. You said that I would hear Your voice and that Your Spirit would testify about You and guide me into the truth. First John 2:20 promises that as Your Spirit teaches me, I will abide in You. Lord, open my spiritual ears to listen as a disciple. I want to hear Your words of life!

1:8 "If you yourself do not know, most beautiful among women, go forth on the trail of the flock, and pasture your young goats by the tents of the shepherds" *[Bridegroom speaking].*

In the previous verse the maiden was seeking to reestablish intimacy in her relationship with the Lord after a season of distraction in which her focus was on "working for Him" instead of service flowing *out of her relationship with Him* (cf. Eph. 2:10, NLT). She acknowledged her error and asked the Lord how to return to the place of intimacy with Him.

In the verse before us Jesus responds to her prayer, beginning with an affirmation that reveals how He sees her—even in her weakness and immaturity. He calls her "most beautiful among women." What an amazing commendation to receive from our Bridegroom, Jesus. This is light years away from the way most of us view ourselves. We focus on all the areas where we are falling short and on the sins we have yet to overcome. Yet the focus of Jesus is just the opposite. He looks at the "yes" in our heart, the desire to love Him with our whole heart, mind, soul, and strength, and declares we are most beautiful in His eyes! If we could begin to see ourselves from the Lord's perspective, we would make no agreements with the enemy's lies. One of the enemy's primary tactics to keep us from intimacy with the Lord is to speak lies to our minds, producing feelings of shame and rejection. These emotions cause us to distance ourselves from the Lord, feeling He is disgusted (or at the very least disappointed) by our shortcomings. *The Song reveals to our hearts the truth of Jesus's emotions toward us. He sees us as "most beautiful," even in our immaturity and our struggle with sin, because He sees the desire in our hearts to be fully His.*

The maiden has just asked the Lord where He feeds His flock, and He responds that if she doesn't know, she should follow the trail of His flock and pasture her young goats by the tents of the shepherds. "The shepherds" symbolize what I describe as "under-shepherds," referring to those He has given revelation and a gift of teaching to feed His sheep. The Lord tells her to follow their trail, or glean from the wisdom He has given them, and to pasture (or feed) her young goats by the tents of these "under-shepherds." "Her young goats" refers to those younger in the Lord that she is discipling. *The Lord advises the maiden to feed these young disciples with the wisdom and revelation of His "under-shepherds" as they are learning His Word and learning to hear His voice.*

> Lord, engrave on my heart the amazing truth that You see me as "most beautiful," even in my immaturity and struggle with sin, because You see the desire in my heart to be fully Yours. Lead me on the trail of Your flock and direct me to the under-shepherds You choose for me and for those You have given me to disciple.

1:9 "To Me, My darling, you are like My mare among the chariots of Pharaoh" *[Bridegroom speaking].*

J. Hudson Taylor writes:

> Those [horses] selected for Pharaoh's own chariot would not only be of the purest blood and perfect in proportion and symmetry but also perfect in training, docile, and obedient; they would know no will but that of the charioteer, and the only object of their existence would be to carry the king wherever he wanted to go.[5]

So it is with us, His bride. We carry the Lord with us wherever we go in the person of the Holy Spirit. We are His witnesses in this world. Whether or not we become like one of Pharaoh's horses—obedient and knowing no will but that of our Master—is our choice. We can cooperate with the Holy Spirit's process of sanctification in our lives so that we become bond-servants (the Greek word is *doulos* and means those whose will is altogether consumed in the will of their Master), or we can claim the Lord's name but retain our own will. He always gives us free choice. We determine how far we progress in the sanctification process that brings us into conformity with His likeness and character. Be that as it may, the wonderful truth is that the deeper we go in our relationship with the Lord, the more our hearts are opened to believe His love for us. The result of this revelation is that we *want* to submit to His process of sanctification in our lives. Jesus loved us so much He gave everything for us, suffering an agonizing, excruciating death *in our place* to pay the penalty for *our* sins! He "humbled Himself by becoming obedient to the point of death, even death on a cross" (Phil. 2:8). This is an extraordinary statement. In the Roman culture the cross was the most despised (and the most cruel and barbarous) form of death known to men. Before the crucifixion itself, the prisoner was scourged. This entailed being tied to a post with the body bent over, while the Roman lictor applied blow after blow on his bared back with a lash intertwined with pieces of bone or steel. This in itself was frequently sufficient to cause death. Then, if the prisoner survived, he was either tied or nailed by his hands and feet to the cross. Because of the abnormal position of the body, being suspended by the two hands, the slightest movement would cause additional torture. Often it would be two or three agonizing days of torture before death would finally occur, so the Roman soldiers would sometimes break the legs of the prisoner to hasten death. That the Son of the Almighty God and Creator of the universes, the Father's equal, would voluntarily submit to that torture—*for our sakes*—to redeem us to the Father should make us fall on our knees, pouring out extravagant love and worship to the One who loved us that much! *There is no greater love than that.* No human love is comparable.

In his book *Rees Howells: Intercessor*, Norman Grubb gives the account of a Jewish man, Maurice Reuben, who became a believer in the Messiah, Jesus. Because of this, he was disinherited by his father and rejected by his wife and his family. To add insult to injury, he was committed to an asylum by his brother because he claimed

THE LOVE SONG OF THE AGES

to have heard the Lord's voice. In the asylum, the bitterness of his position overcame him. He fell on his knees by his bed and poured out his heart to the Lord in prayer. While he was there, a vision of Calvary appeared to him. He said he witnessed every stage of the crucifixion. He forgot his own sufferings in the sufferings of the Savior, and from that hour he was a changed man. He told the Lord that whatever He allowed him to go through, he would never complain again. Maurice's wife became a believer a year later when she heard him preach at a camp meeting but was not willing to make her home with him again unless he gave up the life of faith that the Lord had called him to. She insisted that he earn a living like other Christians did. It was a difficult test, but he would not compromise his calling. He didn't see his wife for another three years, and then she too had a revelation of the Cross. As a result of this revelation she testified that whereas before as a believer she had not been willing to share the sacrificial life of her husband, now if it would be for God's glory, she would beg her bread from door to door.[6]

In this verse the Lord once more affirms the maiden, comparing her to a mare among the chariots of Pharaoh. Even as Pharaoh's mares knew no will but that of the king, the maiden's deepest desire is to become His bond-servant: one whose will is altogether consumed in His will.

> Lord, please give me a revelation of the Cross—of the amazing love that You demonstrated for me there and the incredible price You paid for my sins when You took on Yourself the punishment that was due me. I want to be Your bond-servant, Lord: my will totally consumed in Your will.

1:10 "Your cheeks are lovely with ornaments, your neck with strings of beads" *[Bridegroom speaking]*.

The word for ornaments in this verse is used for round ornaments hanging down in front on both sides of a headband. This kind of ornamentation was worn by wealthy women in ancient times. *Because the cheeks often express the emotions of a person, particularly when flushed or pale, cheeks represent the emotions throughout the Song. The Bridegroom is commending the maiden for the control she has over her emotions in this verse.* She does not allow them to direct her life, understanding that emotions are fueled by our thoughts and past experiences and many times by the lies written on our hearts by the enemy.

The neck symbolizes the will in the Scriptures. When the Lord spoke of His people as being rebellious, He called them "stiff-necked" (cf. Acts 7:51, Exod. 33:5, Deut. 9:13–14, 2 Chron. 30:8). *In this verse, the Bridegroom commends the maiden for the control she has over her will, as symbolized by strings of beads on her neck. Each bead symbolizes an occasion when she made a choice to obey Him, even at great personal cost.*

The reference to ornaments on the cheeks (control over her emotions) and strings of beads on the neck (a strong will) represent two of the natural gifts and abilities the Lord has given the maiden from birth. However, these gifts must still be sanctified by the Holy Spirit to be used in the service of the King.

The scripture speaks of "refining by fire" as one of the Lord's methods of sanctification in our lives. The apostle Peter wrote, "…now for a little while, if necessary, you have been distressed by various trials, so that the proof of your faith, being more precious than gold which is perishable, even though tested by fire, may be found to result in praise and glory and honor at the revelation of Jesus Christ" (1 Pet. 1:6–7). The Greek word for "tested" here is *dokimazo* and means to prove or *bring forth the good in us or to make us good.*

God said to Israel through the prophet Isaiah, "Behold, I have refined you, but not as silver; I have tested you in the furnace of affliction" (Isa. 48:10). The psalmist wrote, "For You have tried us, O God; You have refined us as silver is refined" (Ps. 66:10). The prophet Malachi proclaimed that Jesus is like a refiner's fire, "…and He will purify the sons of Levi and refine them like gold and silver, so that they may present to the LORD offerings in righteousness" (Mal. 3:2–3).

When gold or silver was refined in ancient times, it was heated

17

to a very high temperature, which caused the impurities to rise to the surface. They could then be skimmed off the top of the liquid metal, leaving an unmarred surface that reflected the image of the refiner. This is a wonderful picture of Jesus as the Refiner's Fire in our lives. Although He allows trials and difficult circumstances to test us, their purpose is always to "bring forth the good in us"—to purify our hearts so that we become a clearer reflection of His image.

> Lord, please sanctify the natural gifts and abilities You've given me so that they will produce much fruit for Your kingdom. I ask for Your refining fire in my life so that I will become a clearer reflection of Your image to the lost.

1:11 "We will make for you ornaments of gold with beads of silver" *[Bridegroom speaking].*

The word "make" is the Hebrew word *asah* and means to create in this context. It is used in Scripture to describe *God's creative activity.* The King's gifts are created (or formed) in her by the Holy Spirit.

Gold is used in Scripture to represent the divine nature or holiness, as Exodus makes clear. All of the wood in the tabernacle was overlaid with gold, and the mercy seat, lampstand, and all of the utensils were made of pure gold. The plate on the front of the priest's turban was made of pure gold and engraved "Holiness to the Lord" (cf. Exodus chapters 25 through 30). The entire inside of Solomon's temple and its furnishings, even the floor, was either made of pure gold or overlaid with gold (cf. 1 Kings 6; 2 Chron. 3–4). Even the street of the New Jerusalem will be made of pure gold (cf. Rev. 21:21).

Silver is used in Scripture to speak of redemption (cf. 1 Pet. 1:18–19). To redeem means to buy back, to recover, to set free by paying a ransom. *The Lord says in this verse that "We" (the Trinity) will create in the maiden new gifts that exhibit the divine nature as the result of Our redeeming work in her life.*

Redemption takes place when we are born again, yet it is also a progressive work in our lives as the Lord restores our soul (Ps. 23:3). He is continually at work in our lives to recover what the enemy has stolen, to restore our souls from the damage inflicted on them through sin (both our own sin and the sins of others against us), and to set us free. *In God's economy, silver and gold go together. It is His redeeming work in our hearts, represented by silver beads, which make room for His divine gifts and nature to be imparted to us, represented by ornaments of gold in this metaphor.*

> Lord, thank You for Your redeeming work in my heart—for recovering what the enemy has stolen and for setting me free. Help me cooperate with the Holy Spirit as You restore my soul from the damage of sin—both my own sin and the sins of others against me. And form Your divine nature and gifts in my heart so that I will reflect Your glory.

1:12 "While the King was at His table, my perfume gave forth its fragrance" [Bride speaking].

King Jesus at His table is a picture of our communion—or fellowship—with Him through the indwelling Spirit. A meal taken together at a table in the ancient world was a time of sharing or communion. In New Testament times meals were often taken at a low rectangular table with couches on three sides, the fourth side remaining open for women and servants to serve food. Three or four persons could recline on each couch so that literally one person's head was at another person's chest. The evening meal was the main meal of the day among the Jews and was served after the day's work was completed. The entire family and often guests gathered around the table sharing fellowship (communion) as they ate together. This is a beautiful picture of our communion with the Lord. Communion is defined as intimate conversation, intimate relationship. As we come before the Lord to wait in His presence, we commune with Him and are "fed" by Him through the Person of the Holy Spirit (2 Cor. 13:14).

An additional benefit of communing with the Lord and being fed at His table is that *His fragrance begins to cling to us.* J. Hudson Taylor wrote that it is only in the Lord's presence and through His grace that whatever fragrance or beauty in us comes forth.[7] Just as in a negative sense the smell of smoke clings to us when we enter a smoke-filled room, in a wonderfully positive sense the Lord's own fragrance clings to us as we spend time in His presence.

The word *perfume* in this verse is literally *nard* or *spikenard*, a very costly fragrant ointment. Mary of Bethany anointed Jesus with a pound of pure nard before His crucifixion. This was most likely her entire dowry, or the property she would bring to her husband at marriage. It was worth three hundred denarii according to Judas, or about a year's wages. Yet Mary counted it as nothing compared to the privilege of honoring her Messiah, Jesus, and anointing His body for burial. Therefore, this verse also highlights another great truth: *only as we spend time with Him in intimate communion will we receive the grace to die to self and live for Him, symbolized by nard in this account.*

In speaking about His crucifixion shortly after Mary's act of worship, Jesus said, "Truly, truly, I say to you, unless a grain of wheat falls into the earth and dies, it remains alone; but if it dies, it bears *much fruit*" (John 12:24, emphasis added). Our lives are also like a "grain of wheat." If we ask for the grace to die to "self" and live for Him, He will enable us to produce much fruit for His kingdom.

> Lord, help me make time daily to sit at Your feet, to both share my heart with You and to listen for Your voice to me. As I spend time with You in the "secret place," give me the grace to die to "self" so that I will produce much fruit for Your kingdom.

1:13 "My Beloved is to me a pouch of myrrh which lies all night between my breasts" *[Bride speaking].*

Wealthy women in the ancient world sometimes perfumed their beds with myrrh and fragrant spices (cf. Prov. 7:17) or wore a pouch of spices as a necklace when retiring for the night. *The maiden says that her Beloved, Jesus, is as a fragrant pouch of myrrh that lies over her heart as she sleeps.* Because myrrh was an ingredient of the holy anointing oil used to consecrate the priests (Exod. 30:23–30), it is symbolic of Jesus as our great High Priest who constantly makes intercession for us before the throne of God. *The maiden is confident that even as she sleeps, the incense of His prayers and intercession for her move the heart of the Father.* Romans 8:34 assures us, "…Jesus Christ is He who…is at the right hand of God, who also intercedes for us." Hebrews 7:25 speaks in like manner, "Therefore He is able to save completely those who come to God through Him, because He always lives to intercede for them" (NIV).

As Jesus hung on the cross, He was offered wine mixed with myrrh as a kind of anesthetic, but refused to drink it (Mark 15:23). John 19:39–40 tells us that Nicodemus took Jesus's body after His crucifixion and bound it in linen wrappings with a mixture of myrrh and aloes before laying it in the tomb. Therefore myrrh also speaks of the Cross and the precious sacrifice freely made by the Son of God as our great High Priest to redeem us to God. *The Cross is the irrefutable evidence of our worth to God. As the maiden meditates on the Cross and what Jesus endured because of love for her, she is empowered to love Him in a deeper way.*

> Lord, I ask for revelation of Your role as my great High Priest: the One who always lives to make intercession for me. Give me confidence in Your ability to keep me on the path that You have chosen for me and to perfect and complete that which You have ordained for my life. I also ask for a deeper revelation of Your love for me as I meditate on the Cross. May that revelation empower me to love You in a deeper way.

1:14 "My beloved is to me a cluster of henna blossoms in the vineyards of Engedi" *[Bridegroom speaking].*

Henna was a fragrant yellow and white flower that grew at Engedi, an oasis on the west coast of the Dead Sea in the territory of Judah. Engedi's luxurious vegetation was famous in the days of Solomon. *The Hebrew word for Engedi means "fountain of the lamb."* The Bridegroom is taking pleasure in the beautiful fragrance that clings to the maiden as a result of her communion with Him. As she sits at His feet, drinking from the fountain of the Lamb, her spirit is saturated with His fragrance.

It is interesting to note that Ezekiel prophesied that water from the temple will become a river and flow to Engedi, this water making all the water it flows into fresh water, so that every creature in it will live (Ezek. 47:10). Verse 12 says that by this river will grow all kinds of trees for food. These trees are not ordinary trees; their leaves will not wither and they do not stop producing fruit. "…They will bear every month because their water flows from the sanctuary, and their fruit will be for food and their leaves for healing." Compare this with Revelation 22:1–2, "Then he showed me a river of the water of life, clear as crystal, coming from the throne of God and of the Lamb, in the middle of its street [speaking of the New Jerusalem]. On either side of the river was the tree of life, bearing twelve kinds of fruit, yielding its fruit every month; and the leaves of the tree were for the healing of the nations."

Engedi, or "the fountain of the Lamb," is a beautiful picture of the Holy Spirit. Jesus said, "…If any man is thirsty, let him come to Me and drink. He who believes in Me, as the Scripture said, 'From his innermost being shall flow *rivers of living water.' But this He spoke of the Spirit,* whom those who believed in Him were to receive…" (John 7:37–39, emphasis added).

The Bridegroom uses romantic imagery to describe the beautiful fragrance that clings to the maiden, comparing it to the fragrance of henna blossoms in Engedi. This is, of course, His very fragrance. As a result of her devotion, the time spent sitting at His feet drinking from "the fountain of the Lamb," His own fragrance now clings to her. Not only this, His Spirit flows out of her heart as a river of living water bringing His life and refreshment to those it touches.

> Lord, help me make spending time in Your presence daily my first priority. I want to commune with You and drink from Engedi, the fountain of the Lamb. Cause Your rivers of living water, the precious Holy Spirit, to flow out of my innermost being, carrying Your life and refreshment to those around me.

1:15 "How beautiful you are, My darling, how beautiful you are! Your eyes are like doves" *[Bridegroom speaking].*

Once again, the Lord calls the maiden beautiful. In Song 1:5 He told her she was lovely; in Song 1:8 He called her "most beautiful among women." The Lord constantly affirms her in the truth that *she is beautiful in His eyes,* and this produces in her heart a sense of security that cannot be shaken. Because she feels secure in the knowledge of her beauty and inestimable value in His eyes, she will run *to* Him, not *from* Him, when she falls into sin.

In poetic language, the maiden's eyes are compared to doves' eyes. Doves are known for their loyalty. If their partner dies, they will not seek another mate. *The Lord is affirming her loyalty and devotion to Him alone.* A second distinguishing characteristic of the dove is that it has no peripheral vision, therefore its focus is single. Jesus spoke of our eyes as being the gateway to our soul. He said, "The eye is the lamp of the body; so if your eye is clear, your whole body will be full of light. But if your eye is bad, your whole body will be full of darkness…" (Matt. 6:22–23). The Greek word for "clear" in this verse is *haplous* and means singleness, simplicity, absence of folds. This Greek word is only used here and in the parallel verse in Luke 11:34. It refers to the focus of our spiritual eyes: the eyes of our heart (cf. Ps. 16:8).

When the Holy Spirit descended on Jesus after He was baptized in the Jordan River, He came in the form of a dove. *Doves symbolize purity, innocence, and godly character expressed in the fruit of the Spirit. The Bridegroom speaks of her loyalty and devotion to Him alone, but also of the purity and single focus of the eyes of her heart and the godly character she is developing as she learns to abide in Him, progressively coming to depend on His Holy Spirit living inside her.*

> Lord, make me secure in the knowledge that I am beautiful in Your eyes so that I will run to You, not from You, when I fall into sin. I ask You to give me "doves' eyes"—spiritual eyes in single focus on You and Your kingdom. Help me learn to abide in You, depending more and more on the precious Holy Spirit living in my heart so that Your character will be reflected in my life.

1:16 "How handsome You are, my Beloved, and so pleasant! Indeed, our couch is luxuriant!" *[Bride speaking].*

The maiden is captivated by the beauty of the Bridegroom as His character and personality are revealed to her by the Holy Spirit. Isaiah 33:17 says, "Your eyes will see the King in His beauty..." "See" is the Hebrew word *chazah* and means to behold or *to discern with revelation. The Holy Spirit is enlightening the eyes of the maiden's heart and revealing the character of the Lord to her as He gives her revelation of the Scriptures. She is beginning to see the Lord's beauty as far superior to any of the counterfeits the world has to offer!*

"Our couch is luxuriant" is a metaphor for the richness of their growing relationship. A couch in ancient times was a bed on a raised platform along the wall of a room. They were normally covered with cushions and used as a sofa during the day. *The couch represents the place where the maiden and the Bridegroom meet to spend time together, talking and listening to each other's heart. It symbolizes the "secret place" of His presence* (cf. Ps. 31:20).

> Lord, You said that my spiritual eyes would behold You in Your beauty. I ask You to fulfill this promise in my life. I want to see Your beauty as far superior to any of the counterfeits the world has to offer. Give me a spirit of wisdom and of revelation in the knowledge of You as I spend time with You in the "secret place" of Your presence.

1:17 "The beams of our houses are cedars, our rafters, cypresses" *[Bride speaking].*

Houses can be translated as "rooms in a large house," thus we could say, "The beams of the rooms in our house are cedar, the rafters are cypress."

Beams are long, thick pieces of wood, metal, etc., used as horizontal support for a roof or ceiling. Rafters are beams that slope from the ridge of a roof to the eaves and serve to support the roof. The beams and rafters of a house are the second most important structural element of a house (after the foundation) because they support the ceiling and roof.

"Cedar" is the Hebrew word *erez*, which is from an old Arabic root meaning "a firmly rooted strong tree." The cedars of Lebanon are magnificent evergreens often 120 feet high and 40 feet in girth. They exude a fragrant gum or balsam. The wood does not quickly decay, nor is it eaten by insect larvae. Cypress wood is also very hard and durable. Cedar and cypress were the only types of wood used in Solomon's temple (1 Kings 5:8).

The maiden is saying that their house, their dwelling place (representing their relationship), is strong and durable and cannot be easily overcome by things that would assault it or try to weaken it. This metaphor also relates to spiritual warfare, since the beams and rafters speak of the invisible upper support for the house. Their relationship is protected from the assault of the enemy as the maiden abides under the shadow of the Almighty. David said, "*He who dwells in the secret place of the Most High shall abide under the shadow of the Almighty. I will say of the LORD, 'He is my refuge and my fortress; my God, in Him I will trust'....For you have made the Lord, my refuge, even the Most High, your dwelling place. No evil will befall you, nor will any plague come near your tent.*" (Ps. 91:1–2, NKJV; 9–10, emphasis added).

> Lord, open my spiritual eyes to see You as my Refuge and my Fortress, my Protector from the assaults of the enemy as I abide under Your shadow. Help me learn to dwell in the secret place of Your presence where I am beyond the reach of the enemy's arrows.

Chapter 2

HIS BANNER OVER US IS LOVE

2:1 "I am the rose of Sharon, the lily of the valleys" *[Bride speaking]*.

J. HUDSON TAYLOR WRITES of this verse:

> The last words are often quoted as if they are the utterance of the Bridegroom, but I believe this to be in error. The bride says in effect, "You call me fair and pleasant, but the fairness and pleasantness are Yours; I am but a lowly, scentless rose of Sharon (i.e., the autumn crocus) or lily of the valley." To this the Bridegroom responds, "Be it so; but if a wild flower, yet....like a lily among the thorns, so is my darling among the maidens."[1]

Most authorities think that the rose referred to in Song 2:1 and Isaiah 35:1 is not what we know as the rose today, but a low-growing bulbous plant producing from two to four yellow flowers on each stalk. This flower is noted for its fragrance. Other scholars have suggested the mountain tulip, anemone, saffron, or crocus as the flower in question. All of these flowers grew wild in Palestine.

The maiden is revealing in this verse how she sees herself: she is an ordinary wild flower, one in a field of millions. She does not see herself as particularly gifted or exceptional in any way. Her attitude exemplifies Paul's words in Philippians 2:3, "...with humility of mind regard one another as more important than yourselves."

> Lord, give me the attitude of the maiden in this verse—don't let me think more highly of myself than I should. But please don't let me walk in false humility either, which is just as much a manifestation of "self."

Help me walk in true humility, which is simply agreement with the
truth of how You see me.

The maiden acknowledges she is a simple wildflower, common
and ordinary with no special attributes that draw attention to her.
To this the Bridegroom responds:

2:2 "**Like a lily among the thorns, so is My darling among the
maidens**" *[Bridegroom speaking].*

When we stop to think of all the billions of people on the earth,
both past and present, and the relatively small number that have
sought true intimacy with God (vs. "religion"), it is not difficult to
see why the Lord calls the maiden a "lily among the thorns." He created us for relationship, for fellowship with Himself, yet there are
relatively few who grasp this truth and pursue it above all else. Some
settle into religion and try to earn His love by works (or service), but
they miss the incredible fact that His love can never be earned; it is a
free gift bestowed by His grace (*unmerited* favor) toward us. Nothing
we *do* will ever make Him love us one iota more or less.

This is not to negate the place of service to our fellow man. We
love because He first loved us, and serving is one of the expressions
of true love. Love meets the needs of the one loved and rejoices in
the opportunity to serve. The Lord told us that we prove our love
toward Him by obedience to His Word (John 14:23) and that we
serve Him by serving those He loves, even the least of His brethren
(Matt. 25:31–40).

Be that as it may, we must always remember that the Lord looks
at our hearts, at what is motivating our service. Is it a form of "per-
formance orientation" that we learned growing up—the false belief
that we must perform in order to be loved and accepted? Or is it
love for His people because we understand how precious they are to
Him, even as we know we are precious to Him? If our service is not
grounded in the revelation of the Lord's love for us, and for all of His
brethren, we will eventually burn out. Many have been neutralized
by the enemy in this manner. *In the last analysis, only as we have*

revelation of His love for us are we truly able to love others with His love (cf. 1 John 4:19).

The Lord said through the prophet Jeremiah, "…Don't let the wise boast in their wisdom, or the powerful boast in their power, or the rich boast in their riches. But *those who wish to boast should boast in this alone: that they truly know Me* and understand that I am the LORD who demonstrates unfailing love and who brings justice and righteousness to the earth, and that I delight in these things" (Jer. 9:23–24, NLT, emphasis added).

Jesus emphasized this necessity of truly coming to know Him as a Person (vs. knowing facts about Him) many times in the Scriptures. In His encounter with Mary and Martha recorded in Luke 10:38–42, He called it "the one thing worth being concerned about": "As Jesus and the disciples continued on their way to Jerusalem, they came to a certain village where a woman named Martha welcomed him into her home. Her sister, Mary, sat at the Lord's feet, listening to what He taught. But Martha was distracted by the big dinner she was preparing. She came to Jesus and said, 'Lord, doesn't it seem unfair to you that my sister just sits here while I do all the work? Tell her to come and help me.' But the Lord said to her, 'My dear Martha, you are worried and upset over all these details! *There is only one thing worth being concerned about.* Mary has discovered it, and it will not be taken away from her'" (NLT, emphasis added). *The Lord sees the maiden as a lily among thorns because, like Mary, the passion of her heart is to know Him and to love Him with her whole heart, mind, soul, and strength.*

> Lord, open the eyes of my heart to see myself as Your lily among the thorns. I want my only boast to be that I truly know You. Give me a heart like Mary's that delights in sitting at Your feet, being taught by You. Help me pursue the one thing worth being concerned about—a deepening friendship with You.

2:3 "Like an apple tree among the trees of the forest, so is my Beloved among the young men. In His shade I took great

delight and sat down, and His fruit was sweet to my taste"
[Bride speaking].

The maiden is referring to two aspects of the Lord's character in this verse. First, she says He is shade from the hot sun that she can rest under. This description of the Lord is reminiscent of the "pillar of cloud": a manifestation of the preincarnate Christ who both led the Israelites and provided shade from the sun as they wandered in the desert before entering the Promised Land (Exod. 13:21; Ps. 105:38–39). "His shade" also points to the promise of Psalm 91:1, "He who dwells in the secret place of the Most High shall abide under the shadow of the Almighty (NKJV). *The Lord becomes our covering, our shield from the defilement of the world and the attacks of the enemy, as we learn to dwell in the secret place of the Most High.* The New Testament equivalent to "dwelling in the secret place of the Most High" is "abiding in Him" (John 15:1–8), or we could say "living in the Sabbath rest" (Heb. 4:1–11). This means resting from our own works—the works of the flesh, even good things, but those that did not originate from Him. Then, as we remain connected to Him as a branch abiding in the Vine, He leads us to the good works that we were created to do before the foundation of the world (Eph. 2:10). He said, "I am the vine, you are the branches; he who abides in Me, and I in him, he bears much fruit; for apart from Me you can do nothing (of eternal value is implied)" (John 15:5).

The second aspect of the Lord's character revealed in this verse is His desire to nourish us spiritually. The maiden exclaims, "His fruit was sweet to my taste." Fruit symbolizes spiritual nourishment in this context. David said that God's Word was sweeter than honeycomb to him, that it was more enjoyable to his spirit than something sweet and delicious was to his physical sense of taste (cf. Ps. 19:7–10). *The maiden is delighting in the spiritual nourishment the Lord provides as He feeds her from His Word (cf. John 14:26, 1 John 2:27). Not only that, she delights in His rhema word: the personal words of life that He speaks to her spirit as she communes with Him, talking to Him and listening for His voice to her. (Rhema is Greek for "word," meaning a spoken word.)*

Lord, I ask that the Holy Spirit would teach me even as You promised in Your Word (John 14:26; 1 John 2:27). I ask that He would open my mind to understand the Scriptures even as You did the disciples on the road to Emmaus (Luke 24:45). Teach me to abide in You: to live from my heart and the eternal kingdom of God which is there. Help me remain in Your Sabbath rest so that I will do the good things that You prepared for me to do before the foundation of the world, instead of things that You did not initiate which cannot impart Your life.

2:4 "He has brought me to His banquet hall, and His banner over me is love" *[Bride speaking].*

"Banquet hall" in this verse is literally "the house of wine." Wine represents the Holy Spirit many places in Scripture (cf. Acts 2:13, Matt. 9:17, Eph. 5:18). It is the Holy Spirit who gives us revelation of the Lord's love for us. The apostle Paul wrote, "…the love of God has been poured out within our hearts through the Holy Spirit who was given to us" (Rom. 5:5). The Holy Spirit enlarges our hearts, our spiritual capacity, to believe the Lord's love for us through *revelation, or understanding granted to our spirit.*

Wine is also associated with joy. As we spend time in the Lord's presence, we drink from the wine of the Spirit. King David wrote, "…You make him joyful with gladness in Your presence" (Ps. 21:6), and "…In Your presence is fullness of joy; in Your right hand there are pleasures forever" (Ps. 16:11).

"…His banner over me is love."

A banner is a long strip of cloth bearing a slogan or design, hung in a public place or carried in a demonstration or procession. In ancient times a banquet hall would have the family's banner prominently displayed for all to see. *The bride is saying in this verse that the Lord's banner over her—the overarching message and defining statement of His relationship with her—is love.*

The apostle John, the one who rested his head on Jesus's breast at the last supper, wrote, "…God is love. God showed how much he loved us by sending his one and only Son into the world so that we might have eternal life through him. This is real love—not that we loved God, but that he loved us and sent his Son as a sacrifice to take away our sins" (1 John 4:8–10, NLT). God sacrificed His own sinless Son to redeem us to Himself! As Isaiah said, "But He [Jesus] was pierced through for *our* transgressions, He was crushed for *our* iniquities; the chastening for *our* well-being fell upon Him, and by His scourging we are healed" (Isa. 53:5, emphasis added). *The Cross is the ultimate evidence of God's love for us.*

The apostle John continued in his first letter, "We have come to know and have *believed* the love which God has for us" (1 John 4:16, emphasis added). This "believing" His love for us is possible only through the revelation of the Holy Spirit. It is this revelation of God's love that changes us on the inside, freeing us from the weight and guilt of sin and shame and giving us the desire to live a life that pleases Him. *When our hearts connect with the fact that He truly loves us even though He knows everything about us, every sin we have committed, every character flaw and selfish trait that we possess, and yet He is filled with love for us in spite of it all—our hearts overflow with joy. He is the only One who can love us in this way—totally, unselfishly, and unconditionally.*

> Lord, bring me to Your banquet hall, the house of wine, and fill me with joy in Your presence. Make me secure in the knowledge that You truly love me even though You know every sin I have committed and every character flaw and selfish trait I possess. Enable me to believe the love that You have for me by the revelation of Your Spirit. You are the only One who can love me totally, unselfishly, and unconditionally.

2:5 "Sustain me with raisin cakes, refresh me with apples, because I am lovesick" *[Bride speaking].*

In this verse the maiden is crying out for a deeper revelation of the Lord's character and personality. She asks Him to sustain her with spiritual food, but not only to sustain her (which speaks of having enough to live, but not an abundance); she also asks Him to refresh her. To refresh is to go beyond what is necessary, to make fresh and new and vigorous again. It speaks of new revelation being poured into her heart to augment the foundational truths that sustain her.

In verse 3, the maiden was discovering the Sabbath rest, learning to rest under the Lord's shade and to cease from her own labors so that she could be led by His Spirit. She was reveling in the sweetness of His Word, both the revelation of His written Word and His personal *rhema* word to her heart. In verse 4, she was enjoying being led by Him to the banquet hall, literally the "house of wine." He was filling her heart with joy through the revelation of His love for her poured forth by the Holy Spirit. In the verse before us, she now asks Him to continue feeding her spirit with the foundational truths of the faith, but more than that, to refresh her with more revelation of who He is. She is delighting in each new facet of His personality as He reveals Himself to her and longs for still more; therefore, she describes herself as "lovesick."

> Lord, sustain me with the foundational truths of Your Word, but also refresh me with new revelation of Your character and personality. Open my spiritual eyes to see You as You truly are so that the things of this world will lose their appeal in comparison with Your surpassing beauty.

2:6 "Let His left hand be under my head and His right hand embrace me" [Bride speaking].

This is a picture of the tender embrace of a lover. In such an embrace we feel totally loved, protected, cherished, and secure. The maiden longs to remain in this embrace, never leaving the security and peacefulness of His presence. The Hebrew word for embrace literally means to enfold or envelop. This speaks of the Lord's divine protection and covering, as well as His passionate love for His bride.

The Spanish saint Michael Molinos (and Madame Guyon before him) described this rest in the arms of the Lord as a form of prayer that he called "beholding Him." From this position, we fix our attention on the Lord without requiring anything of Him. Instead, the purpose is to meet with Him in the holy of holies in our hearts, giving Him loving attention in silence and oblivion from every-thing else. Then, as we gaze at Him (cf. Rev. 4, Ezek. 1, Dan. 7:9–10, Isa. 6:1–4), gently expressing our love for Him and rejecting all the thoughts and images that come into our minds, our wills are even-tually surrendered to His divine will. From this position the Lord converses with us and fill us with Himself. This is what the maiden is seeking when she cries, "Let His left hand be under my head and His right hand embrace me."

The Song to this point has described what many have called the "honeymoon stage" in the life of a believer. The Lord covers and pro-tects us from the assaults of the enemy until we are grounded in our relationship with Him. Our hearts are being set to follow Him—for better or for worse, for richer or poorer, in sickness and in health. If this honeymoon period does not take place and a personal relation-ship is not established with the Lord, the believer may fall away at a later time when suffering or the trials and pressures of life overtake them (cf. Matt. 13:20–21).

> Lord, help me learn to rest in Your embrace. Teach me how to quiet my mind and lay aside all concern for outward things so that I can enter the holy of holies in my heart and commune with You. As I do, please conform my will to Your will and fill me with Yourself.

2:7 "I adjure you, O daughters of Jerusalem, by the gazelles or by the hinds of the field, that you will not arouse or awaken My love, until she pleases" *[Bridegroom speaking]*.

Jeanne Guyon wrote concerning this verse:

> You sleep in a spiritual sleep in your Betrothed's arms. You enjoy a holy rest that you have never known before. Previously you rested under His shadow in confidence, but you have never slept on His bosom or in His arms. How strange a thing that people, even spiritual people, are eager to awaken you from this gentle slumber. The daughters of Jerusalem are loving but meddlesome souls. They are anxious to wake you for appar-ently the most valid reasons. But you are so soundly asleep

that you cannot be awakened. The Bridegroom speaks for you, holding you in His arms and charging others not to awaken His dear one. He tells the impetuous daughters that you are more pleasing to Him at rest than in most outward activity. "Do not wake her," He says, "nor disturb her sleep. When I am ready to call her, she will be pleased to awaken and follow."[3]

The Lord adjures (or charges) the daughters of Jerusalem "by the gazelles or by the hinds of the field." This language seems odd to our modern minds, yet the symbolism is rich with meaning. Gazelles and hinds (adult female red deer) are animals which by nature are skittish. The Lord is appealing to the daughters with reference to the gazelles and hinds because they are flighty animals and will spook and run at the slightest provocation. The maiden is not yet mature enough to ignore the distractions that would draw her away from fellowship with Him; therefore, the Lord charges the daughters not to arouse or to distract her until she is ready to leave His presence.

The daughters of Jerusalem are immature believers who love the Lord, but they have not learned to enter His Sabbath rest: the secret place of intimacy with Him where the soul learns to submit to the direction of the Holy Spirit and service is initiated by Him, not by the flesh. Luke records the Lord's words to Martha: "Martha, Martha, you are worried and bothered about so many things; but only one thing is necessary, for Mary has chosen the good part, which shall not be taken away from her" (Luke 10:41–42). The Greek word for "good" in this verse is *agathos* and means good and benevolent, profitable, useful. Contrast this word to another Greek word for good—*kalos*, which means constitutionally good but *not necessarily benefiting others*. The Holy Spirit was not capricious in His use of adjectives in this verse. His choice of *agathos* instead of *kalos* implies that we can do "good" things, but they may not really benefit others in an eternal and spiritual sense. Mary was commended by the Lord for choosing the "good" (Greek *agathos*) part, meaning her choice to sit at His feet and be taught by Him was benevolent in that *it would be used to bless others.*

Lord, I ask for wisdom and discernment to recognize the distractions that undermine my relationship with You. Don't let me be ignorant of the enemy's schemes! Help me prioritize the one necessary thing—an ever-deepening friendship with You.

2:8–9 "Listen! My Beloved! Behold, He is coming, climbing on the mountains, leaping on the hills! My Beloved is like a gazelle or a young stag. Behold, He is standing behind our wall, He is looking through the windows, He is peering through the lattice" *[Bride speaking]*.

Note the change from the previous verse where the maiden was resting quietly in the arms of her Beloved. In this verse she is not with Him but hears His approach. *He is coming in search of her.* The Lord is climbing on the mountains and leaping on the hills like a gazelle or young stag, which speaks of His effortless ability to overcome anything which stands in His way. Nothing can keep Him from the object of His love! Yet when He arrives, He stands behind "their wall" and must look through the windows and the lattice. He is on the outside, seeking to come in and commune with her. The wall is not really "their wall," as the maiden calls it—it is "her wall." She has erected a *wall of separation* between herself and the Lord, perhaps even unknowingly. She may have drawn back because of fear rather than distraction, i.e., "the worries of the world and the desire for other things" (cf. Mark 4:19). Be that as it may, she has drifted away from the depth of fellowship and communion that she once shared with Him, and He is coming in search of her. The Bridegroom is coming to reclaim the heart of His bride!

At this point in her walk with the Lord, the maiden has begun to truly understand and to believe how much He loves her. She knows that He endured the torment of the Cross to redeem her because of His great love for her. But as this revelation begins to take root in her heart, she is also aware that His great love extends to all those who are still bound by the enemy and by sin. She understands that He loves them as much as He loves her. She is beginning to realize that His bride is to be His partner: His hands and feet to those still living in the chains of darkness. I believe the maiden is drawing back not so much from selfishness or worldliness as from immaturity and fear. She is overwhelmed by the great needs of those around her and feels totally ill-prepared to meet those needs, unaware in her immaturity that if she is yoked to Him (abiding in Him) He will enable her to do whatever is required. He will give her the strength and the wisdom she needs, and the gifts and fruit of His Spirit to accomplish His work.

The Lord knows our hearts so much better than we do. He understands that one of the primary barriers that keep us from going deeper in our relationship with Him is fear. We are afraid that if we get too close to Him, He will ask for too much: for more than we are willing (at this point in our journey) to give Him. Most of us have not yet reached a place of trust with the Lord that frees us to give Him our whole heart with nothing held back. *Rees Howells: Intercessor* is an amazing biography that reveals just what lengths the Lord will go to in order to set the captives free. The dealings of the Holy Spirit in Rees's life seemed harsh at times, but Rees came to understand them and even to desire them. He explained:

> A person might think it was a life of bondage and fear. It would be to the flesh, but to the new man in Christ it was a life of fullest liberty. At first I had a tendency to pity myself and grumble at the penalty for disobedience, but *as I saw that I must either lose this corrupt self here or bear the shame of its exposure hereafter, I began to side with the Holy Spirit against myself, and looked on the stripping as a deliverance rather than a loss* (emphasis added).[4]

I remember talking to the Lord after I read *Rees Howells: Intercessor* for the first time. The Lord's dealings with Rees did seem harsh to me and I asked Him about it. He replied that He had only done what Rees *asked* Him to do. There are some who see by revelation the Father's eternal purpose in Christ. This vision so burns in their hearts that they are willing to do whatever it takes to become a vessel the Father can use to bring forth His eternal purpose in the earth. What is this "eternal purpose which He (the Father) carried out in Christ Jesus our Lord" (Eph. 3:11)? Paul wrote that God's eternal purpose in Christ Jesus was that both Jew and Gentile would become "one new man" and through the power of this union would *express His Lordship in the earth*, becoming a witness to the demonic principalities and powers of the manifold (many faceted) wisdom of God (cf. Eph. 2:11–16, 3:8–11).

In His kindness, the Lord has been faithful to remind me that His "perfect love casts out fear" (1 John 4:18). *As we press in to know Him, our hearts will be enlarged to believe His love for us, and His perfect love will drive out the fear in our hearts.* As a result, we will be freed to love Him with our whole heart, mind, soul, and strength. We will be able to trust Him with all that we have and all that we are, unafraid that He will ask for more than we are willing to give. *We will freely give all to the One who gave all for us.*

King David prophesied:

> Your people will offer themselves willingly in the day of Your power, in the beauty of holiness and in holy array out of the womb of the morning; to You [will spring forth] Your young men, who are as the dew.
>
> —PSALM 110:3, AMP

Lord, thank You for Your relentless pursuit of me! I ask that Your perfect love would drive out the fear in my heart so that I can love You with my whole heart, mind, soul, and strength. As I glimpse the depths of Your incredible love for me, enable me to fulfill King David's prophecy—I want to offer myself willingly in the day of Your power, in the beauty of holiness.

2:10–13 "My Beloved responded and said to me, 'Arise, My darling, My beautiful one, and come along. For behold, the winter is past, the rain is over and gone. The flowers have already appeared in the land; the time has arrived for pruning the vines, and the voice of the turtledove has been heard in our land. The fig tree has ripened its figs, and the vines in blossom

have given forth their fragrance. Arise, My darling, My beautiful one, and come along!'" *[Bride speaking, quoting the Bridegroom's words to her]*.

In verse 7 of this chapter the maiden is resting in the Bridegroom's arms, and He charges the daughters of Jerusalem not to awaken her. In verse 8, He is coming in search of her. They have been separated, but she hears His approach as He climbs on the mountains and leaps on the hills—He is coming to reclaim her heart! In verse 9, the Lord has come for her but there is a wall of separation between them and He is on the outside, looking in through the windows and peering through the lattice. As Jesus stands behind the wall of separation He calls to her, gently appealing to her to follow Him. He speaks to her of a new season beginning in her walk with Him: one of pruning the vines and catching the little foxes that are ruining their vineyards (verse 15). He is challenging her to leave the "comfort zone" and follow Him in service, yet the emphasis in this season is still on their relationship and the character work that He wants to do in her heart. "Pruning the vines" refers to the character issues that the Lord desires to transform so that she can bear more fruit for His kingdom. Jesus said, "I am the true vine, and My Father is the vinedresser. Every branch in Me that does not bear fruit, He takes away; and every branch that bears fruit, He prunes it so that it may bear more fruit" (John 15:1–2).

The winter season represents rest in the Lord's presence while He is establishing the foundation of her faith—a personal and intimate relationship with Him. She is not "working" in the winter season, even as the farmer does not work but lets the ground rest or lie fallow until the warmer weather of spring arrives. The new spring season she is entering is one of pruning or sanctification. "The time has arrived for pruning the vines" refers to the vineyard of her heart. There are sin areas in her life that hinder her ability to minister to others with His love and His nature flowing through her.

"My Beloved responded and said to me, 'Arise, My darling, My beautiful one, and come along'" [verse 10, Bride speaking, quoting the Bridegroom].

Once again the Lord affirms the maiden in the knowledge that she is beautiful and precious in His sight. Yet even as He affirms her with words of love, He now woos her to rise up and follow Him in service as He works in His vineyards. The Lord's sanctification process in her life will continue in this season as she works alongside Him. He will use the relationships and situations she encounters to reveal sinful attitudes, hidden motives, and judgments in her heart. Then, as she repents of these sinful attitudes, the Holy Spirit will purify her heart and her motives, conforming her more to His image.

"...For behold, the winter is past, the rain is over and gone" [verse 11, Bride speaking, quoting the Bridegroom].

Here the Lord speaks of the new season that is beginning in her walk with Him. He says winter, with its latter rain, has passed and a new season has arrived. In the land of Palestine, the rain falls chiefly in autumn and winter. The "early" rain (or autumn rain) falls from about mid-September to sowing time in November or December; the "latter" rain (or winter rain) falls in January or February.

"...The flowers have already appeared in the land; the time has arrived for pruning the vines, and the voice of the turtledove has been heard in our land" [verse 12, Bride speaking, quoting the Bridegroom].

The flowers appearing and the voice of the turtledove singing were sure signs that a new season had arrived after the latter rain of winter. The turtledove in Palestine was a migrating wild pigeon, similar to our mourning dove, which sang early in the spring.

The key phrase is "the time has arrived for pruning the vines." The Lord is speaking to the maiden about the pruning that He is going to perform in her heart so that she can bear more fruit for His kingdom. Jesus used this symbolism when speaking to His disciples just before

His crucifixion. He said, "I am the true vine, and My Father is the vinedresser. Every branch in Me that does not bear fruit, He takes away; and every branch that bears fruit, He prunes it, that it may bear more fruit" (John 15:1–2). The Lord then continued His teaching by using the symbolism of the vine and the branches to show them what their relationship with Him was to look like after His resurrection. He said, "Abide in Me, and I in you. As the branch cannot bear fruit of itself unless it abides in the vine, so neither can you unless you abide in Me. I am the vine, you are the branches; he who abides in Me and I in him, he bears much fruit, for apart from Me you can do nothing…If you abide in Me, and My words abide in you, ask whatever you wish, and it will be done for you. My Father is glorified by this, that you bear much fruit, and so prove to be My disciples" (John 15:4–8). (Regarding the promise in verse 7, "…ask whatever you wish, and it will be done for you," it is important to remember that if we are *abiding in Him* we will not ask Him for something that is not His will. His Spirit will enable us to know His mind and His heart, and our prayers will reflect that knowledge.)

> "'…The fig tree has ripened its figs, and the vines in blossom have given forth their fragrance. Arise, My darling, My beautiful one, and come along!'" [verse 13, Bride speaking, quoting the Bridegroom].

The New King James version translates this, "The fig tree puts forth her green figs." In other words, the fruit is there, but it has not yet ripened or matured. This reflects the sanctification process that is taking place in the maiden's life. She has the fruit of the Spirit growing in her heart, but her vine needs pruning by the loving hand of the Lord so that she can bear more fruit (cf. John 15:1–2).

Once again, the Lord affirms the maiden. "The vines in blossom have given forth their fragrance" is a metaphor illustrating how He sees the devotion and sincerity of her heart. Even though the mature grapes are not yet evident on her vine, He sees her life blossoming under the tutelage of the Holy Spirit. He smells the fragrance of her prayers and her devotion as a sweet aroma, one that brings pleasure to His heart (cf. Rev. 5:8). The Lord calls the maiden to arise and come with Him, not simply by issuing a command to her, but by affirming once more her beauty and inestimable worth to Him. He is speaking words of life to her heart, establishing her "spiritual DNA" and transforming the way she sees herself. He affirms not only her beauty, but adds the term of endearment "My darling" to convey how precious she is to His heart. The word *darling* means a person much loved by another, one who is very dear or beloved. This is how our Bridegroom feels about each one of us!

> Lord, I want to say yes to You when You beckon me to follow You. Give me a heart that is quick to obey, Lord. Help me cooperate with the pruning of Your Spirit as You reveal wrong motives and sinful attitudes in my heart so that I can bear more fruit for Your kingdom.

2:14 "O My dove, in the clefts of the rock, in the secret place of the steep pathway, let Me see your form, let Me hear your voice; for your voice is sweet, and your form is lovely" *[Bridegroom speaking].*

The Lord specifically uses the term of endearment "My dove" because of its rich symbolism. As mentioned earlier, doves are known for their loyalty. If their partner dies, they will not seek another mate. Since they have no peripheral vision, their eyes are of single focus. The Lord is affirming once more both the maiden's loyalty and devotion to Him and the single focus of her heart.

The Bridegroom's reference to the cleft of the rock brings to mind Moses's encounter with the Lord as recorded in Exodus:

> So the LORD spoke to Moses face to face, as a man speaks to his friend.... And [Moses] said, "Please, show me Your glory." Then [the Lord] said, "I will make all My goodness pass before you, and I will proclaim the name of the LORD before you. I will be gracious to whom I will be gracious, and I will have compassion on whom I have compassion." But He said, "You cannot see My face; for no man shall see Me, and live." And the LORD said, "Here is a place by Me, and you shall stand on the rock. So

it shall be, while My glory passes by, that *I will put you in the cleft of the rock*, and will cover you with My hand while I pass by. Then I will take away My hand, and you shall see My back; but My face shall not be seen."

—EXODUS 33:11, 18–23, NKJV, EMPHASIS ADDED

Although Moses had an intimate relationship with the Lord and was allowed to glimpse the Lord's glory, this was the exception, not the norm under the old covenant. It is an amazing truth that under the new covenant, all believers can behold the Lord's glory (although imperfectly as with an ancient mirror) when we spend time in His presence (cf. 2 Cor. 3:18). An intimate relationship with the Lord is now available not to certain leaders, but to every believer through the Holy Spirit!

The "clefts of the rock and the secret place of the steep pathway" symbolize the holy of holies in the maiden's heart where the Lord dwells in the person of the Holy Spirit. This is where she retreats to meet with Him and enter His presence. Psalm 31:20 confirms that the secret place is the presence of the Lord: "You hide them in *the secret place of Your presence…*"

In the verse before us the Lord is expressing His pleasure and delight in their growing relationship, assuring the maiden that He loves spending time with her, listening for her voice in the secret place of prayer and communion. The Lord not only meets her in the secret place, He speaks His words of life to her heart! *What an amazing truth that the Lord, the Creator and ruler of the universes, would truly enjoy spending one-on-one time with us!*

Lord, open my spiritual eyes to see what You made available to us at the Cross—that because of Your sacrifice, my heart has become the holy of holies where You dwell by Your Spirit. Teach me to live in the reality of that awesome truth. Please draw me to the secret place of Your presence and speak Your words of life to my heart. Allow me to behold Your glory as I fellowship with You, Lord, so that I will be transformed into Your image with ever-increasing glory by Your Spirit.

2:15 "Catch us the foxes, the little foxes that spoil the vines, for our vines have tender grapes" (NKJV) *[Bridegroom speaking].*

J. Hudson Taylor writes:

> The intruders may be small, but the mischief done is great. A little spray of blossom so tiny as to be scarcely perceived is easily spoiled, but thereby the fruitfulness of a whole branch may be forever destroyed. And how numerous the little foxes are! A little compromise with the world; disobedience to the still small voice in little things; little indulgences of the flesh to the neglect of duty; small neglects, doing evil in little things that good may come; and the beauty and fruitfulness of the vine are sacrificed![4]

In this season, the Lord is gently shining the light of the Holy Spirit on areas of the maiden's life that need to be brought into conformity with His will and His righteousness. He loves her too much to allow her to stay where she is; therefore, He speaks tenderly to her heart, calling her to a deeper level of consecration. As she spends time with Him in "the secret place," or holy of holies in her heart, the Holy Spirit gently points out the "little foxes" or areas of sin and compromise in her life. Then, as she repents of these sinful attitudes, hidden motives, and judgments, the Lord cleanses her heart, washing it with His Word (Eph. 5:16).

It is important to remember that the Holy Spirit is loving and kind—He gently *convicts* our hearts of sin. Paul wrote that *the kindness of God leads us to repentance* (Rom. 2:4). However, when the enemy speaks to our minds, he *condemns* us; his purpose is to produce shame which will never move us toward righteousness. Shame makes us feel like we are hopeless hypocrites, but this is exactly the opposite of how the Lord views us. He knows our spirit is willing but our flesh is weak. He sees the "yes" in our heart and the desire to be fully His. He wants us to run *to Him*, not from Him when we fall into sin! Even the apostle Paul experienced feelings of unworthiness in his struggle with sin (cf. Rom. 7:14–25). Yet he was convinced that the Lord's mercy always triumphs over judgment when there is sincere repentance. He wrote to the church at Philippi, "I want to *know Christ*...so that one way or another I will experience the resurrection from the dead! I don't mean to say that I have already achieved these things or that I have already reached perfection. But I press on to possess that perfection for which Christ Jesus first possessed me. No, dear brothers and sisters, I have not achieved it, but *I focus on this one thing: forgetting the past and looking forward to what lies ahead, I press on to reach the end of the race and receive the heavenly prize* for which God, through Christ Jesus, is calling us" (Phil. 3:10–14, NLT, emphasis added).

> Lord, help me say yes to You as You draw me to a deeper level of consecration. Open my spiritual eyes to see my sin as You see it. Give me the attitude of Paul when I do sin, Lord—help me press "delete" on the past and look forward to what lies ahead. Help me run to You, not from You when I sin.

2:16 "My Beloved is mine, and I am His; He pastures His flock among the lilies" *[Bride speaking].*

Although the Lord has extended an invitation to the maiden to go with Him to work in the vineyards (Song 2:10–15), she does not immediately respond to His invitation. She says, in effect, "The Lord is mine and I am His, and no one can snatch me out of His hand. Although He has called me to go with Him, I know where He pastures His flock and I can go with Him at a more convenient time."

"My Beloved is mine, and I am His..."

Her first statement is the language of complete assurance: of security in the knowledge that she is accepted in the beloved (Eph. 1:3–6, NKJV). The Holy Spirit has given her revelation of Paul's stunning words in Ephesians 1:4–8 (NLT):

> Even before he made the world, God loved us and chose us in Christ to be holy and without fault in his eyes. God decided in advance to adopt us into his own family by bringing us to

himself through Jesus Christ. This is what he wanted to do, and it gave him great pleasure. So we praise God for the glorious grace he has poured out on us who belong to his dear Son. He is so rich in kindness and grace that he purchased our freedom with the blood of his Son and forgave our sins. He has showered his kindness on us, along with all wisdom and understanding.

This revelation from the Lord is a wonderful gift, yet as often happens, the maiden has begun to take this awesome truth for granted.

"...He pastures His flock among the lilies."

Lilies are white and symbolize purity. This statement is a poetic way of saying that the Lord feeds His sheep where there are pure and honest hearts. Jesus commended Nathanael as one who was "without guile" (John 1:45–51). Guile means deceit or dishonesty, something that is false. *When our hearts are pure or "without guile," we can hear the voice of the Holy Spirit with much less distortion* (cf. John 7:17, 14:26).

The Lord defined a person with an "honest heart" for me once as "someone that is willing to embrace the truth, no matter what it *costs* them." In other words, the motives of our hearts affect our ability to perceive truth. When we are willing to embrace the truth "no matter what it costs us," we know that we have come to love truth for Truth's sake. Conversely, when the motives of our hearts are not pure, for instance, when we have come into agreement with a particular brand of theology, we often feel we must make the Scripture fit that "theological box" and our ability to know truth is compromised. We are, in effect, wearing "colored glasses" that distort the truth. A wise person once said, "It's not what we don't know that keeps us from the truth. It's what we think we do know that keeps us from the truth."

Lord, give me a heart that is quick to say yes when You extend an invitation to me. Don't allow me to take my relationship with You for granted but help me treasure it above all else. Please give me an honest heart like Nathanael: one that is pure—without guile and deceit.

2:17 "Until the cool of the day when the shadows flee away, turn, my Beloved, and be like a gazelle or a young stag on the mountains of Bether" *[Bride speaking]*.

Bether means *separation* in the Hebrew language. The maiden is, in essence, saying to the Lord, "I am occupied now with other things so go Your way until evening, and then I will make time to spend with You." She has not yet reached the place of maturity in her relationship with the Lord where she can say, as David did, "My heart has heard you say, 'Come and talk with me.' And my heart responds, 'LORD, I am coming'" (Ps. 27:8, NLT). She is still compartmentalizing her life into "secular" and "sacred," not understanding that the Lord's number one priority for her life is that she learn to abide in Him in unbroken communion.

The maiden's focus at this early stage in her walk with the Lord is still on herself and on *her inheritance in Him*, or how He can benefit her. However, by the end of the Song her focus changes to *His inheritance in her*. She comes to understand the Father's eternal purpose which He carried out in Christ Jesus and begins to walk it out, yoked in service with Him as a bond-servant: one whose will is totally consumed in the will of her Master.

> Lord, open my heart to understand that nothing I do is secular if it is done unto You. Help me learn to live from the eternal kingdom of God which is in my heart, and teach me to abide in You in unbroken communion as I learn to fellowship with Your Spirit.

Chapter 3

SETTING OUR EYES ON THE ETERNAL THINGS

3:1 "On my bed night after night I sought Him whom my soul loves; I sought Him but did not find Him" *[Bride speaking].*

I N THE PREVIOUS verse the maiden, in effect, sent the Lord away until evening when she could make time to spend with Him. However, when it was convenient for her to meet Him at their trysting place (the secret place or holy of holies in her heart), she was unable to feel His presence or hear His voice speaking to her heart.

The maiden is now learning by experience that the Lord does not desire a relationship of convenience with her. She has been occupied with other things, possibly even legitimate things, but when she finds time to seek Him, she is no longer able to sense His presence and commune with Him easily as before. While the maiden loves the Lord's presence, she doesn't fully realize that she wants it on her own terms. She is satisfied with sensing His presence in her emotions when she is alone with Him in her "quiet time," yet she confuses this *feeling of His presence* with the *reality of His indwelling presence*. She is not yet able to maintain her communion with Him in the busyness of her everyday life or while she is serving with Him in the "vineyards." Therefore, *the Lord must withdraw from her in order to woo her to the place of abiding in Him in unbroken communion: a communion that continues even in the midst of her daily commitments.*

> Lord, I want to know the reality of Your indwelling presence. Please teach me to abide in You in unbroken communion—a communion that continues even in the midst of my busy day. Help me learn to fellowship

with Your Spirit—to talk to You throughout my day and to be sensitive to Your promptings, Your impressions, and Your still small voice.

3:2 "I must arise now and go about the city; in the streets and in the squares I must seek Him whom my soul loves. I sought Him but did not find Him" *[Bride speaking].*

The maiden has been seeking the Lord "on her bed"—in her devotional time with Him—but He has withdrawn from her in order to teach her. He called to her to arise and come with Him earlier (Song 2:10–13), but she did not immediately respond to His invitation. She was confident that she knew where to find Him and sent Him away until evening when it was convenient for her to spend time with Him.

In the verse before us the maiden now accepts the Lord's invitation to rise and follow Him since she cannot recover the sense of His presence in the usual way. She begins her search for Him "in the city streets and squares," knowing that He leaves the ninety-nine sheep to go after the one that is lost. Yet the Lord is still hiding Himself from her. *He is training her by taking away the sense of His presence that she only experiences in her devotional time in order to move her beyond a communion with Him that depends on time and place.* He wants her to learn to carry the reality of His presence by faith into the activities of her daily life—in other words, to "abide in Him" or fellowship with His Spirit on a continual basis.

There is also the intimation in this verse that the maiden has withdrawn from fellowship with the body, which the Scripture warns against. She seems to be seeking the Lord in isolation. The Holy Spirit said through the writer of Hebrews, "And let us consider how to stimulate one another to love and good deeds, not forsaking our own assembling together, as is the habit of some, but encouraging one another..." (Heb. 10:24–25). One of the most important lessons the Lord must teach us is our need for one another as members of His body, just as Paul set forth in 1 Corinthians 12:12–27 (cf. Eph. 4:15–16, NIV).

Lord, help me to be quick to respond when You call. I want to have a heart like David's—when You asked him to come and talk with You, he immediately responded, "Lord, I am coming" (Ps. 27:8, NLT). Help me learn not to separate the secular and the sacred in my life, but to fellowship with Your Spirit throughout my day—so that I can carry the reality of Your presence by faith into the activities of my daily life.

3:3 "The watchmen who make the rounds in the city found me, and I said, 'Have you seen Him whom my soul loves?'" *[Bride speaking].*

The maiden humbles herself and turns to His body. She asks the watchmen of the city if they have seen the One she loves. "Watchman" is from the Hebrew word *shamar,* meaning to guard or protect. In the New Testament, those God has given the responsibility to guard and protect His people are the overseers or elders. The Greek word for overseers is derived from the word *episkopeo,* meaning to look after; this word is used in 1 Peter 5:2 exhorting the elders to shepherd the flock of God and to protect them from the "savage wolves" Peter knew would eventually infiltrate the flock. *Episkopos* (overseer) is also used in Acts chapter 20, which records Paul's exhortation to the elders of the church at Ephesus to "be on guard for yourselves and for all the flock, among which the Holy Spirit has made you overseers, to shepherd the church of God which He purchased with His own blood" (Acts 20:28). Therefore, the watchmen in this verse symbolize the elders of the body the maiden is in fellowship with. The maiden wisely humbles her heart and requests their help in reestablishing her intimacy with the Lord.

Lord, help me see my need of Your body and the need of submission to those You have placed in authority over me. Help me follow the example of the maiden—and of the centurion, who walked in humility and understood submission to authority, which produced great faith in his heart (Matt. 8:5–10).

3:4 "Scarcely had I left them when I found Him whom my soul loves; I held on to Him and would not let Him go until I had brought Him to my mother's house, and into the room of her who conceived me" *[Bride speaking].*

When the maiden rose from her bed to follow the Lord, humbling her heart to seek help from His body, He returned to her in sweet fellowship. However, only part of her lesson in faith has been learned. Although she has risen from her bed, she has not yet gone away with Him. She still thinks that the best experience of the Lord is the feeling of His presence and so she holds tightly to it, unwilling to risk losing it again. She speaks symbolically of bringing the Lord into her mother's house and into her room. This is reminiscent of Song 1:16–17 where she speaks of their couch and the beams and rafters of their rooms. Since the maiden is unmarried, she would be living at home with her father and mother. The meeting place with her Beloved would be somewhere private and quiet, a place where she can enter the holy of holies in her heart and hear His still small voice. This room represents their trysting place or "the secret place of His presence" spoken of in Song 2:14 and Psalm 31:20.

Although the Lord has graciously granted the maiden the sense of His presence once more, He is gradually leading her step by step into a deeper walk of faith. He wants her to cherish the time with Him in the secret place and the feeling of His presence when He chooses to grant it, but more than that, He wants her to learn to abide in Him—communing with Him not only in her devotional time, but in the activities of her daily life. *He wants her to walk in the revelation of the incredible gift that she carries in her heart: the Person of the Holy Spirit*—one member of the Godhead but fully equal to the Father and to the Son. Whether she *feels* His presence or not, He is always with her, dwelling in the holy of holies in her heart. The Holy Spirit is within her to open the Scriptures that she may find Christ there, to direct her prayer, to govern her life, and to reproduce in her the character of the Lord.

Lord, help me learn to walk by faith. I want to cherish the feeling of
Your presence when You choose to grant it, but more than that, I want
to learn to abide in You. Help me come to know Your Spirit as a Person,
the third person of the Trinity, fully equal to You and to the Father.
Teach me to depend on Him to open the Scriptures to me so that I will
find You there, to direct my prayer, to govern my life, and to reproduce
in me Your character.

3:5 "I adjure you, O daughters of Jerusalem, by the gazelles or
by the hinds of the field, that you will not arouse or awaken
My love, until she pleases" *[Bridegroom speaking].*

The Lord repeats the same exhortation to the daughters of
Jerusalem that He gave in Song 2:7 when the maiden was resting
quietly in His embrace. She has just regained her communion with
the Lord after a season of interrupted fellowship and is "holding
Him tightly" or guarding their relationship above all other things.
As mentioned earlier, the Lord refers to the gazelles or hinds of the
field because these animals are skittish by nature. They will spook
and run at the slightest provocation. The maiden is not yet mature
enough to ignore the distractions that would draw her out of the
Lord's presence as she has just demonstrated. Therefore, the Lord
again charges the daughters of Jerusalem not to arouse or to distract
her until she is ready to leave His presence.

Lord, help me learn to rest in Your embrace and to resist the distractions that constantly assault me. Don't let me be ignorant of the
enemy's schemes to lure me from the secret place of Your presence. But
also help me learn to fellowship with Your Spirit not only in my devotional time, but in the midst of my busy day.

3:6 "Who is this coming up from the wilderness like columns
of smoke, perfumed with myrrh and frankincense, with all
scented powders of the merchant?" *[Unidentified speaker].*

(The New American Standard Bible used as the primary translation throughout this book translates this verse: "What is this coming

up from the wilderness..." but notes in the margin that the literal translation is "*Who* is this coming up from the wilderness..." I have chosen to use the literal translation of the verse.)

In the preceding verse, the Lord has just admonished the daughters of Jerusalem not to disturb the maiden while she rests in His embrace. Suddenly an unidentified speaker interrupts the narrative with a vivid description of the royal procession of King Solomon (a type of Jesus) on the day of his wedding. The speaker is not identified in the Song but represents the Holy Spirit. The Spirit gives an impassioned fourfold description of Jesus's character and commitment to His bride, which will be crucial to anchor her soul in the difficult seasons ahead.

The Holy Spirit first describes the Lord Jesus in this metaphor as "coming up from the wilderness like columns (or pillars) of smoke." Exodus 13:21 and Exodus 40:34–38 both give similar pictures of the Lord:

> The LORD went ahead of them. He guided them during the day with a pillar of cloud, and he provided light at night with a pillar of fire. This allowed them to travel by day or by night.
> —EXODUS 13:21, NLT

> Then the cloud covered the Tabernacle, and the glory of the LORD filled the Tabernacle. Moses could no longer enter the Tabernacle because the cloud had settled down over it, and the glory of the LORD filled the Tabernacle. Now whenever the cloud lifted from the Tabernacle, the people of Israel would set out on their journey, following it. But if the cloud did not rise, they remained where they were until it lifted. The cloud of the LORD hovered over the Tabernacle during the day, and at night fire glowed inside the cloud so the whole family of Israel could see it. This continued throughout all their journeys.
> —EXODUS 40:34–38, NLT

This is a picture of the pre-incarnate Christ, long ago manifested as a pillar of cloud, leading the children of Israel through the wilderness.

The wilderness in Scripture represents the place of testing where God is determining whether or not we will obey Him. Moses wrote, "You shall remember all the way which the LORD your God has led you in the wilderness these forty years, that He might humble you, testing you, to know what was in your heart, whether you would keep His commandments or not" (Deut. 8:2). Even the Son of God was tested in the wilderness by the devil before He began His earthly ministry (cf. Matt. 4:1-11, Mark 1:12-13, Luke 4:1-14). Luke's Gospel tells us that after this time of testing by Satan, "...Jesus returned to Galilee *in the power of the Spirit...*" (Luke 4:14, emphasis added). As T. Austin Sparks has said, our self-life is the ground of Satan's power. Therefore the Lord takes us through times of testing in the wilderness, applying the principle of the Cross to our self-life so that Satan "has nothing in us" (cf. John 14:30). As Satan loses ground in our lives we become a cleansed temple for the Holy Spirit to dwell in, vessels which can hold the Lord's own power and authority.

It is important to note that this does not mean that only when we are without sin we can walk in power, or that God is endorsing us because we do walk in a measure of His power. God grants manifestations of His power because of His great love for His children, in order to bless and heal them—not to endorse the vessel through whom His power flows. Jesus said even some of those who cast out demons and perform miracles would be rebuked and sent away from His presence because they "practice lawlessness" (Matt. 7:21-23). The Greek word for "lawlessness" in this verse means opposition to or contempt for the will of God. If we walk in sin on a continual basis without sincere repentance and determination to turn away from our sin, we are showing contempt for the will of God. As a result, even if we cast out demons or perform miracles in His name, the Lord will tell us that He never knew us on the judgment day. The apostle John wrote, *"By this we know that we have come to know Him, if we keep His commandments"* (1 John 2:3, emphasis added). Truly knowing God produces in our hearts a *desire* to obey Him. In his letter to the church at Rome, Paul wrote that the Lord had given him grace and authority as an apostle to bring about "the obedience of faith" or, we might say, the obedience resulting from faith. *True faith (i.e., knowing God) produces the fruit of obedience in our lives.*

> "…perfumed with myrrh and frankincense, with all scented powders of the merchant?"

Frankincense was an ingredient in the incense used in the tent of meeting, and myrrh was an ingredient in the holy anointing oil used to consecrate the priests (cf. Exod. 30:22–30, 34–35). In the New Testament, Revelation 5:8, 8:3, and 8:4 all speak of incense in conjunction with the prayers of the saints. Therefore, myrrh and frankincense speak of the priestly ministry of Jesus as our great High Priest and the One who always lives to make intercession for us (cf. Heb. 3:1, 7:25).

Combining the elements above, the first revelation of Jesus given by the Holy Spirit in this passage of Scripture is Jesus as the living Word who directs our path, leading us step by step as we go through our wilderness seasons and the times of testing in our lives, constantly offering intercession to the Father on our behalf as our great High Priest. Truly, it is His intercession for us that strengthens us and keeps us from falling. The Lord told Peter on the night of His betrayal, "…'Simon, Simon! Indeed, Satan has asked for you, that he may sift you as wheat. But I have prayed for you, that your faith should not fail; and when you have returned to Me, strengthen your brethren'" (Luke 22:31–32, NKJV).

> Lord, thank You for leading me through the times of testing in my life, strengthening me through Your prayers. Please give me revelation of Your role as my great High Priest: the One who always lives to make intercession for me—who is able to keep me from stumbling and to stand in the presence of Your glory blameless with great joy (Heb. 7:25, Jude 24).

3:7–8 "Behold, it is the traveling couch of Solomon; sixty mighty men around it, of the mighty men of Israel. All of them are wielders of the sword, expert in war; each man has

his sword at his side, guarding against the terrors of the night" *[Unidentified speaker].*

The second revelation of Jesus given by the Holy Spirit in this passage of Scripture is Jesus as our Defender and Protector, our "Dread Champion" surrounded by His warrior angels. The Lord said through the prophet Jeremiah, "But the LORD is with me like a dread champion; therefore my persecutors will stumble and not prevail..." (Jer. 20:11). The psalmist wrote, "The LORD is my light and my salvation; whom shall I fear? The LORD is the defense of my life; whom shall I dread?" (Ps. 27:1).

One of the names given to Jesus in the Old Testament is "the Lord of Hosts"; or, we could say, Commander of the Angelic Armies. Second Kings 6:16–17 gives us a glimpse of these angelic hosts:

So he [Elisha] answered, "Do not fear, for those who are with us are more than those who are with them." Then Elisha prayed and said, "O LORD, I pray, open his eyes that he may see." And the LORD opened the servant's eyes, and he saw; and behold, the mountain was full of horses and chariots of fire all around Elisha.

Paul wrote to the church at Colossae, "He [Christ] canceled the record of charges against us and took it away by nailing it to the cross. In this way, he disarmed the spiritual rulers and authorities. He shamed them publicly by his victory over them on the cross" (Col. 2:14–15, NLT). To disarm someone is to take away their weapons. Ephesians 1:22 tells us, "And He [God] put *all things* in subjection under His [Christ's] feet..." (emphasis added). These verses clearly demonstrate the sovereignty of our Lord and His victory at the Cross over the enemy of our souls. He is indeed our Dread Champion and the Commander of the Angelic Armies, those ministering spirits sent out to render service for our sake (Heb. 1:14).

King David, who was a type of Jesus, had thirty-seven "mighty men of valor" in his army who did great exploits of courage because the Lord was with them (cf. 2 Sam. 23:8–39; 1 Chron. 11:10–47). These mighty men were renowned for their strength, fearlessness, and dedication. The Lord is looking for mighty men and women of valor in our day who will not wrestle with flesh and blood, but those who will wrestle in prayer. These "warriors" will take hold together with the Holy Spirit in intercession until the victory is assured, releasing the angelic armies to do warfare with the demonic powers who hold humanity in bondage. (For an excellent description of this kind of intercession, see *Rees Howells: Intercessor*, chapter 9.)

> Lord, open my spiritual eyes to see You as my Dread Champion, the Commander of Angelic Hosts. Give me revelation of what You accomplished at the Cross when You disarmed the principalities and powers in the heavenly realm. And teach me to wrestle in prayer—taking hold together with Your Spirit in intercession—which will release the angelic armies to do warfare on Your behalf.

3:9 "King Solomon has made for Himself a sedan chair from the timber of Lebanon" *[Unidentified speaker]*.

Note that Song 3:7 speaks of the "traveling couch" of King Jesus, while this verse speaks of the "sedan chair" that Jesus made for Himself. In the Hebrew text, these are different words; therefore, they do not symbolize the same thing. The sedan chair (or *palanquin*, NKJV and ASV) referred to in this verse was a portable chair enclosed with curtains that was carried on poles by royal attendants. Its interior was very luxurious and large enough to recline in comfortably. It would have been customary in the ancient world for the king to send his sedan chair to gather the bride-to-be on the day of their wedding.

This royal chair is said to have been constructed of timber from Lebanon. Scripture notes that King Solomon contracted with Hiram king of Tyre to cut down cedars from Lebanon to use in the construction of the temple (cf. 1 Kings 5:1–6). This is significant to this metaphor because the temple housed the presence of God in the holy of holies, which was, of course, a manifestation of the Holy Spirit.

Combining these metaphors, I believe this royal chair, or palanquin, represents the Holy Spirit. It is the Spirit who seals us for the day of redemption (or we could say, the marriage supper of the Lamb): "In Him you also trusted, after you heard the word of truth, the gospel of your salvation; in whom also, having believed, you were sealed with the Holy Spirit of promise, who is the guarantee of our inheritance" (Eph. 1:13–14, NKJV; also cf. 2 Cor. 1:22; Eph. 4:30). *It is the Holy Spirit who seals us and "carries us" to our Bridegroom and the marriage supper of the Lamb.*

The apostle John wrote, "'Let us rejoice and be glad and give glory to Him, for the marriage of the Lamb has come and His bride has made herself ready.' It was given to her to clothe herself in fine linen, bright and clean; for the fine linen is the righteous acts of the saints. Then he said to me, 'Write, "Blessed are those who are invited to the marriage supper of the Lamb..."'" (Rev. 19:7–9). *We are being prepared for a wedding and our Bridegroom, Jesus, has sent a royal chair (symbolizing the Holy Spirit) to transport us to the wedding. He has surrounded this "royal chair" with angelic hosts to ensure that we reach our destination safely.*

> Lord, thank You for sealing me with the Holy Spirit of promise, who is transporting me to the marriage supper of the Lamb. Thank You for surrounding me with Your angelic escorts: those ministering spirits sent to render service for me and to ensure that I reach my destination safely.

3:10 "He made its posts of silver, its back of gold and its seat of purple fabric, with its interior lovingly fitted out by [or 'for'] the daughters of Jerusalem" *[Unidentified speaker].*

King Solomon (symbolizing Jesus) had this royal chair or palanquin constructed with posts of silver, symbolizing redemption (1 Pet. 1:18), and a back of gold, which symbolizes deity (Exodus chapters 25–30). Its seat was upholstered with purple fabric, symbolizing royalty or kingship (Judg. 8:26, Esth. 8:15).

The interior of the royal chair is said to have been lovingly fitted out by the daughters of Jerusalem. The King James Version translates this, "...the midst thereof being paved with love, *for* the daughters of Jerusalem" (emphasis added). I agree with Mike Bickle, who believes the King James Version is the correct translation, because redemption is Jesus's work *for* the daughters, not the daughters' work for Jesus. The Holy Spirit reveals Christ's work of redemption for us (silver for redemption); He is the third person of the Godhead (gold for deity); He is the Spirit of Christ, who is our King (purple for kingship). And finally, it is the Holy Spirit who reveals the love of God to the daughters of Jerusalem and to all those whom the Father calls (Rom. 5:5).

In verses 9 and 10 of this chapter, the Holy Spirit gives a third revelation of Jesus as the Author and Perfecter of our faith—the One who gives us His very own Spirit to carry us to our goal—the marriage supper of the Lamb (cf. Heb. 12:2; Rev. 19:7–9).

> Lord, thank You for giving me the most precious gift of salvation, Your very own Spirit, to live in my heart. He is the third person of the Trinity—fully equal to You and to the Father—He is my Redeemer, and He is my King. Thank You that He is the guarantee of my inheritance until the redemption of Your purchased possession, Your blood-bought bride (Eph. 1:14)!

3:11 "Go forth, O daughters of Zion, and gaze on King Solomon with the crown with which His mother has crowned Him on the day of His wedding, and on the day of His gladness of heart" *[Unidentified speaker].*

The names Zion and Jerusalem are used interchangeably in the Old Testament; however, Zion is technically one of the hills on which Jerusalem stands. David brought the ark to Zion, and Solomon later moved it to the temple on Mt. Moriah; the name Zion was then extended to take in the temple mount. Eventually, the name Zion came to be used for the whole of Jerusalem. In the Song of Songs, the Holy Spirit refers to the "daughters of Jerusalem" in 1:5, 2:7, 3:5, 3:10, 5:8, 5:16, and 8:4; He calls them the "daughters of Zion" in 3:11 only. The Holy Spirit is not indiscriminate in His choice of titles. While "daughters of Jerusalem" refers to immature believers throughout the Song, I believe the title "daughters of Zion" in this verse refers to immature believers (since Zion and Jerusalem came to be used inter-changeably) but also specifically to the remnant of Israel whom the Lord is calling, as I will attempt to demonstrate below. I believe the Holy Spirit is making a point through His choice of titles, reminding His predominantly Gentile church that He has never stopped loving His firstborn children, the Jews, and that He will fulfill every promise made to them in Scripture.

Isaiah 49:5–6 is a Messianic passage, referring to the Lord Jesus as God's Servant: "And now says the LORD, who formed Me from the womb to be His Servant, *to bring Jacob back to Him, so that Israel might be gathered to Him* ... He says, 'It is too small a thing that You should be My Servant to raise up the tribes of Jacob and to restore the preserved ones of Israel; I will also make You a light of [literally "to"] the nations so that My salvation may reach to the end of the earth'" (emphasis added).

Isaiah continues, "But Zion said, 'The LORD has forsaken me, and the Lord has forgotten me.' Can a woman forget her nursing child and have no compassion on the son of her womb? *Even these may forget, but I will not forget you. Behold, I have inscribed you on the palms of My hands; your walls are continually before Me. ... For I will contend with the one who contends with you, and I will save your sons*" (Isa. 49:14–16, 25, emphasis added).

The Lord prophesied again through Isaiah regarding the salvation of Israel, saying:

> ...Loose yourself from the chains around your neck, O cap-tive *daughter of Zion*. For thus says the LORD, "You were sold for nothing and *you will be redeemed* without money." ... But I will reveal my name to my people, and they will come to know its power. Then at last they will recognize that I am the one who speaks to them. How beautiful on the mountains are the feet of the messenger who brings good news, *the good news of peace and salvation*, the news that the God of Israel reigns! ... For the LORD has comforted His people, *He has*

> redeemed Jerusalem... [so] that all the ends of the earth may
> see the salvation of our God.
>
> —ISAIAH 52:2-3, 6-7 (NLT), 9-10, EMPHASIS ADDED

In these verses "daughter of Zion" refers to the Jews who accept their Messiah, who hear the announcement of salvation and receive the good news (cf. Micah 2:12, 7:18-20).

Luke 23:28 is the only reference to the daughters of Jerusalem in the New Testament. Jesus was being led to Golgotha after Pilate pronounced His sentence, granting the Jews' request to release Barabbas instead of Him. Following the Lord was a great crowd of people, including women, who were mourning over Pilate's decision. "But Jesus turned and said to them, 'Daughters of Jerusalem, don't weep for me, but weep for yourselves and for your children. For the days are coming when they will say, 'Fortunate indeed are the women who are childless, the wombs that have not borne a child and the breasts that have never nursed.' People will beg the mountains, 'Fall on us,' and plead with the hills, 'Bury us.' For if these things are done when the tree is green, what will happen when it is dry?'" (Luke 23:28-31, NLT). The significant point is that *Jesus called "daughters of Jerusalem" the women who had accepted Him as their Messiah!* The daughters of Jerusalem in this New Testament account were the women following Jesus, weeping because of the sentence pronounced by Pilate that He be crucified. They represent the remnant of Jews who accepted their Messiah at His first coming.

Therefore, I believe the titles "daughters of Zion" and "daughters of Jerusalem" in the Song include the remnant of Israel, those whom the Lord will call through the witness of the true church. The daughters are watching the maiden throughout the Song and are usually portrayed as interested bystanders. This is certainly true for the Jews whom the Lord is calling into His kingdom. Whether we realize it or not, they are observing our lives and must see in us a love that is willing to sacrifice for the sake of the ones loved, following the example of their Messiah. Rick Joyner has said:

The Lord made the Jew the greatest test of whether or not we are preaching a true gospel. *Only the true gospel will move the Jews to jealousy as it was commissioned to do. The ability of our gospel to move the Jew is the acid test meant to determine if we are preaching the undiluted truth.*[1]

Repeating 3:11:

"Go forth, O daughters of Zion, and gaze on King Solomon with the crown with which His mother has crowned Him on the day of His wedding, and on the day of His gladness of heart" [Unidentified speaker].

In the ancient Near Eastern culture, the bridegroom would dress himself in festive garments and wear a crown of gold, silver, or flowers presented to him by his mother on the day of his wedding. In the verse before us, *the Holy Spirit is exhorting the daughters of Zion to go out and behold King Jesus wearing His royal crown on the day of His wedding.* The royal crown is said to be given to Jesus by "his mother," which often symbolizes the church in Scripture. However, the church does not give Jesus the authority to rule and reign (symbolized by the crown), the Father does. Therefore, "his mother" is symbolic of God in this verse. God is portrayed with *both* motherly and fatherly qualities throughout the Scripture (cf. Ps. 91:4, Isa. 66:10–13; 46:3–4, etc.).

"The day of his wedding" and "the day of His gladness of heart" is once more referring to the marriage supper of the Lamb spoken of in Revelation 19. This is the glorious future day when we will see Him as He truly is, when every tear will be wiped away and there will be no more death or pain, and Jesus will be given His inheritance— us—His bride, those who have made themselves ready and clothed themselves in fine linen, which is the righteous acts of the saints (Rev. 19:7–9). *While this is yet future, we are told to set the eyes of our heart on eternal things.* Paul wrote to the church at Corinth, "Since we consider and look not to the things that are seen but to the things that are unseen; for the things that are visible are

temporal (brief and fleeting), but the things that are invisible are deathless and everlasting" (2 Cor. 4:18, AMP). *It is this conscious setting of the eyes of our hearts on the everlasting (or eternal) things which enables us to walk worthy of our calling* (cf. Eph. 4:1, Col. 1:10, 1 Thess. 2:12). *As we cultivate this "eternal perspective" we will even begin to rejoice in our trials, which are allowed to help keep us on the path of life.* This is what the apostle Paul was alluding to when he wrote, "For I consider that the sufferings of this present time are not worthy to be compared with the glory that is to be revealed to us" (Rom. 8:18).

The fourth and final revelation of Jesus in this passage of Scripture is the sovereign Bridegroom King. The Lord Jesus is a sovereign King because He possesses absolute power and authority (cf. Eph. 1:20–22, Col. 2:9–10). Yet at the same time, He is a Bridegroom who is lovesick for us, His bride! The prophet Isaiah wrote, "...As the bridegroom rejoices over the bride, so your God will rejoice over you (Isa. 62:5). Hosea wrote, "'It will come about in that day,' declares the Lord, 'That you will call Me Ishi [my husband] and will no longer call Me Baali [my master]....I will betroth you to Me forever; yes, I will betroth you to Me in righteousness and in justice, in lovingkindness and in compassion, and I will betroth you to Me in faithfulness. Then you will know the Lord'" (Hos. 2:16, 19–20). The apostle John wrote, "He who has the bride is the bridegroom; but the friend of the bridegroom, who stands and *hears Him*, rejoices greatly because of the bridegroom's voice..." (John 3:29, emphasis added). Our Bridegroom not only rejoices over us and betroths us to Himself forever, He shares His heart with us as we listen for His voice! He is the blessed and only Sovereign, our passionate Bridegroom, and our glorious King, the supreme Ruler of the universes, who is worthy of all glory and honor and praise forever!

> Lord, please open the eyes of my heart to see You as my Bridegroom King. You are a Bridegroom who rejoices over me, who sent Your Spirit to carry me to the marriage supper of the Lamb. But You are also my

King, the One who possesses all power and authority—the One to which every knee will eventually bow. I also ask You for revelation concerning the "one new man" You desire as Your bride. Please impart to me Your heart for Your people Israel, and cause Your love in me to draw them to their Messiah.

Chapter 4

THE LORD'S RAVISHED
HEART FOR HIS BRIDE

4:1 "How beautiful you are, My darling, how beautiful you are!
Your eyes are like doves behind your veil; your hair is like a
flock of goats that have descended from Mount Gilead" *[Bride-
groom speaking].*

THE HOLY SPIRIT has just finished His stunning description of
four distinct aspects of the Lord's character that will stabilize the
maiden's heart in the trials ahead. Suddenly the speaker changes and
the Lord Himself begins to speak, revealing to the maiden what He
sees when He looks at her heart. He exclaims, "How beautiful you
are!" and then repeats His compliment for emphasis. First Samuel
16:7 reminds us, "...For the LORD does not see as man sees; for man
looks at the outward appearance, but the LORD looks at the heart"
(NKJV). The Lord sees the maiden's heart and the budding virtues
there which will one day be in full bloom as He walks with her
through the sanctification process and conforms her to His image.
*He sees her as a father sees the child he adores. Even though a father
knows his child's character flaws and sins, those things can never
diminish his love for his child. So it is with the Lord. Although He
sees the sin areas in our lives, He loves us just as much* now *as He
will love us when we are fully mature.*

The Lord speaks first of the maiden's eyes and compares them to
dove's eyes. As mentioned before, doves are extremely loyal to their
mate. If their partner dies, they will not seek another mate. Since
they have no peripheral vision, their eyes are in single focus on the
object of their vision.

A veil symbolizes modesty, thus the phrase "behind your veil" speaks of the maiden's modest or humble behavior. When Rebekah met Isaac for the first time, "she took her veil and covered herself" (Gen. 24:65). A veil also conveys the idea that however attractive physical appearances may be, the soul and character are paramount. *The Lord is commending the maiden in this verse for the single focus of her eyes, her loyalty and devotion to Him alone, and for her modest and humble behavior.*

> "...your hair is like a flock of goats that have descended from Mount Gilead."

The Lord compares the maiden's hair to a flock of goats who have descended the mountain after feeding at the famous pastures of Mount Gilead. The goats of that region were renowned for their shiny black hair due to the superior pastures found on the mountain. Hair in the Scripture is associated with God-given strength, as in the life of Samson (Judges chapters 13–16), and with the Nazirite vow (Numbers chapter 6).

The angel of the Lord (or preincarnate Christ) appeared to Samson's mother, who was barren, and told her that the child she would bear would be a Nazirite to God from the womb and that no razor would come upon his head (Judg. 13:3–5). Because of Samson's dedication to God from birth, "the Spirit of the Lord would come upon him mightily" when he encountered certain situations, and he was given supernatural strength over his enemies (cf. Judg. 14:6, 19; 15:14).

A Nazirite was an Israelite who took a vow of separation and self-imposed abstinence for the purpose of dedicating himself or herself to the Lord. The word Nazirite means "separated" or more specifically, "one who is separated unto the Lord." The regulatory laws for the vow of a Nazirite are found in Numbers 6:1–23. Three principal marks distinguished a Nazarite: 1) a renunciation of wine and all products of the vine, including grapes; 2) prohibition of the use of a razor (the hair could not be cut during the prescribed time of the vow); and 3) avoidance of contact with a dead body. While the Nazirite vow seems odd to our modern minds, as does much of the ritual prescribed by the Law, there is significance if we search for it. God does not require His people to do things that have no purpose or meaning. We know the Old Testament has many types and shadows that are fulfilled in the New Testament (cf. Col. 2:16–17, Heb. 10:1). With this in mind, I asked the Holy Spirit to teach me about the Nazarite vow. This is what He said (taken from my journal):

The Nazirite vow was a set time when one of My children consecrated themselves to Me. The word consecrate means to set aside for sacred use. It was a period of drawing close to Me under the old covenant by denying the flesh. Each of the stipulations had deep symbolic meaning, which are actually fulfilled in the new covenant through the indwelling Spirit as one learns to abide in Me. The prohibition of wine or any product of the vine was a statement of complete dependence on Me. As I said in John 15, I am the true Vine and My desire is that My children "abide"—gain their life and all that sustains them—in Me. Refusing to partake of the fruit of the natural vine symbolized dependence on Me, the true Vine. My Word also says that wine makes the heart glad. An even deeper joy can be found in remaining united to Me, the true Vine. Nothing pleases My heart more than when My children find their joy in Me, rather than seeking it from worldly things that have no eternal value. The prohibition of the use of a razor symbolized dependence on My strength vs. reliance on human strength. As long as Samson's hair was not cut (no razor touched his head), he walked in the supernatural strength of My Spirit. A razor, or metal, symbolizes man's strength and ingenuity. This requirement of the vow was a statement of dependence on My strength and ingenuity rather than natural human strength and ingenuity. The prohibition regarding going near a dead body was symbolic of drawing life only from Me. This is eternal life, that they may know My Father and I through the indwelling Spirit. Eternal life is not a future event, it is a present tense relationship with Me through My Spirit. The specific commandment that even if a family member died the vow was not to be broken was meant to show that the most important relationship you have in this life is with Me. It supersedes even love for parents and family. Did I not say to the one desiring to follow Me, "Let the dead bury their own dead?"

The Lord also reminded me of the verse in 1 Kings 6:7 that says, "And the temple, when it was being built, was built with stone finished at the quarry, so that no hammer or chisel or any iron tool was heard in the temple while it was being built" (NKJV). Iron was used to make both a razor and the tools to finish the stone for the temple. In both cases iron represents reliance on man's strength and ingenuity, in contrast to reliance on God's strength and ingenuity.

The Lord speaks of the maiden's hair as being beautiful and shiny, symbolizing the dedication of her heart to Him and her desire to minister to others with the wisdom and strength that He provides, not her own wisdom and strength.

> Lord, open my heart to believe that You love me in my immaturity and weakness just as much as You will love me when I am fully mature. You see me just as a father sees the child he adores. Make me secure in this amazing truth so I will run to You, not from You, when I fall into sin. Give me spiritual eyes in single focus on You and Your kingdom, and teach me to remain united to You, the True Vine, drawing my life and strength from You.

4:2 "Your teeth are like a flock of newly shorn ewes which have come up from their washing, all of which bear twins, and not one among them has lost her young" *[Bridegroom speaking].*

This verse is rich with symbolism. Teeth are used for chewing and symbolize long and loving meditation on the meat of God's Word. The Lord first compares the maiden's teeth to a flock of newly shorn ewes, or female sheep. When sheep are shorn, their wool is removed using a sharp-edged instrument or shears. The sheep become, in a sense, "naked." Thus, *the Lord is commending the maiden's determination to shed her preconceived ideas and biases as she approaches God's Word in order to discover the true meaning of the text.* A. W. Tozer spoke to this truth in *The Knowledge of the Holy*:

The scholar has a vitally important task to perform within a carefully prescribed precinct. His task is to guarantee the purity of the text, to get as close as possible to the Word as originally given. He may compare Scripture with Scripture until he has discovered the true meaning of the text. But right there his authority ends....*After the meaning is discovered, that meaning judges him; never does He judge it.*[1]

The Lord also compares the maiden's teeth to ewes that have born twins. Since sheep normally bear only one offspring, *this metaphor refers to her reproductive ability, i.e., her ability to draw others into the kingdom and to disciple them so that they are able to assimilate the meat of God's Word and do not remain "babes in Christ," or fleshly believers* (cf. 1 Cor. 3:1–3).

Finally, the Lord compares her teeth to sheep that have just come up from their washing. In Ephesians 5:26 Paul tells us that the Lord sanctifies and cleanses us by washing with the water of the Word. *The Lord is commending the maiden for her faithfulness to first submit her heart and actions to the washing of His Word before she teaches others.* She does not want to teach others to do what she herself is not doing, being mindful of James's warning: "My brethren, let not many of you become teachers, knowing that we shall receive a stricter judgment" (James 3:1, NKJV).

> Lord, I want to practice the discipline of long and loving meditation on the meat of Your Word. Help me lay aside my preconceived ideas and biases as I approach Your Word so that I can discover the true meaning of the text. Help me submit my own heart and actions to the washing of Your Word before I teach others. And help me look to the Holy Spirit as my Teacher, Lord. You promised He would teach me and bring to my remembrance all that You said to me in Your Word. Help me train those I disciple to do this as well, so they will grow up to be mature believers able to digest the meat of Your Word.

4:3 "Your lips are like a scarlet thread, and your mouth is lovely. Your temples are like a slice of pomegranate behind your veil" *[Bridegroom speaking].*

The color scarlet is used many places in the Scripture to symbolize redemption. The Lord spoke through the prophet Isaiah, "'Come now, and let us reason together,' says the LORD, 'Though your sins are as scarlet, they will be white as snow; though they are red like crimson, they will be like wool'" (Isa. 1:18).

Joshua chapter 2 also points to scarlet as a symbol of redemption. It gives the account of Rahab the prostitute, who gave shelter to the spies sent to view the land of Canaan. She made them vow that they would not harm her or her family when they returned to conquer the land in exchange for hiding them from the king of Jericho, who wanted to kill them. The spies gave her a cord of scarlet thread as a sign and told her to tie it in her window. When they returned to conquer Jericho, they promised they would "pass over" her home, not harming anyone in her family when they saw the scarlet thread.

The writer of Hebrews explained, "For after Moses had read each of God's commandments to all the people, he took the blood of calves and goats, along with water, and sprinkled both the book of God's law and all the people, using hyssop branches and scarlet wool. Then he said, 'This blood confirms the covenant God has made with you.' And in the same way, he sprinkled blood on the Tabernacle and on everything used for worship. In fact, according to the law of Moses, nearly everything was purified with blood. For without the shedding of blood, there is no forgiveness" (Heb. 9:19–22, NLT). We know, of course, that the blood of Jesus is the fulfillment of this type and shadow in the Old Testament. Only the blood of the spotless Lamb of God can make our sins, which are as wool dyed scarlet, become as pure and white as snow or natural wool. Wool dyed scarlet speaks of fallen man; wool that is pure and white speaks of man redeemed by the blood of the Lamb, the "new creation" Paul spoke of in his letter to the Corinthians: "Therefore, if anyone is in Christ, he is a new creation; old things have passed away; behold, all things have become new" (2 Cor. 5:17, NKJV).

"You lips are like a scarlet thread" speaks of her words which have been influenced by redemption. James wrote, "…If anyone does not stumble in what he says, he is a perfect man, able to bridle the whole body as well," and "If anyone thinks himself to be religious, and yet does not bridle his tongue but deceives his own heart, this man's religion is worthless" (James 3:2 and 1:26). Paul wrote to the church at Ephesus, "Don't let words come out of your mouth that are corrupted by evil motives (for example judgment or superiority), but only speak words that promote the spiritual growth of others, according to the need of the moment, so that you may extend God's grace (unearned and undeserved favor) to those who hear you" (Eph. 4:29, my personal translation combining the New American Standard and Wuest translations of the New Testament).

Mike Bickle has said, "Godly speech is the final frontier of deep spirituality." *The Lord is commending the maiden's godly speech in this verse and her desire to speak only what is pleasing to Him in obedience to His Word.*

"…Your temples are like a slice of pomegranate behind your veil."

The temples are the area between the eyes and the hairline on either side of the forehead. They represent the thought life, since this is where the organ of thought—the brain—is located. Jewish tradition teaches that the pomegranate is a symbol for righteousness because it is said to have 613 seeds, which corresponds to the 613 mitzvot or commandments of the Torah. *Combining these metaphors, the Lord is commending the maiden for the control she has over her thought life. She is learning to walk in His righteous ways, even in her thought life, which is the key to every other area of her life.*

The apostle Paul had much to say about our thought life. He exhorted us to bring every thought captive to the obedience of Christ (2 Cor. 10:5) and to set our minds on what the Spirit desires (Rom. 8:5; cf. Rom. 12:2, Eph. 4:22–23, Col. 3:2). Every sin we commit starts as a thought. If we allow a thought regarding some sinful action to germinate, it will eventually give birth to sin. But if we take those thoughts captive, refusing to allow them to grow and replacing them with the truth of God's Word, we can learn to walk in His righteous ways.

> Lord, I commit to set my mind on the things of Your Spirit. Help me learn to take every thought captive: to make my thoughts obedient to You and to Your Word. Sanctify my speech, Lord, and teach me to bridle my tongue so that I only speak words that promote the spiritual growth of others.

4:4 "Your neck is like the tower of David, built with rows of stones on which are hung a thousand shields, all the round shields of the mighty men" *[Bridegroom speaking].*

The neck in Scripture symbolizes the will. Throughout Scripture, when the Lord rebuked His people for their stubbornness and resistance to His will (or disobedience to His commandments), He called them "stiff necked" (cf. Deut. 31:27, 2 Chron. 36:13, Prov. 29:1, Isa. 48:4, Jer. 7:26, 17:23). By contrast, the Greek word for bond-servant in the New Testament means one who is in a permanent relation of servitude to another, his will altogether consumed in the will of the other. The Lord Jesus, Paul, Peter, James, Jude, and Epaphras are all spoken of as bond-servants in the New Testament (Phil. 2:7; Rom. 1:1; 2 Pet. 1:1; James 1:1; Jude 1; Col. 4:12).

The tower of David was a lofty stronghold or inner fort strategically built into the wall surrounding Jerusalem. Its purpose was to provide a place for watchmen who guarded the city to distinguish whether those approaching were enemies or friends but more importantly, as fortification for the defense of the city.

The New King James version translates this verse, "Your neck is like the tower of David, built for an armory, on which hang a thousand bucklers, all shields of mighty men." An armory was a storehouse for weapons; a buckler was a small, round shield held by a handle or worn on the arm. The tower fortress of David would have included an armory housing weapons, including the shields of David's mighty men. The apostle Paul described our spiritual armor in his letter to the Ephesians: "Put on the whole armor of God, that you may be able to stand against the wiles of the devil. For we do not wrestle against flesh and blood, but against principalities, against powers, against the rulers of the darkness of this age, against spiritual hosts of wickedness in the heavenly places...Stand therefore, having girded your waist with truth, having put on the breastplate of righteousness, and having shod your feet with the preparation of the gospel of peace; above all, taking the shield of faith with which you will be able to quench all the fiery darts of the wicked one. And take the helmet of salvation, and the sword of the Spirit, which is the Word of God" (Eph. 6:11–17, NKJV). Paul also referenced the weapons of our righteousness in his letter to the church at Corinth, "...We use the weapons of righteousness in the right hand for attack and the left hand for defense" (2 Cor. 6:7, NLT).

Combining these metaphors, the Lord is commending the maiden for her resolute will, which is conformed to His will, and her growing authority in the spiritual realm as one who is learning to use the shield of faith, the weapons of righteousness, and the sword of the Spirit—the Word of God.

> Lord, I ask You to conform my will to Your will so that I will become Your bond-servant. Give me revelation of the authority You purchased for me at the Cross, and teach me to skillfully use the shield of faith, the weapons of righteousness, and the sword of Your Spirit.

4:5 "Your two breasts are like two fawns, twins of a gazelle which feed among the lilies" *[Bridegroom speaking].*

The breast symbolizes the ability to feed and nurture others. *The Lord is commending the maiden in this verse for her skill in training the younger disciples in the ways of His kingdom.* Song 2:16 says, "...He [the Lord] pastures his flock among the lilies," meaning *He feeds His sheep where there is purity of heart. The lily is a symbol of purity and in this metaphor refers to the heart that is without guile.* Because the maiden's heart is pure (free from false motives) the Lord is able to teach her from the rich storehouse of His Word. She is not approaching the Scripture wearing "colored glasses," i.e., teaching which forces the Word of God to conform to a particular theological "box."

"Your two breasts are like two fawns, twins of a gazelle…"

I believe this verse also points to a somewhat cryptic statement Jesus made that is recorded in the Gospel of Matthew: "…Therefore every teacher and interpreter of the Sacred Writings who has been instructed about and trained for the kingdom of heaven and has become a disciple is like a householder who brings forth out of his storehouse *treasure that is new* and *[treasure that is] old*…" (Matt. 13:52, AMP, emphasis added). In this statement, Jesus was looking ahead and referring to the truth contained in both the "Old Testament" and the "New Testament," which of course had not yet been written. He was saying that those who are instructed about the kingdom of God embrace and teach the truth of the entire counsel of Scripture, knowing that the "new" covenant does not *replace* the "old" covenant in the economy of God but is actually a *fulfillment* of it. Jesus said, "Don't misunderstand why I have come. I did not come to abolish the law of Moses or the writing of the prophets [what we know as the Old Testament]. No, I came to accomplish their purpose" (Matt. 5:17, NLT, emphasis added). Some in the church today seem to ignore the first part of Jesus's statement. He clearly said that He did not come to abolish (to put an end to, to make null and void) the law of Moses or the writing of the prophets. Instead, He came to accomplish (to succeed in doing) their purpose. In other words, *He came to model the "new covenant" for us*. He lived His earthly life as a perfect Man, in complete dependence on the Holy Spirit.

O. Palmer Robertson writes:

> The cumulative evidence of the Scriptures points definitely toward the unified character of the biblical covenants. God's multiple bonds with His people ultimately unite into a single relationship. Particular details of the covenants may vary. A definite line of progress may be noted. Yet the covenants of God are one.… The Abrahamic, Mosaic, and Davidic covenants

do not present themselves as self-contained entities. Instead, each successive covenant builds on the previous relationship, continuing the basic emphasis which had been established earlier.... *Instead of "wiping the slate clean" and beginning anew, each successive covenant with Abraham's descendants advanced the original purposes of God to a higher level of realization.... The new covenant, promised by Israel's prophets, does not appear as a distinctive covenantal unit unrelated to God's previous administrations. Instead, the new covenant as promised to Israel represents the consummate fulfillment of the earlier covenants"* (emphasis added).[2]

The Lord spoke through the prophet Jeremiah, "'But this is the covenant which I will make with the house of Israel after those days,' declares the LORD, 'I will put My law within them and on their heart I will write it; and I will be their God, and they shall be My people'" (Jer. 31:33). This is the "new" covenant, the *fulfillment* of God's earlier covenants to the nation of Israel! How would the Lord put His law within His people and write it on their hearts? Through the Person of the indwelling Holy Spirit! Paul confirmed this truth in his letter to the church at Galatia: "Christ redeemed us from the curse of the Law [or the curse resulting from not obeying the Law—see Gal. 3:10 and Deut. 27:26]...in order that...the blessing of Abraham might come to the Gentiles, *so that we might receive the promise of the Spirit through faith*" (Gal. 3:13–14, emphasis added). What was the blessing of Abraham referenced in this verse? Paul says it was the promise of the Holy Spirit! The Abrahamic covenant given by God to Abraham (Gen. 12:1–3, 22:16–18) states that in Abraham all the families of the earth would be blessed and that Abraham's seed (Christ) would possess the gate of His enemies. (Paul makes it clear that this "seed" was Christ: "Now the promises were spoken to Abraham and to his seed. He does not say, 'And to seeds,' as referring to many, but rather to one, 'And to your seed,' that is, Christ" [Gal. 3:16]). Paul continued his explanation to the Galatians, reminding them that "...the Law, which came four hundred and thirty years later, does not invalidate a covenant previously ratified by God, so as to nullify *the promise*" (Gal. 3:17, emphasis added). He states that the Law was given because of sin "*until the seed would come to whom the promise had been made*" (Gal. 3:19, emphasis added). This Seed, Christ, was given to us in the fullness of God's time, accomplished His work of redemption, ascended to the Father, and then poured out the promised Holy Spirit, the One who enables us to keep the Law. Paul continued in his letter to the church at Galatia, "...the Law has become our tutor to lead us to Christ..." (Gal. 3:24). *The purpose of the Law was to show us our utter inability to keep it on our own. In this way, it served as a tutor* (Greek *paidagogos*, a teacher of children) *pointing us to Christ and our need of the Holy Spirit.*

Paul wrote to the church at Rome, "For what the Law could not do, weak as it was through the flesh, God did: sending His own Son in the likeness of sinful flesh and as an offering for sin, He condemned [deprived of strength] sin in the flesh, *so that the requirement of the Law might be fulfilled in us, who do not walk according to the flesh but according to the Spirit*" (Rom. 8:3–4, emphasis added). *Paul asked these same Christians, "Do we then nullify the Law through faith? May it never be! On the contrary, we establish [or demonstrate] the Law*" (Rom. 3:31, emphasis added). The New Living Translation crystallizes this verse for our modern minds: "Well then, if we emphasize faith, does this mean that we can forget about the law? Of course not! In fact, *only when we have faith do we truly fulfill the law*" (Rom. 3:31, NLT, emphasis added).

When Jesus was asked by a Pharisee which was the great commandment in the Law, He replied, "'You must love the Lord your God with all your heart, all your soul, and all your mind.' This is the first and greatest commandment. A second is like it: 'Love your neighbor as yourself.' The entire law and all the demands of the prophets are based on these two commandments" (Matt. 22:37–40 combining the New Living and New American Standard translations). The ancient rabbis isolated 613 separate commandments in the entire Law of Moses, but the Ten Commandments are the principles upon which the rest are based. (The Holy Spirit called the Ten Commandments the "words of the covenant" in Exodus 34:28; the remaining laws were "ordinances" according to Exodus 21:1, meaning any aspect of civil or religious government.) Jesus took what started out as 613 commandments, which were summed up in ten in the Law of Moses, and reduced them to two. All of God's commandments under the old covenant as to how His people should live may be abbreviated simply as to have love for God and love for man. This is what Paul also taught regarding love for our fellow man when he said, "Owe nothing to anyone except to love one another; for he who loves his neighbor has fulfilled the law...Love does no wrong to a neighbor; therefore love is the fulfillment of the law" (Rom. 13:8, 10).

Jesus (our example) fully performed the Law, but not as the Son of God. Philippians 2:7 tells us that He emptied Himself of His divine privileges and took the form of a bond-servant, being born as a man. Instead, Jesus fully performed the Law as *a man dependent on the Holy Spirit*. We too are to fulfill the Law (which Jesus boiled down to loving God and loving people) as men and women who "walk according to the Spirit," or as the New Living Translation renders it, *those who no longer follow our sinful nature but instead follow the Spirit* (Rom. 8:4, NLT).

It is important to note that the Holy Spirit defines God's covenant with man in the Scripture as an everlasting or eternal covenant. He said through the prophet Jeremiah, "The earth is also polluted by its inhabitants, for they transgressed laws, violated statutes, broke the *everlasting covenant*" (Isa. 24:5, emphasis added). The Holy Spirit also said in the New Testament, through the writer of the letter to the Hebrews, "Now the God of peace, that brought again from the dead our Lord Jesus, that great shepherd of the sheep, *through the blood of the everlasting covenant*" (Heb. 13:20, KJV, emphasis added). This is not semantics as some would argue. It is critical to our understanding as there is much false teaching in the church today because of this forced dichotomy between the "old" and "new" covenants. Some in the church promote "replacement theology," which asserts that the church has replaced Israel in the purposes of God rather than being grafted in among the Jews and becoming a partaker *with them* of the rich root of the olive tree, as Paul explained so clearly in his letter to the church at Rome. Paul asked, "Did God's people stumble and fall beyond recovery?" and then answered his own question emphatically, "Of course not! They were disobedient, so God made salvation available to the Gentiles. *But he wanted his own people to become jealous and claim it for themselves.* Now if the Gentiles were enriched because the people of Israel turned down God's offer of salvation, think how much greater a blessing the world will share when they finally accept it" (Rom. 11:11–12, NLT, emphasis added). The church has not replaced Israel in the purposes of God, we have been grafted into their rich olive tree! Paul continued in his letter to the church at Rome, "But if some of the branches [unbelieving Jews] were broken off, and you, being a wild olive, were grafted in among them and *became partaker with them* of the rich root of the olive tree [Messiah], do not be arrogant toward the branches; but if you are arrogant, remember that it is not you who supports the root, but the root supports you" (Rom. 11:17–18, emphasis added; cf. Rev. 5:5, 22:16).

Paul also addressed this issue of the church being grafted in among the Jews in his letter to the church at Ephesus, calling it "...the mystery of Christ, which in other generations was not made known to the sons of men...to be specific, that the Gentiles are *fellow heirs* and *fellow members of the body,* and *fellow partakers of the promise [the Holy Spirit] in Christ Jesus through the gospel*" (Eph. 3:4–6, emphasis added). (It is important to note that the Greek word for "mystery" is *musterion* and means a sacred thing hidden or secret which is naturally unknown to human reason and is only known by the revelation of God. In the ordinary sense a mystery implies knowledge withheld; its scriptural significance is *truth revealed*.) Especially in light of Paul's teaching in Romans chapter 11 referenced above, doesn't it seem like we in the church have gotten it backwards at best? Do we see ourselves in this way—as fellow heirs with the Jews and partakers with them of the rich root of the olive tree (Christ)—or have we substituted our "precepts of men" for the truth that Paul so clearly taught that through the Cross, Jews and Gentiles have become "one new man" (cf. Matt. 15:9, Eph. 2:11–18)?

In like manner, other streams in the body of Christ have adopted alternate brands of theology which, in effect, completely discount the Old Testament. (Old "covenant" is the more accurate translation of the Greek word *diatheke* rendered "testament" in our Bibles.) They teach that what Jesus accomplished on the cross completely supersedes and renders obsolete the Old Testament (i.e., Old "Covenant"). An example of this forced dichotomy between the "old" and "new" covenants is the teaching that God no longer judges us because of what Jesus did on the cross, that Jesus fully absorbed the wrath of God toward man until the final day or the "great and terrible day of the Lord." This teaching presumes that God dealt with His people one way under the "old" covenant and deals with them in a completely different way under the "new" covenant, because we are under the "rule of grace." One pastor wrote to me, "Jesus bore our sins and all of God's wrath against them (citing John 12:32 to substantiate this claim). And this doesn't only apply to believers. First John 2:2 says Jesus, 'is the propitiation for our sins: and not for ours only, but also for the sins of the whole world.' So, God isn't personally judging nations today for their sins." I believe this is an example of scriptural presumption: of adding to or going beyond the written Word of God.

Another trend in the body of Christ is the "hyper grace" message, or what Dietrich Bonhoeffer called "cheap grace." Paul warned of this in his letter to Timothy, "For a time is coming when people will no longer listen to sound and wholesome teaching. They will follow their own desires and will look for teachers who will tell them whatever their itching ears want to hear" (2 Tim. 4:3, NLT). These people ask, "If God is good and a God of love, how can He bring judgment?" It's really the other way around—if God did not judge what is evil, He could not be good. *Love must oppose what is evil. And yet the message of the Bible is that this same Love put Himself in the place of those being judged in order to open the way for them to be restored to fellowship with God.* I love what Derek Prince wrote in this regard: "Christians who question the reality of God's judgment on sin should ponder afresh the significance of the crucifixion. Even Jesus could not make sin acceptable to God, but had to endure the full outpouring of His wrath."[3]

"Your two breasts are like two fawns, twins of a gazelle which feed among the lilies."

The Lord is commending the maiden in this verse for feeding from the rich truth of His Word, both old and new covenants (or what the Holy Spirit calls the "eternal covenant"), and then passing on those gems of truth and wisdom to those she disciples. She is becoming a disciple of the kingdom who brings forth, out the storehouse of her heart, treasure that is "old" and treasure that is "new" (Matt. 13:52).

> Lord, give me a pure heart, one that is free from false motives, so that You can feed me from the rich storehouse of your Word, Your eternal covenant. Make me a disciple of the kingdom who is able to bring forth out of the storehouse of my heart treasure that is "old" and treasure that is "new." Equip me to disciple those You assign to me, and help me lead them to You, the living Truth.

4:6 "Until the cool of the day when the shadows flee away, I will go my way to the mountain of myrrh and to the hill of frankincense" *[Bride speaking].*

The Lord has just used glowing words to tell the maiden how lovely she is in His eyes, taking great care to acknowledge and to bless the budding virtues He sees in her heart. He has commended her loyalty and devotion (eyes, Song 4:1); consecration and reliance on His strength, not her own (hair, Song 4:1); spiritual capacity to receive the meat of God's Word and to nourish new disciples (teeth, Song 4:2); godly speech (lips, Song 4:3); righteousness even in her thought life (temples, Song 4:3); resolute will and authority in the Spirit (neck, Song 4:4); and skill in drawing out the deep truths of His Word and in nurturing younger disciples (breasts, Song 4:5).

As a result of the Lord's loving patience and words of encouragement, the maiden's heart has been opened to believe His love for her on a deeper level. As a result, she now resolves to go with Him in service, regardless of what it might cost her. She would rather be with Him—even serving in difficult obscure places if He calls her there—than have a life of ease without Him. The psalmist wrote, "For a day in Your courts is better than a thousand outside. I would rather stand at the threshold of the house of my God than dwell in the tents of wickedness" (Ps. 84:10).

In the verse before us, the maiden tells the Lord that she is now willing to go to the mountain of myrrh and to the hill of frankincense. *The mountain of myrrh symbolizes death to our self-life and the sacrifice of service when it is costly and difficult.* Myrrh was an ingredient used by the Jews to embalm a dead body. John 19:39 tells us that Nicodemus anointed Jesus's body with myrrh and aloes before His burial. Therefore, myrrh in this context speaks of the Cross, the death to our self-life, which alone enables us to bear "much fruit." Jesus alluded to this truth when He said, "...Unless a grain of wheat falls into the earth and dies, it remains alone; but if it dies, it bears much fruit" (John 12:24).

Paul wrote to the church at Corinth that we are "always carrying about in the body the dying of Jesus, so that the life of Jesus also may be manifested in our body. For we who live are constantly being delivered over to death [of self] for Jesus's sake, so that the life of Jesus also may be manifested in our mortal flesh. So death works in us, but life in you" (2 Cor. 4:10–12). In other words, as Paul embraced the Cross and died to his self-life (as a grain of wheat falls into the earth and dies), the *resurrection life of Christ* flowed through him producing much fruit in the church (cf. Col. 2:11–13).

Paul wrote to the church at Rome, "We were buried therefore with Him [Christ] by the baptism into death, so that just as Christ was raised from the dead by the glorious [power] of the Father, so we too might [habitually] live and behave in newness of life. For if we have become one with Him by sharing a death like His, we shall also be [one with Him in sharing] His resurrection [by a new life lived for God]" (Rom. 6:4–5, AMP). L. E. Maxwell crystallized the essence of these verses when he wrote:

> There must be a living participation by the Spirit through a new death to self. I cannot draw upon the life of the Crucified

without admitting a new vital fellowship with Him in His death. *I have the new life as I refuse the old—at the Cross.*[4]

"...I will go my way to the mountain of myrrh and to the hill of frankincense."

As stated earlier, *frankincense was an ingredient used in the incense for the temple; therefore, it speaks of the priestly ministry of intercession.* The apostle John saw the four living creatures and the twenty four elders falling down before Jesus, each holding golden bowls full of incense, which are the prayers of the saints (Rev. 5:8). Exodus 30:34–38 recounts the Lord's instructions to Moses regarding the fashioning of the incense for the temple. This was so important to the Lord that He stipulated that if the ingredients for incense were mixed in the same proportions as the temple incense but used in a secular way, the offending person would be cut off from his people (meaning either exiled or put to death). In the New Testament, Revelation 5:8 and 8:3–4 both speak of incense in conjunction with the prayers of the saints. *The maiden is saying that she will not only go with Him in the costly way of service to others (the mountain of myrrh), but she will follow Him in the service of intercession (the hill of frankincense). She understands that without the preparation of hearts through prayer, the seed of the Word will fall beside the road, on rocky places, or among thorns; in other words, it will fail to produce fruit in the lives of those she serves* (cf. Matt. 13:3–9, 18–23).

Mike Bickle has said, "Our prayer life empowers our soul to embrace the cross in self-denial." Therefore, the intercession portrayed in this metaphor is actually twofold: the Holy Spirit prays through us and *for us* so that we can "embrace the cross" in self-denial, and we pray in agreement with the Spirit *for others* that their hearts would be prepared to receive the seed of His Word.

> Lord, help me go with You to the hill of frankincense—the place of intercession—to prepare the hearts of those I serve. Cause Your Spirit to pray through me for others but also for me, so I can embrace the cross in self-denial. As I do this, pour Your resurrection life into me and

strengthen me to go to the mountain of myrrh—the place of service—
even when it is costly and difficult.

4:7 "You are altogether beautiful, My darling, and there is no
blemish in you" *[Bridegroom speaking]*.

The Lord affirms the maiden once more, declaring she is "altogether beautiful"; or, we could say, "wholly or completely beautiful."
He emphasizes this statement by adding, "there is no blemish in
you." As Mike Bickle says, this does not mean that she is without
sin; instead, *He is defining her in terms of her willing spirit, not in
terms of her weak flesh.*

> Lord, open my heart to believe that You see the desire of my heart to
> please You. You know that I want to love You with my whole heart,
> mind, soul, and strength, and that makes me altogether beautiful in
> Your eyes. Engrave on my heart the awesome truth that when You look
> at me, You see my willing spirit, not my weak flesh.

4:8 "Come with Me from Lebanon, My bride, may you come
with Me from Lebanon. Journey [or 'look'] down from the
summit of Amana, from the summit of Senir and Hermon,
from the dens of lions, from the mountains of leopards"
[Bridegroom speaking].

It is significant that this is the first time in the Song that the Lord
calls the maiden His bride. This title of honor is bestowed on her
after her commitment in verse 6 to go with Him in the costly way
of service to others, symbolized by the mountain of myrrh, and to
follow Him in the service of intercession, symbolized by the hill of
frankincense. Of course, she became His bride the moment she was
born again, yet her response to the Lord in verse 6 shows movement
from the positional truth that she is the bride of Christ to the experiential truth, or "living expression," of that position. Paul wrote to the
church at Ephesus, "As the Scriptures say, 'A man leaves his father
and mother and is joined to his wife, and the two are united into
one.' This is a great mystery, but it is an illustration of the way Christ

and the church are one" (Eph. 5:31–32, NLT). Her life is now a demonstration of the "great mystery" Paul alluded to in his letter to the Ephesians. She is joined to the Lord in both heart *and will* and is "one spirit with Him" (1 Cor. 6:17).

In poetic language the Lord calls her to come with Him from Lebanon. Lebanon is significant because it was part of the land the Lord promised to the sons of Israel (cf. Deut. 1:7; Josh. 1:4, 13:1–5). Its southernmost promontory is Mount Hermon, which rises over 9,000 feet above sea level. *The Book of Judges tells us that God left the people who lived in Mount Lebanon in the land to teach the Israelites war:* "These are the nations that the LORD left in the land to test those Israelites who had not experienced the wars of Canaan. *He did this to teach warfare to generations of Israelites who had no experience in battle.* These are the nations: the Philistines (those living under the five Philistine rulers), all the Canaanites, the Sidonians, and the Hivites living in the mountains of Lebanon from Mount Baal-hermon to Lebo-hamath" (Judg. 3:1–3, NLT, emphasis added). *These verses suggest Lebanon is a metaphor for training in spiritual warfare.*

> "...Journey [or look] down from the summit of Amana, from the summit of Senir and Hermon, from the dens of lions, from the mountains of leopards."

This sentence is packed with symbolism: a summit is the highest elevation in a mountain range; the name Amana means *truth*; Senir was an alternate name for Hermon (cf. Deut. 3:9), which means *destruction*. Jesus is the Way, *the Truth*, and the Life (John 14:6) and appeared for this purpose: to *destroy* the works of the devil (1 John 3:8). The dens of *lions* and mountains of leopards symbolize the spiritual hosts of wickedness in the heavenly places. First Peter 5:8 tells us that our enemy, the devil, roams around like a roaring *lion* seeking someone to devour. Ephesians 6:12 tells us that the principalities, powers, and rulers of the darkness of this age are spiritual hosts of wickedness in the heavenly places (demons). Combining these metaphors, *this verse speaks of partnering with the Lord in spiritual warfare from the place of ascension with Him.* The highest elevation (or summit) in the heavenly realm is with Christ, the Truth (Amana) and Destroyer of the works of the devil (Senir, Hermon). From that exalted perspective, seated with Him in the heavenly places (Eph. 2:6), we look down on the dens of lions and mountains of leopards, i.e., spiritual hosts of wickedness in the heavenly places, and He enables us to partner with Him in spiritual warfare.

As Watchman Nee said, heavenly things can be clearly discerned only in heavenly places, and *earthly things can be clearly discerned only from a heavenly perspective. It is from this place of ascension with Christ that we gain true discernment (i.e., a heavenly perspective) to understand earthly things.* Paul wrote to the church at Ephesus, "But God—so rich is He in His mercy! Because of and in order to satisfy the great and wonderful and intense love with which He loved us, even when we were dead (slain) by [our own] shortcomings and trespasses, He made us alive together in fellowship and in union with Christ; [He gave us the very life of Christ Himself, the same new life with which He quickened Him, for] it is by grace (His favor and mercy which you did not deserve) that you are saved (delivered from judgment and made partakers of Christ's salvation). *And He raised us up together with Him and made us sit down together [giving us joint seating with Him] in the heavenly sphere [by virtue of our being] in Christ Jesus (the Messiah, the Anointed One)*" (Eph. 2:4–6, AMP, emphasis added).

Paul wrote to the church at Corinth, "We prove ourselves by our purity, our understanding, our patience, our kindness, by the Holy Spirit within us, and by our sincere love. We faithfully preach the truth. God's power is working in us. *We use the weapons of righteousness in the right hand for attack and the left hand for defense*" (2 Cor. 6:6–7, NLT, emphasis added). As Paul both taught and demonstrated, *the way to walk in spiritual authority is to be conformed to the image of God's Son.* He wrote to the church at Rome that *God predestined us to be conformed to the image of His Son* so that Jesus would be the firstborn Child among many brothers and sisters (Rom. 8:29). To the church at Corinth he wrote, "For we who live are constantly being delivered over to death for Jesus' sake [we are dying to our self-life to be conformed to His image], *so that the [resurrection] life [and authority] of Jesus also may be manifested in our mortal flesh*" (2 Cor. 4:11, emphasis added). *The path to spiritual authority is the way of the Cross, i.e., death to our self-life.* The account of the seven sons of Sceva in Acts 19:13–17 clearly demonstrates this truth. These men were trying to cast out demons using the authority of Jesus by saying, "I adjure you by Jesus whom Paul preaches." A demon answered them, "I recognize Jesus, and I know about Paul, but who are you?" The evil spirit then leaped on the men, overpowering all seven of them, and they fled from the house naked and wounded. Demons recognize and submit only to the authority of Jesus. *As we abide in Him, armed with weapons of righteousness and the sword of His Word, He enables us to share His authority and push back the kingdom of darkness.*

> Lord, I want to be raised up to sit with You in the heavenly places so that I will discern earthly things from that position of ascension—Your heavenly perspective. Help me die to my self-life, being conformed to Your image, so that I can share Your authority and partner with You in intercession to push back the kingdom of darkness.

4:9 "You have made My heart beat faster, My sister, My bride; you have made My heart beat faster with a single glance of your eyes, with a single strand of your necklace" *[Bridegroom speaking].*

The New King James version renders this: "You have ravished My heart, My sister, [My] spouse; you have ravished My heart with one [look] of your eyes, with one link of your necklace." Webster's Dictionary defines ravish: *to transport with great joy or delight; to enrapture!*

I love what Mike Bickle teaches regarding this verse:

> Paul encouraged the church to break strongholds of the mind (2 Cor. 10:4–5). A stronghold in the mind is a collection of thoughts that are in agreement with the devil, and not in agreement with God. Wrong ideas that exalt themselves against

the truth of Who God is, and who we are to God. *We destroy strongholds by agreeing with how God thinks and feels about us. False ideas about the knowledge of God damage our intimacy with God.* This knowledge about God's heart enables us to be passionate about Him, with extravagant love and gratitude.[5]

Mike continues:

At the Last Supper (John 13–17), Jesus was preparing His disciples to fervently love God under the pressures of immanent disappointment, persecution, temptation, and service. On this occasion, He repeatedly spoke of God's loving desire for them. However, He also told them that they would *all* deny Him that very night (Matt. 26:31). In other words, these affirmations of His love were spoken to weak, yet sincere believers, not just to mature believers. *At the Last Supper, Jesus emphasized that the measure of God's love and affection for them was no less than the measure of love and affection that He has for His Son.*[6]

Mike highlights these three staggering affirmations made by Jesus at the Last Supper:

- The Father's love and affection for Jesus is the standard of the Son's love and affection for us. Jesus declared, "Just as the Father has loved Me, I have also loved you…" (John 15:9a).

- The Father's love and affection for Jesus is equal to the Father's love and affection for us. Jesus prayed that the world might know that the Father loves the church as much as He loves Him (John 17:23d).

- The Father's love and affection for Jesus will be the quality of love and affection imparted to the church to love Jesus. Jesus prayed that the love with which the Father loved Him would be in the church (John 17:26c).[7]

"You have ravished My heart, My sister, My spouse; you have ravished My heart with one look of your eyes, with one link of your necklace" [NKJV, Bridegroom speaking].

Jesus calls the maiden both His sister and His bride in this verse, emphasizing the depth of their relationship. A sister is not an acquaintance; I know my sister intimately and she knows me in the same way. We are bound by love, loyalty, and commitment to one another. The Lord also calls the maiden His bride, emphasizing her maturing partnership with Him. She is progressively learning to abide (or remain) in Him as a branch drawing its life from the vine.

The phrase "one look of your eyes" refers to the movement of our heart toward the Lord: the time we set aside to pray, to worship, to meditate on His Word, and to talk to Him and listen for His voice. "With one link of your necklace" refers to our will being submitted to His will or, we could say, His Lordship in our lives. Mike Bickle writes that the neck is symbolic of the will throughout the book, and the necklace around the neck, or the links of the necklace, speak of the individual acts of submission to His will or instruction (cf. Prov. 1:8–9).

This portion of Scripture reveals how Jesus sees us even in our weakness and sin. It reveals His emotional makeup: the intense passion of His heart for His people who are sincere in their devotion to Him even in their immaturity. The Lord is saying to us in this verse: *With one movement of your heart toward Me, with every act of worship or obedience to My Word, with every step you take toward knowing Me in a deeper and more intimate way, My heart is ravished (transported with great joy and delight) over you!* Selah! (From the Psalms, meaning "pause, and meditate on that!")

> Lord, I ask You for faith to believe that Your heart is ravished over me— that You are filled with great joy and delight with every movement of my heart toward You. Please open my heart to believe that You love me as much as the Father loves You (John 15:9) and that He loves me as much as He loves You (John 17:23). Please continue to reveal the Father's character to me, described by His names, so His love for You will be imparted to me (John 17:26).

4:10 "How beautiful is your love, My sister, My bride! How much better is your love than wine, and the fragrance of your oils than all kinds of spices!" *[Bridegroom speaking].*

The Lord repeats the titles given to the maiden in the previous verse: My sister and My bride. In the designation "sister," He is emphasizing His identification with us. Hebrews 2:17 reminds us, "Therefore, it was necessary for him to be made in every respect like us, his brothers and sisters, so that he could be our merciful and faithful High Priest before God…" (NLT). In the designation "My bride," the Lord is emphasizing His desire for bridal partnership with His people.

The prophets Isaiah and Hosea both compared the Lord's love for His people to a husband's love for his bride:

> "It will come about in that day," declares the LORD, "That you will call Me Ishi ['my husband'] and will no longer call Me Baali ['my master'].…I will betroth you to Me forever; yes, I will betroth you to Me in righteousness and in justice, in lovingkindness and in compassion, and I will betroth you to Me in faithfulness. Then you will know the LORD."
>
> —HOSEA 2:16, 19–20

> For your husband is your Maker, whose name is the LORD of hosts; and your Redeemer is the Holy One of Israel, who is called the God of all the earth.
>
> —ISAIAH 54:5

What exactly does it mean when we say God desires "bridal partnership" with His people? Just as a husband and wife work together as partners in a marriage, the Lord desires our partnership with Him to be marked by the same qualities that make a marriage commendable: loyalty, trust, fidelity, honor, respect, friendship and a sharing of hearts, teamwork, and love for others expressed in actions.

"…How much better is your love than wine…"

As already discussed, wine represents the best the world has to offer. Zechariah 10:7 says wine makes the heart glad. *The Lord is communicating to His bride that her love for Him is more precious to Him than anything in the world He created, and it "makes His heart glad" above all other things.*

"...and the fragrance of your oils than all kinds of spices!"

Spices in ancient times were valuable and expensive and were considered a luxury among the Jewish people. They emitted a particular fragrance and were used to make incense, the holy anointing oil, cosmetics, perfume, and to prepare bodies for burial. The principal Hebrew word for spice, *besem*, refers to any aromatic vegetable compound such as myrrh, cinnamon, cassia, and so forth. However *a rare spice, bosem—meaning "creating desire"—is indicated only in Song of Songs 5:13 and 6:2 in reference to the fragrance of Jesus that "creates desire" in our hearts to know Him.*

In this verse when the Lord speaks of the bride's fragrance, He is referring to her heart, to the essence of who she is, which is not visible to the physical eye but is plainly visible to the Lord's eyes. First Samuel 16:7 tells us, "...God sees not as man sees, for man looks at the outward appearance, but the LORD looks at the heart." Mike Bickle writes that a fragrance is invisible to the eye, but expresses the inner quality of a wood or plant. Thus, *the Lord uses "fragrance" as a metaphor to express how lovely her heart is in His eyes. He sees and cherishes the inner quality of her heart, her desire to be His, even in her weakness and immaturity.*

Second Corinthians 2:14–15 declares that we are the fragrance of Christ to God and that we spread everywhere the fragrance of what it means to know Him (by the testimony of our life, my addition). This verse suggests that our spiritual man emanates a fragrance, whether we realize it or not, which is perceived by the spirit of others. Just as in a negative sense the smell of smoke clings to our clothes when we enter a smoke-filled room, in a positive sense the Lord's fragrance begins to cling to us as we spend time in His presence.

Lord, open my heart to believe that my love for You makes Your heart glad above all other things. Engrave this truth on my heart so that it is "heart knowledge" and not just "mental assent." Help me learn to fellowship with Your Spirit so that I can walk with You in bridal partnership. And cause Your fragrance to cling to me as I spend time in Your presence so that I will spread everywhere the fragrance of what it means to know You.

4:11 "Your lips, My bride, drip honey; honey and milk are under your tongue, and the fragrance of your garments is like the fragrance of Lebanon" *[Bridegroom speaking].*

The Book of Proverbs is helpful in interpreting this verse. Proverbs 10:21 tells us, "The lips of the righteous feed many." Proverbs 15:7 declares, "The lips of the wise disperse knowledge" (KJV). *Therefore, lips in this metaphor symbolize godly speech, whether teaching which nourishes the spirit, encouragement, or reproof which helps keep us on the path of life* (cf. Prov. 10:17; 2 Tim. 4:2; Rev. 3:19).

Honey is often used in Scripture as a metaphor for pleasant things; it was also a common food staple in biblical times. God repeatedly spoke of the land that He was giving to the Israelites as "a land flowing with milk and honey." This was a metaphor for a land of abundance: one that would readily yield all that was necessary to sustain them. *"Your lips, [My] bride, drip honey" is a lovely and poetic way of saying "Your words, My Beloved, are pleasing to Me; they dispense wisdom and knowledge to nourish My sheep, they bless and encourage, and they give reproof when necessary to help keep My loved ones on the path of life."*

The phrase "under your tongue" is used in Scripture to refer to the things hidden in the heart. Compare Job 20:12, "Though evil is sweet in his mouth, and he hides it under his tongue," and Psalm 10:7, "His mouth is full of curses and deceit and oppression; under his tongue is mischief and wickedness." Jesus made this connection between our words and our hearts when He said, "Out of the abundance of the heart the mouth speaks" (Matt. 12:34; Luke 6:45). Therefore, *the phrase "honey and milk are under your tongue" refers to the godly abundance of the bride's heart: the spiritual treasures of wisdom and knowledge she has gleaned from His Word and hidden in her heart to nourish others.*

> "…and the fragrance of your garments is like the fragrance of Lebanon."

Lebanon was well known in biblical times for its groves of cedar trees, whose wood was extremely hard and resistant to decay and gave off a wonderful fragrance. As mentioned before, cedar and cypress were the only types of wood used in Solomon's temple (1 Kings 5:8). Garments in Scripture are often a metaphor for deeds or acts of service (cf. Rev. 19:8, "And to her it was granted to be arrayed in fine linen, clean and bright, for the fine linen is the righteous acts of the saints," NKJV). Combining these metaphors, *"the fragrance of your garments is like the fragrance of Lebanon"* is the Lord's commendation for the bride's acts of service, which are a sweet-smelling aroma, an acceptable sacrifice that brings joy to His heart. Paul used this same imagery when he spoke of the financial help the Philippian church sent to him as "a sweet-smelling aroma, an acceptable sacrifice, well pleasing to God" (Phil. 4:18, NKJV).

> Lord, may honey and milk be under my tongue: I ask You to give me spiritual treasures of wisdom and knowledge to nourish others as You teach me from Your Word. May my lips drip honey: may my words be pleasing to You and may they nourish and bless others, even bringing life-giving reproof when necessary. And may the fragrance of my garments be like the fragrance of Lebanon: may my acts of service ascend like a sweet-smelling aroma, an acceptable sacrifice that brings joy to Your heart.

4:12 "A garden locked is My sister, My bride, a rock garden locked, a spring sealed up" *[Bridegroom speaking]*.

To understand this verse, it is helpful to know the historical context for a garden in biblical times. King Solomon made gardens and parks for himself, as noted in Ecclesiastes 2:4–6. The gardens of a king would normally be enclosed with a fence of stone to keep out trespassers and animals that might trample and muddy the spring that watered the garden. A king's garden was a retreat: a place for him to go to withdraw from the demands of his position and to relax and enjoy the beauty of nature. (The Garden of Gethsemane was a public garden and a favorite place of prayer for the King of kings, Jesus.)

In the verse above, when the Lord refers to His bride as a "locked garden," He is using the phrase as a metaphor for her heart. Proverbs 4:23 counsels us to "Watch over your heart with all diligence, for from it flow the springs of life." The Lord is commending the bride for her diligence in guarding her heart from the contamination and defilement of the world and sin. Proverbs says we must watch over our heart diligently because it contains the "springs of life" or "rivers of living water" as Jesus called them: "He who believes in Me, as the Scripture has said, out of his heart will flow rivers of living water. But this He spoke of the Spirit..." (John 7:38–39, NKJV). *These "rivers of living water," or "springs of life," are the Spirit of Christ who dwells in our heart.* Paul admonished us not to grieve the Spirit, by whom we are sealed for the day of redemption (Eph. 4:30). *When we guard our hearts from the defilement of the world, we are honoring our King by doing whatever is necessary to avoid grieving His Spirit. As a result, His Spirit is able to flow freely from our hearts to meet the needs of others as "rivers of living water."*

> Lord, teach me to fellowship with Your Spirit throughout my day, and help me to be quick to obey His voice and His promptings. Help me guard my heart from the contamination of the world and sin so He will flow freely from my heart as a river of living water to meet the needs of others.

4:13–14 "**Your shoots are an orchard of pomegranates with choice fruits, henna with nard plants, nard and saffron, calamus and cinnamon, with all the trees of frankincense, myrrh and aloes, along with all the finest spices**" *[Bridegroom speaking].*

The New Living Translation renders this: "[You are like a lovely orchard bearing precious fruit, with the rarest of perfumes] nard and saffron, fragrant calamus and cinnamon…myrrh, and aloes [perfume from every incense tree], and every other lovely spice."

The Lord is commending the bride's fruitfulness by comparing her to a lovely orchard. He said in John 15:8, "My Father is glorified by this, that you bear much fruit, and so prove to be My disciples." He explained in the parable of the sower that the one who receives the Word of God in good ground (a heart that is not hard; one that is "plowed" and ready to receive the seed) is the one who hears the Word and understands it, producing fruit—some one hundred times, some sixty times, and some thirty times what was sown (Mark 4:2–20).

As a branch abiding in the Vine, the bride is learning to abide in Jesus, thus bearing "lasting fruit." The summation of all that Jesus taught His disciples about living life in the kingdom (as it is expressed in the earth through the lives of those who know Him) is found in John chapter 15. This chapter is part of the final teaching Jesus gave His disciples just before He was arrested in the Garden of Gethsemane. He said, "Remain in me, and I will remain in you. For a branch cannot produce fruit if it is severed from the vine, and you cannot be fruitful unless you remain in me. Yes, I am the vine; you are the branches. Those who remain in me, and I in them, will produce much fruit. *For apart from Me you can do nothing*….You didn't choose me. I chose you. I appointed you to go and produce lasting fruit…" (John 15:4–5, 16, NLT, emphasis added).

"Your shoots are an orchard of pomegranates…"

The pomegranate speaks of the fruit of righteousness in the bride's life. According to Jewish tradition, the pomegranate is a symbol for righteousness because it is said to have 613 seeds corresponding to the 613 mitzvot or commandments of the Torah. Under the new covenant, we fulfill the righteous requirement of the Law as we abide in the Lord, following His Spirit. Paul wrote to the church at Rome, "For the law of the Spirit, of life in Christ Jesus, has set you free from the law of sin and death. For what the Law could not do…God did: sending His own Son in the likeness of sinful flesh and as an offering for sin, He condemned [Greek *katakrino*—to deprive of strength] sin in the flesh, *so that the requirement of the Law might be fulfilled in us, who do not walk according to the flesh but according to the Spirit"* (Rom. 8:2–4, emphasis added; commas in first verse mine). The "law of the Spirit" *is* "life in Christ Jesus—abiding in Him."

> [You are like a lovely orchard bearing precious fruit, with the rarest of perfumes] nard and saffron, fragrant calamus and cinnamon…myrrh, and aloes [perfume from every incense tree], and every other lovely spice.
> —SONG OF SOLOMON 4:13–14, NLT

The plants that are listed as "the rarest of perfumes" in the New Living Translation are those that were used in making incense or anointing oils. The apothecary would dry the spices and mix them with resins to burn as incense or with oils to use as a perfume to anoint the body. *Incense, as mentioned before, speaks of the bride's prayer life, which is precious to the Lord. The plants used to make perfumes speak of her inward adornment which cannot be seen but is experienced by others as "the hidden person of the heart, with the incorruptible beauty of a gentle and quiet [lit. "undisturbed, peaceful"] spirit, which is very precious in the sight of God"* (1 Pet. 3:3–4). The bride is clothed with His righteousness as she abides in Him, even in the "hidden person of the heart"—her thought life, attitudes, and motives.

Highly significant is the inclusion of nard in the plants mentioned above. *Nard speaks of the bride's devotion and worship. The Lord is commending the bride for having a heart like Mary's, one that freely pours out all that she has and all that she is in extravagant worship to the Son of God.* Both Matthew's Gospel and John's Gospel document Mary of Bethany's extravagant act of worship just before the Lord's crucifixion (cf. Matt. 26:6–13 and John 12:3–8). Mary anointed Jesus with nard, an extremely costly perfume, in keeping with the Jewish custom of anointing a body for burial. This perfume was probably her dowry and was worth almost a year's wages. Because the custom of giving a dowry is not practiced in our Western culture, it is easy for us to miss the significance of Mary's sacrifice. A dowry was a gift given by the parents to their daughter at her marriage, rather than at their death, which was to provide an endowment, or income, for her in the event she was widowed. In ancient times, widows were in an especially difficult position because employment for women was not readily available, nor were there any secular institutions to provide for them. Some received help through family or friends, but many lived in abject poverty. As Mary poured the extremely expensive perfume on Jesus's head and anointed His feet, wiping them with her hair, her actions spoke much louder than words. She was, in effect, saying, "You are the Pearl of great price, and I am relinquishing all that I have and all that I am to follow You. I have no back-up plan. I place my life completely in Your hands."

> Lord, I want my heart to be a lovely orchard bearing precious fruit for You, even one hundred times what is sown in it for Your kingdom. I ask You to clothe me with Your righteousness as I learn to abide in You, even in the hidden person of my heart: my thought life, attitudes, and motives. Most of all, give me a heart like Mary's who held back nothing but poured out all that she had and all that she was in extravagant worship to You.

4:15 "You are a garden spring, a well of fresh [literally 'living'] water, and streams flowing from Lebanon" *[Bridegroom speaking].*

As mentioned earlier, the spring in a king's garden would normally be enclosed with a fence of stone to keep out trespassers and animals that might trample and muddy the water. Therefore, *a garden spring in this metaphor refers to His Spirit in the garden of the bride's pure and undefiled heart.*

A well of fresh or "living water" refers to her present-tense relationship (or fellowship) with the Holy Spirit. Paul wrote to the church at Corinth, "The grace of the Lord Jesus Christ, and the love of God, and the *fellowship of the Holy Spirit,* be with you all" (2 Cor. 13:14, emphasis added). "Fellowship" is the Greek word *koinonea* and means communion or fellowship. Webster's Dictionary defines fellowship as companionship and mutual sharing; communion is defined as intimate conversation, intimate relationship. Therefore we could translate this verse using the definition of fellowship as, "The grace of the Lord Jesus Christ, and the love of God, and the *mutual sharing and intimate relationship with the Holy Spirit* be yours."

"Streams flowing from Lebanon" refers to the fast-moving streams formed by the melting snow that covers the towering mountains of Lebanon. Mountains in Scripture often symbolize the heavenly realm; thus, *"streams flowing from Lebanon" is a metaphor for the Holy Spirit as a fast-moving stream flowing unhindered from the bride's innermost being as she remains united to Christ, seated with Him in the heavenly realm* (cf. Eph. 2:4–6).

In contrast to the Lord's praise for the bride, Jeremiah records the Lord's rebuke to the Israelites: "For My people have committed two evils: they have forsaken Me, the fountain of living waters, to hew for themselves cisterns, broken cisterns that can hold no water" (Jer. 2:13). The Lord identifies Himself in this verse as *"the fountain of living waters"* and says His people have abandoned Him. The second evil they committed was to substitute cisterns they had made (underground tanks for storing water), but the cisterns were broken and the water leaked away. In other words, the Israelites had abandoned a vital, living relationship with the Lord for "religion." They had chosen to obey the Law in their own strength, which, of course, was not possible. Paul taught that the purpose of the Law was to show us our complete inability to keep it outside of a vital relationship with the Lord (cf. Gal. 3:21–5:26). The righteous requirement of the Law is fulfilled in us only as we follow (or fellowship with) His Spirit. Paul wrote to the church at Rome, "For what the Law could not do...God did: sending His own Son in the likeness of sinful flesh and as an offering for sin, He condemned [Greek *katakrino*—to deprive of strength] sin in the flesh, so that the requirement of the Law might be fulfilled in us, who do not walk according to the flesh but according to the Spirit" (Rom. 8:3–4).

The Lord uses poetic language in this verse to praise the bride for her devotion and desire to walk in His ways. He says, "You guard your heart in obedience to My Word; therefore, the spring in the garden of your heart is pure and undefiled (referring to her spirit, which is joined to the Holy Spirit). *Because My Spirit is not grieved, He can flow freely from your heart to meet the needs of others as a well of living water and streams flowing from Lebanon."*

> Lord, help me guard my heart above all else so that the Springs of Life, Your precious Holy Spirit, can flow freely from my heart to meet the needs of others. Help me learn to remain in continual fellowship with the Holy Spirit, abiding in You, so that I can walk in Your righteous ways.

4:16 "Awake, O north wind, and come, wind of the south; make my garden breathe out fragrance, let its spices be wafted abroad. May my Beloved come into His garden and eat its choice fruits!" *[Bride speaking].*

Proverbs 25:23 tells us, "The north wind brings forth rain…" *In Israel, the north wind brings rain, thunder, lightening, and hail. Spiritually, this represents times of adversity and disappointment in our lives. The south winds in Israel bring the heat, which ripens the fruit. They bring warmth and refreshing after the cold of winter. The bride understands that in order to become like her Beloved, she needs both the warm south winds and the cold north winds of adversity to blow on her heart—her "garden" in this metaphor.* As Mike Bickle teaches, some issues of God's training in our lives can only be the result of difficult circumstances. Deep pockets of unperceived pride, ambition, anger, etc., are uncovered as we work through difficult circumstances.

Proverbs 16:2 says, "All the ways of a man are clean *in his own sight*, but the LORD weighs the motives" (emphasis added). The Lord knows our hearts so much better than we do. We may think our hearts are pure regarding a certain issue, but the Lord knows our true motives. In His great love for us, He uses trials and difficult circumstances to bring the "dross" in our hearts to the surface. Even as silver and gold were heated to a very high temperature in order to cause the impurities (dross) to rise to the surface, so the

Lord uses the heat of trials and circumstances to allow us to see the dross in our own hearts. He then gives us the opportunity to allow the Holy Spirit to blow that dross away, even as a bellows was used by a smith to blow the dross from the surface of the molten silver or gold. If we are willing to repent of our unforgiveness, selfish ambition, or whatever the particular sin may be which rises to the surface of our hearts, He is "faithful and righteous to forgive us our sins and to cleanse us from all unrighteousness" (1 John 1:9).

"...make my garden breathe out fragrance, let its spices be wafted abroad."

Watchman Nee wrote a wonderful book called *The Release of the Spirit* describing the process the Lord takes us through for this verse to be fulfilled in our lives, using the terms "inward man" for our spirit where God's Spirit lives and "outward man" for the soul. He writes:

Just as we are dressed in clothes, so our inward man [spirit] "wears" an outward man [the soul].[8]

Whether our works are fruitful or not depends upon whether our outward man [soul] has been broken by the Lord so that the inward man [spirit] can pass through that brokenness and come forth....The Lord Jesus tells us in John 12, "Except the grain of wheat falling into the ground die, it abides alone; but if it dies, it bears much fruit." Life is in the grain of wheat, but there is a shell, a very hard shell on the outside. As long as that shell is not split open, the wheat cannot sprout and grow. "Except the grain of wheat falling into the ground die..." What is this death? It is the cracking open of the shell through the working together of temperature & humidity in the soil. Once the shell is split open, the wheat begins to grow. So the question here is not whether there is life within, but whether the outside shell is cracked open.[9]

The Holy Spirit has not ceased working. One event after another...comes to us. Each disciplinary working of the Holy Spirit has but one purpose: to break our outward man [soul] so that our inward man [spirit] may come through.[10]

The Lord longs to find a way to bless the world through those who belong to Him. Brokenness is the way of blessing, the way of fragrance, the way of fruitfulness, but it is also a path sprinkled with blood.[11]

When we really understand the cross we shall see it means the breaking of the outward man [soul]. The cross must break all that belongs to our outward man—our opinions, our ways, our cleverness, our self-love, our all.[12]

"May my Beloved come into His garden and eat its choice fruits!"

This is the first time in the Song that the bride calls her heart "His garden," not "my garden." Since "His garden" in this metaphor is her heart, "choice fruits" are the fruit of His Spirit: love, joy, peace, patience, kindness, goodness, faithfulness, gentleness, and self control (Gal. 5:22). The greatest of these is love: both love for the Lord and love for her fellow man. But she is coming to understand that *"unfeigned" love for her fellow man is only possible as an overflow of her love for Him* (cf. 1 Pet. 1:22, KJV).

Paul wrote to the church at Corinth that God manifests through us the sweet aroma of the knowledge of Him in every place (2 Cor. 2:14). The Greek word for "knowledge" here is *gnosis*, from the word *ginosko*, meaning to know experientially (or by experience). It is from the place of intimacy with Him, from the place of our deepening friendship with Him, that we manifest the sweet aroma of the *experiential* knowledge of God wherever we go. We don't just use words to tell others about Him, our life *demonstrates* His character to those around us. We become "living letters," written not with pen and ink, but with the power of the Holy Spirit in a transformed life (2 Cor. 3:3).

The Lord told us clearly that when we love others, we are loving Him:

Then the King will say to those on His right, "Come, you who are blessed by my Father, inherit the Kingdom prepared for you from the creation of the world. For I was hungry, and you fed me. I was thirsty, and you gave me a drink. I was a stranger, and you invited me into your home. I was naked, and you gave me clothing. I was sick, and you cared for me. I was in prison,

and you visited me." Then these righteous ones will reply, "Lord, when did we ever see you hungry and feed you? Or thirsty and give you something to drink? Or a stranger and show you hospitality? Or naked and give you clothing? When did we ever see you sick or in prison and visit You?" *And the King will say, "I tell you the truth, when you did it to one of the least of these my brothers and sisters, you were doing it to me!"*
—MATTHEW 25:34–40, NLT, EMPHASIS ADDED

This verse demonstrates how the Lord is able to "eat" or enjoy the choice fruits of the garden of our hearts: as the fruit of His Spirit is manifested in our lives to bless others, we are blessing Him as well. Whatever we do for the least of His brothers and sisters, we are doing for Him—our beloved Bridegroom King.

> Lord, I echo the bride's prayer in this verse. I ask for both the warm winds of the south, for times of refreshing in Your presence, and for the cold winds of the north, the times of trial and adversity that conform me to Your image. Help me cooperate with the discipline of Your Spirit, and enable me to see His stripping as a deliverance rather than a loss. I ask You to break the hard outer shell of my soul so that the life of Your Spirit can be released to bless others.

Mike Bickle teaches that there are two primary sections in the Song: the first four chapters of the Song focus on the bride understanding and enjoying *her inheritance in Christ*. These chapters emphasize how God views and cherishes us—His bride. The last four chapters, beginning with the verse above, focus on *Jesus's inheritance in the bride*. The Father promised to give Jesus an inheritance (cf. Ps. 2:8, Eph. 1:18). One aspect of this inheritance is the mandatory obedience of all creation (cf. Phil. 2:9–11); however, Jesus wants more than this. *He longs for an eternal companion or bride who voluntarily chooses to be equally yoked to Him in love* (Eph. 5:31–32, Rev. 19:7). *We (the bride of Christ) are the great prize of all the ages that Jesus awaits!*

Chapter 5

UNVEILING THE MAGNIFICENCE OF CHRIST JESUS

5:1 "I have come into My garden, My sister, My bride; I have gathered My myrrh along with My balsam. I have eaten My honeycomb and My honey; I have drunk My wine and My milk. Eat, friends; drink and imbibe deeply, O lovers" *[Bridegroom speaking]*.

IN THE PREVIOUS verse the bride invited her Lord to come and enjoy the fruit of His garden (her heart). She asked for the refining fire of the Holy Spirit and assured the Lord that she would be content with whatever circumstances He placed her in—whether pleasant circumstances (the warm south wind) or with trials to conform her to His image (the cold north wind). *Her deepest desire is that His fruit would be formed in her heart and His very fragrance would exude from her, drawing others to Him.*

Watchman Nee speaks of the bride's prayer in Song 4:16 as a consecration of the first fruits of the garden of her heart. Even as the Israelites were to bring the first fruits of their soil into the house of the Lord (Exod. 23:19), so the bride desires to dedicate the first fruits of her heart to Jesus.

In the verse before us the Lord replies to the bride's prayer and consecration, accepting the first fruits of her heart joyfully. He describes three specific activities in this passage:

"...I have gathered My myrrh along with My balsam..."

The Lord Jesus gathers His myrrh and His balsam (or "spices" in other translations) from her garden: this is a metaphor for the fruit of the Cross or death to "self." Myrrh was an aromatic gum that was used as a spice, as a perfume when mixed with oil, and with other spices for embalming a dead body in biblical times. Nicodemus took a mixture of myrrh and aloes and wrapped Jesus's body in linen wrappings with the spices after His crucifixion (John 19:39–40). Therefore, myrrh and spices in this verse symbolize the death to self, or death of her soul life, that the Holy Spirit has accomplished in the bride's heart. The Lord taught that whoever wishes to save his life (Greek *psuche* or soul) would lose it, but whoever would lose (Greek *apollumi*—to destroy) his life (literally soul) would save it (Mark 8:35). Therefore, *the Lord gathers or accepts from her heart the fruit of the Cross which has transformed her from being "self" centered to being "kingdom" centered.*

"...I have eaten My honeycomb and My honey..."

In Song 4:11, the Lord praises the bride by telling her that her lips drip as the honeycomb, and honey and milk are under her tongue. Proverbs 16:24 tells us that pleasant words are like a honeycomb: sweet to the soul and healing to the bones. *In this metaphor the Lord is commending the bride for her godly speech which gives grace to those who hear her.* The apostle Paul gave us this exhortation in his letter to the Ephesians: Don't let words come out of your mouth that are corrupted by evil motives (ex. judgment, superiority), but only speak words that promote the spiritual growth of others (according to the need of the moment), that you may extend God's lovingkindness and grace (unearned favor) to those who hear you (Eph. 4:29, my own expanded translation of the verse). As the Lord Himself told us, out of the abundance of the heart the mouth speaks (Luke 6:45). *The Lord "eats" or partakes of the first fruits of the bride's godly speech. He is blessed by the purity of her heart which produces words full of grace for others.*

"...I have drunk My wine and My milk..."

Wine in this verse represents the Lord's blood, which He called "My blood of *the covenant*" when He gave the disciples the cup of wine to drink in celebrating the last Passover with them (Matt. 26:27–28). Wine also represents the Holy Spirit. Luke records in Acts chapter 2 that the disciples were filled with the Spirit and began to speak in languages they did not know. Verse 13 records, "But others were mocking and saying, 'They are full of sweet wine.'" Thus, *wine in this verse represents knowledge of our covenant with God, given by the revelation of the Spirit, or what New Testament writers called "solid food"* (1 Cor. 3:2; Heb. 5:12–13). *Milk represents "the introductory teaching about Christ" or the foundation of our faith as described in Hebrews 6:1–2.* Both are essential in training disciples and laying a strong foundation for their faith. *The Lord commends the bride for being able to give the needed nourishment to those she relates to, whether to babes in Christ (milk) or to mature believers (wine).*

The prophet Isaiah alluded to this same truth:

> Ho! Every one who thirsts, come to the waters; and you who have no money come, buy and eat. Come, buy *wine and milk* without money and without cost. Why do you spend money for what is not bread, and your wages for what does not satisfy? Listen carefully to Me, and eat what is good, and delight yourself in abundance. Incline your ear and come to Me. Listen, that you may live; and I will make an *everlasting covenant* with you, according to the faithful mercies shown to David.
>
> —ISAIAH 55:1–3, EMPHASIS ADDED

"Eat, friends; drink and imbibe deeply [literally *become drunk*], O lovers."

Only after the Lord receives the first fruits of the bride's heart are others given the invitation to enjoy her garden. The Hebrew words for *friends* and *lovers* in this verse are noteworthy. "Friends" is the Hebrew word *rea* or *reya* and refers to a close friend or an occasional one; a chance acquaintance or an intimate companion. "Lovers" is the Hebrew word *dowd* and means *one beloved. Friends* is a general term with a range of meanings, while *lovers* is a specific term implying intimacy. These two Hebrew words encompass the full spectrum of those who love the Lord. *To the babes in Christ, represented by the word "friends," the Lord extends the invitation to partake of the milk of the Word in the bride's garden (or heart): the "elementary teaching about the Christ" which is able to lay a strong foundation in their lives. To those who are lovesick, the "ones beloved," the Lord extends the invitation to partake of myrrh and spice in the bride's garden (heart) representing death to self (the fruit of the Cross) that they might be conformed to His image. The Lord extends the invitation to drink deeply of the wine—or revelation of our covenant with God given by the Spirit—literally, to "become drunk" to those who are lovesick.*

> Lord, I offer to You the "first fruits" of my heart. May You find myrrh there, representing death to my self-life; honeycomb, representing godly speech which gives grace to those who hear; and wine and milk, representing both the milk and meat of Your Word. May the fruit of my garden bring joy to Your heart first, and after You have enjoyed its fruit, may it nourish those You love.

5:2 "I was asleep but my heart was awake. A voice! My Beloved was knocking; 'Open to Me, My sister, My darling, My dove, My perfect one! For My head is drenched with dew, My locks with the damp of the night" *[Bride speaking].*

The bride is speaking to the daughters of Jerusalem in the next seven verses. She begins by telling them that she was asleep, but her heart was awake, and in this dreamlike state she heard the voice of the Bridegroom calling to her. Once again He speaks words of life to her, calling forth the virtues He sees in her heart. She is "His sister": His intimate companion and friend. She is "His darling" or "His love" in other translations: the object of His heart's devotion and the one who ravishes His heart with one glance of her eyes (i.e., one movement of her heart toward Him). She is "His dove": His loyal one whose eyes are focused only on Him. And she is "His perfect one":

one whose heart is blameless toward Him, who is quick to obey and quick to repent of sin.

In this dreamlike state the bride hears the Lord's voice and the sound of His knock on the door of her heart, beckoning her to open her heart wide to Him. However, this is a new revelation of the Lord—she now sees Him as the Jesus of Gethsemane. "For My head is drenched with dew, My locks with the damp of the night" is reminiscent of our Lord on the night before His crucifixion, as He went to the Garden of Gethsemane to pray:

> And having fallen upon His knees, He was praying, saying, "Father, if You are willing, remove this cup from Me. Nevertheless, not my desire but yours, let it keep on being done." And there appeared to Him an angel from heaven, strengthening Him. And having entered a state of severe mental and emotional struggle to the point of agony, He was praying more earnestly. And His perspiration became like great drops of blood [by reason of the fact that His blood burst through the ruptured walls of the capillaries, the latter caused by agony, coloring the perspiration and enlarging the drops] continually falling down upon the ground.
>
> —LUKE 22:41–44, WUEST

Watchman Nee wrote of this verse that the Lord is now calling the bride to go through a new experience of the Cross or one she has only experienced in a shallow way. He is now asking her to open the door of her heart to Him as the Man of Sorrows. Even as Jesus was rejected not only by men, but seemingly by God as well, the bride must learn what it means to be (seemingly) rejected by God and to suffer the deeper misunderstanding and shame of the Cross.[1]

> Lord, help me to be quick to open the door of my heart to You even when You come to me as the Jesus of Gethsemane. I ask for grace to embrace whatever cross You ask me to carry even if it means "being despised and forsaken of men" as You were (Isa. 53:3).

5:3 "I have taken off my dress, how can I put it on again? I have washed my feet, how can I dirty them again?" *[Bride speaking]*.

The bride said yes to the Lord's request to go with Him in service in Song 4:8 and prayed for the refining work of the Holy Spirit in her life in Song 4:16. Yet she does not give the Lord instant obedience as He calls to her in this encounter as the Jesus of Gethsemane. *She must face the fear in her own heart before she can follow Him in this new season. She does not refuse Him but wrestles with this new revelation of the Lord as the Man of sorrows.* She is at first unwilling to leave the place of spiritual rest as symbolized by the removal of her dress and washing of her feet. Yet the Lord patiently calls her to a deeper revelation of the Cross and to the fellowship of His sufferings (Phil. 3:10). The bride is counting the cost before saying yes to this new revelation of her Lord and what He may be requiring of her in this new season.

> Lord, help me to love the revelation of You as the Jesus of Gethsemane as much as I love the Jesus of unfailing love and the Jesus of resurrection power. Cause Your perfect love to cast out the fear in my heart. Help me to count the cost but then to say yes to You, no matter what You ask of me.

5:4 "My Beloved extended His hand through the opening, and my feelings were aroused for Him" *[Bride speaking]*.

The Lord is not in the least bit dissuaded by the bride's fear. He knows her spirit is willing but her flesh is weak. *He extends His hand to her, symbolizing His strength and sustaining power.* The Holy Spirit said through the psalmist, "I have found David my servant; with my sacred oil I have anointed him. *My hand will sustain him; surely my arm will strengthen him*" (Ps. 89:20–21, NIV, emphasis added). Truly, it is the Lord's grace, His strength and sustaining power, that *enables* us to embrace the cross. When the Lord finds a heart that is willing, He supplies the grace and strength to do what is required.

Lord, thank You for Your hand upon my life, which sustains me and strengthens me. Thank You for pouring out grace to help me embrace the Cross and follow You even in the difficult and painful seasons of my life.

5:5 **"I arose to open to my Beloved; and my hands dripped with myrrh, and my fingers with liquid myrrh, on the handles of the bolt"** *[Bride speaking].*

The Lord's love for the bride and His complete confidence in her strengthen her resolve, and she rises to open the door of her heart to Him. His perfect love has cast out the fear in her heart that hindered her from completely abandoning her life to Him (1 John 4:18). As mentioned earlier, myrrh was used in combination with spices to embalm Jesus's body before it was placed in the tomb; therefore, myrrh symbolizes the Cross (cf. John 19:39). *The reference to hands dripping with myrrh on the handles of the bolt speaks of the costly decision to humble herself to the point of death—the death of her self-life on the cross* (cf. Phil. 2:8).

There is something in the human heart that wants to focus on the "big" things we will do for God, like being a missionary to a remote village or dying a martyr. Art Katz (a Messianic Jew, prophet, and author) wisely wrote:

> Martyrdom is easy when it comes as a final moment, but the truth of the Cross for the church is the *daily* dying.[2]

In other words, it is only through embracing the daily dying of our self-life in the "small" things that we gain spiritual strength to embrace the "bigger" sacrifices that the Lord might call us to.

Lord, You know my spirit is willing but my flesh is weak, so You extend Your hand of grace to me, strengthening me to say yes to the cross. Help me to arise and open the door of my heart to You when You call, my fingers dripping liquid myrrh—symbolizing the death of my self-life on the cross.

5:6 "I opened to my Beloved, but my Beloved had turned away and had gone! My heart went out to Him as He spoke. I searched for Him but I did not find Him; I called Him but He did not answer me" *[Bride speaking]*.

The bride is now experiencing what the mystics called the "dark night of the soul"—*the darkness of the withdrawn sense of the presence of God.* Isaiah 50:10 speaks of this divine darkness: "Who is among you that fears the LORD, that obeys the voice of His servant, that walks in darkness and has no light? Let him trust in the name of the LORD and rely on his God." The child of God described in this verse fears the Lord and obeys His Son yet still walks in divine darkness—the dark night of the soul. This darkness is given *by God*, and it will not dissipate until it has accomplished His work in our hearts. The encouragement of the latter half of the verse is to "trust in the name of the Lord and rely on his God." *It is possible to fear God and to obey Him without fully trusting in His name (meaning His character represented by His many names) and without fully relying on Him.* The work that the Lord desires to do in each of our hearts is summarized by Job at the end of his trial: "I have heard of You by the hearing of the ear; but now my [spiritual] eye sees You" (Job 42:5). The Lord wants to bring us to the place where we no longer rely on our knowledge of Him (knowing Him by the hearing of the ear) or even our ministry for Him. Instead, He wants us to see Him as He truly is ("but now my eye sees Thee"). *God uses the experiences in our lives, particularly our trials, to remove the veils from our faces so that we can see Him more clearly.* Trials have a way of forcing us to become more honest with ourselves and with God. They remove the masks we hide behind and the things we use to justify ourselves if we choose to walk in humility. Paul wrote to the church at Corinth that we behold the glory of the Lord (or see Him as He truly is) as we gaze at Him with an *unveiled* face (2 Cor. 3:18).

Michael Molinos wrote:

> Do not be deceived in the midst of tribulation...there is *no time* in your life when you are nearer to God than in the time

when He has deserted you! The sun may be hidden behind the clouds, yet the sun has not changed its place, nor has one bit of its brightness been lost. *The Lord allows a painful desertion of His presence from within you to purge and to polish you, to cleanse you and to despoil the self! Your Lord does this so that you might have a clear-cut opportunity to give your whole being up to Him without any notice of personal gain... but rather only to be His delight.*[3]

Lord, help me to accept everything from Your hand equally—the times of blessing and the times of divine darkness when even Your presence seems to be withdrawn. Help me to remain faithful even when I don't understand what You're doing in my life. Remove the veils from my face through the trials You allow me to walk through so that I will see You more clearly. Purge my heart until its one desire is to love You with my whole heart, mind, soul, and strength and to love others as an overflow of my love for You.

5:7 "The watchmen who make the rounds in the city found me, they struck me and wounded me; the guardsmen of the walls took away my shawl from me" *[Bride speaking].*

The bride encountered watchmen, or spiritual authorities in the church, the first time she lost the sense of the Lord's presence. In this earlier encounter (Song 3:3) she humbled herself to ask for their help in finding the Lord, i.e., restoring her fellowship with Him. However, her second encounter with the watchmen in the church is not at all like the first. In this encounter, *they strike her and wound her, symbolizing rejection and persecution by those in authority over her.* Perhaps she disagreed with them concerning a doctrinal issue, or perhaps she felt called by God to serve His people in a way that her fellowship was not called to. Perhaps she simply wanted to leave her current fellowship to learn from a different stream in the body of Christ. Or perhaps she is a prophetess and gave a "hard" word that they did not want to receive. Regardless of the reason, those in authority over her are offended and unjustly accuse her. This deeply wounds her spirit. Not only do they unjustly accuse her, *they remove her spiritual covering represented by the taking away of her shawl or veil.* With her spiritual covering removed, she is unable to do ministry in the body she was related to. She has been stripped of the two main desires of her heart: "draw me after you," or draw me into an intimate relationship with You, and "let us run together," or let me be yoked to You, serving Your people alongside You (Song 1:4).

Even beyond this disappointment, she experiences the shame of rejection as described of the Lord in Isaiah 53:4, "... Yet we ourselves esteemed Him stricken, smitten of God, and afflicted." Watchman Nee writes that the Lord's call in Song 5:2, as the Jesus of Gethsemane, is beyond many believers expectations:

> They do not realize that there is the aspect of shame to the cross....Although they have suffered a little for the cross and met some persecution and shame, they have always felt that the cross was their glory, their life, and their power. It never occurred to them that the cross would become their shame...that others would consider that God has rejected them, and that God would put them through trials and strip them of comfort and sympathy from those whom they know, who would think that they were smitten by God. They may have suffered shame from the world, but spiritual shame is something new to them. This kind of misunderstanding will touch their feeling in a deep way, because it has to do with the relationship between God and them. Only then will they know what it means to "fill up on my part that which is lacking of the afflictions of Christ" (Col. 1:24)....If God allows her to be misunderstood, stripped of her good name, shamed, and considered by others as being in an argument with God, how can she glorify Him any longer?...She does not realize that her concerns revolve around how she can glorify God. She must be stripped by God to the point that even this good self-intention to glorify God is removed. *The cross must work so deeply on her until she is content with the portion that God has allotted for her and until she lets God take care of His own glory.*[4]

The bride has encountered what Mike Bickle describes as the "Saul type leaders" in the body of Christ. These leaders are insecure, which gives rise to jealousy and fear. They feel the need to protect their reputation instead of allowing God to defend them. In contrast to the leaders just described, those with the heart of David realize it is the Lord's vineyard and they have no spiritual "rights" over the people under their care. They seek first to lead their people into an intimate relationship with the Lord, teaching them to hear His voice. Only after that foundation is established do they seek to help them find their place of service in the body and to grow in the gifting that the Lord has given them. Rather than becoming jealous, these leaders are happy when someone they have discipled is given honor or advances beyond them, because they are helping to establish the Lord's kingdom, not building their own. We would all love to serve under the authority of David type leaders, but as Mike Bickle wisely says, we need the Saul type leaders in our lives. God uses them to refine us and to work humility in us so that we become more like His Son.

> Lord, give me Your grace to forgive when I encounter the Saul type leaders in Your body. Help me realize that You allow encounters of this kind to work humility in me and to make me more like You. Give me Your "eternal" perspective, Lord, so that I can respond to "temporary" offenses in a way that pleases You.

5:8 "I charge you, O daughters of Jerusalem, if you find my Beloved, that you tell Him I am lovesick!" (NKJV, *Bride speaking*).

In her "dark night of the soul" the bride is strengthened as she realizes her Lord experienced the same twofold test she has experienced. He endured profound rejection from the spiritual leaders of His time because He sought only the approval of His Father, not the approval of men. As the Prophet, He fearlessly confronted the religious leaders for their duplicity and misuse of the Scriptures. The miracles He performed exposed the jealousy in their hearts, and

Matthew records that even Pilate knew that it was because of envy that they delivered Jesus to him for crucifixion (Matt. 27:18). When they committed the ultimate rejection, nailing Him to a cross, He too experienced the pain of feeling abandoned by the Father, crying out, "My God, My God, why have You forsaken Me?" As the bride looks to the example of her Beloved, her spirit is infused with His divine strength. She humbles herself, enlisting the help of the immature daughters to find her Beloved.

The psalmist wrote, "...I know, O LORD, that Your judgments are righteous, and that in faithfulness You have afflicted me" (Ps. 119:75). The Hebrew word for "faithfulness" in this verse is *emuwnah* or *emunah* and means *God's covenant faithfulness*. The psalmist had undoubtedly gone through some severe dealings with the Lord, but he was able to see that only God's covenant faithfulness was behind these judgments. He understood that the Lord cannot ignore our sin, because sin is never only a private matter. Sin not only brings forth "death" or destruction in our lives but also in the lives of those around us. Because the psalmist trusted God's faithfulness, he was able to see from an "eternal perspective" and to agree with God's refining process in his life.

The bride understands that the unjust treatment by those in authority over her is allowed by God to refine her and to train her in humility. Instead of becoming bitter and running from God, she runs to Him even though she feels nothing. It is easy to love Jesus when we feel His presence and the tokens of His affection and when our circumstances are pleasant. Such was the bride's experience in Song 2:5, "Sustain me with raisin cakes, refresh me with apples, because I am lovesick." But in this new season, her circumstances are painful and difficult. Only those who are fully His, who are in it for Him and not for themselves, can love Him through the times of pain and suffering when even the sense of His presence is taken from them. It is in these times of spiritual darkness and pain that the gold of our faith is refined and purified.

Lord, give me the psalmist's unshakeable confidence in Your covenant faithfulness. Enable me to see from Your eternal perspective so that I will cooperate with Your refining process in my life. I'm in this for You, Lord, not for myself. Help me to rejoice even in the trials You allow so that the proof of my faith, being more precious than gold which is perishable—even though tested by fire—may be found to result in praise and glory and honor at Your coming (1 Pet. 1:6–7).

5:9 "What kind of beloved is your Beloved, O most beautiful among women? What kind of beloved is your Beloved, that thus you adjure us?" *(Daughters of Jerusalem speaking).*

The New Living Translation renders this, "Why is your lover better than all others, O woman of rare beauty? What makes your lover so special that we must promise this?" The daughters of Jerusalem are perplexed by the bride's response to her Beloved in this trial. They don't understand her unshakeable love for Him in light of His presumed treatment of her. In their eyes, He has abandoned her and allowed her to be deeply wounded by the leaders of the church when He could have protected her. Because their love is conditional, based on how they are treated by others, they have no frame of reference for her extravagant love in the face of heartbreak and suffering. In contrast to their love, the bride's life demonstrates the pure *agape* love of the Father that is defined in 1 Corinthians 13:4–7. It is this love which adorns her with true beauty: the inward beauty of the spirit.

In addition to the unconditional love for the Lord demonstrated by the bride through this trial, the daughters see in her life a living demonstration of Peter's exhortation, "You should clothe yourselves instead with the beauty that comes from within, the unfading beauty of a gentle and quiet spirit, which is so precious to God" (1 Pet. 3:4, NLT). The Greek word for "gentle" is *prautes*, often translated "meek." Vine's Expository Dictionary of Old and New Testament Words defines *meek* as follows:

> An inwrought grace of the soul; the exercises of it are first and chiefly towards God. *It is that temper of spirit in which we accept*

His dealings with us as good, and therefore without disputing or resisting; it is closely linked with the word "tapeinophrosune" [humility]... *This meekness, however, being first of all a meekness before God, but also in the face of men, even of evil men, out of a sense that these, with the insults and injuries which they may inflict, are permitted and employed by Him for the chastening and purifying of His elect.* The meaning of *prautes* is not readily expressed in English, for the terms meekness, mildness, commonly used, suggest weakness and pusillanimity (timidity) to a greater or less extent, whereas prautes does nothing of the kind.... It must be clearly understood, therefore, that *the meekness manifested by the Lord and commended to the believer is the fruit of power. The common assumption is that when a man is meek it is because he cannot help himself; but the Lord was "meek" because He had the infinite resources of God at His command. Described negatively, meekness is the opposite to self-assertiveness and self-interest; it is an equanimity of spirit that is neither elated nor cast down, simply because it is not occupied with self at all* (emphasis added).[5]

The bride is clothing herself with the Lord's agape love and meekness as she learns to abide in Him. She is walking in the reality of Paul's beautiful benediction and promise: "The grace of the Lord Jesus Christ, and the love of God, and the fellowship of the Holy Spirit, be with you all" (2 Cor. 13:14). *We come to know the Lord in an intimate way through our fellowship with the Holy Spirit: by talking to Him and expecting Him to answer us, either by impressions, gentle pictures seen by our spiritual eyes, dreams, through His Word, or by His still small voice to our spirits.* Through the bride's intimate relationship with the Holy Spirit, the Lord's agape love begins to replace the conditional love of her fallen nature. As a result, the "fragrance" of her relationship with the Lord awakens in the daughters a desire to know Him in a deeper way. They are, in effect, asking, "What kind of Man is this Jesus that causes you to love Him so passionately? What is it that you know about Him that we don't know?"

Lord, I want to have a heart like the bride that loves You even in the face of heartbreak and suffering. Give me the unshakeable confidence in Your character that David had, who went into the temple to worship You after his child by Bathsheba died. Teach me to abide in You so that Your fragrance will cling to me and awaken in others a desire to know You in a deeper way.

5:10 "My Beloved is dazzling and ruddy, outstanding among ten thousand" *[Bride speaking]*.

Mike Bickle describes the next seven verses of the Song as one of the most outstanding expressions of worship in the Word of God; a magnificent poetic unveiling of the splendor of Christ Jesus. He believes this passage of Scripture is meant to equip our souls to effectively worship God in times of testing, asserting that knowledge of these ten attributes will stabilize our hearts in the midst of the storms of life. Mike encourages believers to speak these attributes back to God in worship and prayer as a practical way of growing in our understanding of the Lord's character.

The bride's first proclamation in this section is a general description of the Lord's majesty, which is followed by ten specific attributes of the Lord's personality and character conveyed as metaphors using the human body. The Holy Spirit used the imagery of the temple (gold, precious stones, ivory, cedars of Lebanon) because they are things that would have been familiar to the people of that day but also as a prophetic signpost pointing to Jesus: "And I saw no temple in it [the new Jerusalem in the new heavens and new earth], *for the Lord God the Almighty and the Lamb are its temple*" (Rev. 21:22, emphasis added).

Since the Holy Spirit is the true author of the Song, He is the only One who can unlock the mysteries of the symbolic language. Even then, there are levels of revelation that could not be mined in a lifetime. Our prayer can only be to ask the Lord to fulfill in our lives the prophecy of Isaiah: "*Your eyes will see the King in His beauty*" (Isa. 33:17, emphasis added).

When asked by the daughters why she loves the Bridegroom

115

unconditionally, in spite of her mistreatment by the leaders in the church, the bride exclaims, "He is dazzling and ruddy!" Dazzling is also variously translated as white, brilliant, or radiant. This brings to mind the revelation of the Lord that John the apostle was given on the island of Patmos: "And His head and His hair were white like white wool, like snow...and His face was like the sun shining in its strength" (Rev. 1:14, 16). Dazzling may be defined as overpowering as with very bright light. *The Lord is dazzling white, which speaks of His purity and holiness. He is blameless, undefiled by sin, and perfect in His character.*

When the prophet Isaiah was given a vision of the Lord in the year of King Uzziah's death, he saw the Lord sitting on a throne with the train of His robe filling the temple. Seraphim stood above Him, calling out to each other, "Holy, Holy, Holy, is the LORD of hosts, the whole earth is full of His glory" (Isa. 6:3). The New Bible Commentary notes that the name *seraphim* means "fiery ones." Although these winged creatures are man-like with a face, hands, and feet (Isa. 6:2, 6), the point of their description is to re-emphasize the holiness of God, in whose presence even the sinless angels hesitate to look at Him (cf. Isa. 6:2—with two wings they cover their face). Isaiah's response was, "Woe is me, for I am ruined! Because I am a man of unclean lips..." The New Living Translation renders this, "My destruction is sealed, for I am a sinful man..." *Isaiah was so completely overwhelmed by the holiness of the Lord and devastated by the contrast of His own sinfulness that he felt he would die simply from gazing at the holy God!*

When the prophet Ezekiel was given a vision of the Lord (Ezekiel chapter 1), he fell on his face as a dead man. It was necessary for the Holy Spirit to enter him and strengthen him, setting him on his feet, so that the Lord could speak with him. In like manner, when the apostle John was given a vision of the Lord on the island of Patmos, he too fell at His feet as a dead man (Rev. 2:9–17).

The reactions of these men when allowed to glimpse the holiness of God should alert us to our own lack of reverence. By contrast, in many churches today members carry coffee into the sanctuary to sip while they "worship" the holy and majestic God. A. W. Tozer spoke to this condition in *The Knowledge of the Holy*:

> The church has surrendered her once lofty concept of God and has substituted for it one so low, so ignoble, as to be utterly unworthy of thinking, worshipping men. This she has done not deliberately, but little by little and without her knowledge; and her very unawareness only makes her situation all the more tragic....Before the Christian church goes into eclipse anywhere there must first be a corrupting of her simple basic theology. She simply gets a wrong answer to the question, "What is God like?" and goes on from there....The idolatrous heart assumes that God is other than He is...and *substitutes for the true God one made after its own likeness.*[6]

"My Beloved is dazzling and ruddy, outstanding among ten thousand."

The bride's further description of the Lord as "ruddy" refers to the wholeness or perfection of His character. A synonym for ruddy would be rosy, which implies health and attractiveness, as in rosy cheeks. The Lord is whole or complete in His nature and personality, lacking nothing. The perfection of His nature, or the qualities that make Him who He is, draw her to Him. Included in those qualities are perfect love, faithfulness, goodness, compassion, wisdom, mercy, grace, truth, righteousness, and justice. But as A. W. Tozer wrote, there can be no conflict in God's attributes. His being is unitary; therefore, He cannot act at a given time from one of His attributes while the rest remain inactive. His justice is always present in mercy and His love in judgment and so with all of God's attributes.[7]

The adjective *ruddy* also refers to the Lord's humanity. First Samuel 16:12 describes David as "ruddy, with beautiful eyes and a handsome appearance." *The combination of dazzling and ruddy speaks both of Christ's divine and His human nature: dazzling white in His purity and holiness as God, and ruddy referring to the human form He voluntarily took upon Himself as the son (or descendant) of David.*

"Outstanding among ten thousand" indicates He is completely

distinguished from any other: in a class of His own. The word *outstanding* literally means "lifted up as a banner" in the original language. A banner in ancient times was a piece of cloth bearing an insignia that was attached to a pole and used as a battle standard or flag symbolizing a leader, people, military unit, etc. The prophet Isaiah spoke prophetically of Jesus as a "banner to the people": "And in that day there shall be *a Root of Jesse, who shall stand as a banner to the people*; for the Gentiles shall seek Him, and His resting place shall be glorious. . . . He will set up a banner for the nations, and will assemble the outcasts of Israel, and gather together the dispersed of Judah from the four corners of the earth" (Isa. 11:10, 12, NKJV). Jesus Himself said, "And I, if I am lifted up from the earth, will draw all men to Myself" (John 12:32).

Numbers 21:4–9 gives the account of the bronze serpent, which Jesus also applied in reference to Himself. The king of Edom had refused to allow the Israelites to pass through his land, forcing them to go through the wilderness by the Red Sea. The people became impatient and spoke against God and Moses, saying, "Why have you brought us up out of Egypt to die in the wilderness? For there is no food and no water, and we loathe this miserable food" (Num. 21:5). As a consequence of their rebellion, God sent serpents that bit the people so that many of them died. When the people repented of their sin and asked Moses to intercede for them, God told Moses to make a bronze serpent and set it on a standard or pole. When someone who had been bitten looked at it, he would live. Jesus referenced this account when speaking to Nicodemus, saying, "As Moses lifted up the serpent in the wilderness, even so must the Son of Man be lifted up; so that whoever believes will in Him have eternal life" (John 3:15–16).

Therefore, "outstanding among ten thousand" also refers to the Lord's unique role as the Suffering Servant of Isaiah 53 who paid the price for our sins with His own precious blood in order to redeem us to God. Paul gave an eloquent summary of the atonement in his letter to the church at Philippi: "Though He was God, He did not think of equality with God as something to cling to. Instead, He gave up His divine privileges, taking the form of a bond-servant and being made in the likeness of men. Being found in appearance as a man, He humbled Himself by becoming obedient to the point of death, even death on a cross" (Phil. 2:6–8, using both the NLT and the NAS).

> Lord, open my spiritual eyes to see You, my King, in Your beauty! You are dazzling in purity and holiness; sinless and perfect in character. You are perfect love; You are faithful, good, compassionate, righteous, merciful, wise, just, and full of grace. You are truth embodied. You are "ruddy" in Your humanity Lord: gentle and humble in heart. You didn't cling to Your rights as God but gave up Your divine privileges for my sake. You humbled Yourself to the point of death, even the torture and shame of death on a cross for me. You voluntarily became like me in all things that You might be a faithful and merciful High Priest on my behalf. You are outstanding among ten thousand, Lord; far superior to all others and worthy of all blessing and honor and glory and dominion forever and ever (Rev. 5:13)!

5:11 "His head is like gold, pure gold; His locks are like clusters of dates, and black as a raven" *[Bride speaking].*

The bride begins her specific description of the Lord's personality and character by referring to His sovereignty and authority. Jesus is designated as the "head" referring to His sovereignty in many places in Scripture: "…He [Christ] is the head over all rule and authority" (Col. 2:10). The Father "…seated Him at His right hand in the heavenly places, far above all rule and authority and power and dominion, and every name that is named, not only in this age but also in the one to come. And He [God] put all things in subjection under His [Jesus's] feet, and gave Him as head over all things to the church, which is His body, the fullness of Him who fills all in all" (Eph. 1:20–23; cf. 1 Cor. 11:3; Eph. 4:15, 5:23; Col. 1:18). The writer of Hebrews tells us, "In these last days [God] has spoken to us in His Son, whom He appointed heir of all things, through whom also He made the world. And He [Jesus] is the [exact representation] of His [God's] nature, and upholds all things by the word of His power" (Heb. 1:2–3). What a statement! Jesus upholds (supports, holds together) all things in the universe by His Word! Consider what this says about the *power* of His Word! Selah (i.e., pause and think about that)!

The bride describes the Lord's authority as being "like gold." Gold is valued because it is enduring and retains its beauty. In the Scripture gold symbolizes holiness, as Exodus makes clear. All of the wood in the tabernacle was overlaid with gold, and the mercy seat, lampstand, and all of the utensils were made of pure gold. The plate on the front of the priests' turban was made of pure gold and engraved "Holiness to the Lord." (See Exodus chapters 25 through 30.) The entire inside of Solomon's temple and its furnishings, even the floor, was either made of pure gold or overlaid with gold (cf. 1 Kings 6; 2 Chron. 3–4). Even the street of the New Jerusalem will be made of pure gold (Rev. 21:21).

The Lord's authority is like pure gold: pure in that it is free from defilement, a lust for power, or evil motives as is often the case with human authority. His authority has only our good as its motivation; therefore, we can submit to His Lordship over our lives with complete confidence. It is never a struggle to submit to someone's authority when we know we are loved and cherished by them. Our Bridegroom will one day exercise His authority over every person; however, until that time He is seeking voluntary lovers.

"…His locks are like clusters of dates, and black as a raven."

Other translations render this, "His locks are wavy, and black as a raven." Hair in the Scripture symbolizes the Nazarite vow of dedication (Num. 6:2–5). A Nazarite was someone who was consecrated, or set apart to God, either from birth by his parents or as a self-imposed vow. During the time of the vow the hair could not be cut. John the Baptist, the forerunner of the Lord, was a Nazarite from birth (cf. Luke 1:15). Although Jesus Himself was not a Nazarite, His entire life was consecrated to His Father. He did only what He saw His Father doing and spoke only what His Father gave Him to speak (cf. John 5:19, 30; 8:28; 12:50; 15:15). He lived his entire earthly life as a Man dependent upon the Holy Spirit so that He could be both our High Priest and our example (cf. Heb. 2:17; 1 Pet. 2:21). Therefore, *hair in this verse speaks of the Lord's dedication to both His Father and to His Bride. Black wavy hair is a metaphor that suggests the strength and energy of youth. Taken together, these metaphors assure us that the Lord's dedication to us is vigorous and strong and can never weaken with time.*

> Lord, Your authority in my life is like pure gold—it is free from evil motives and has only my good as its motivation. I can submit to Your authority without question because I know that I am loved and cherished by You. Your dedication to both the Father and to me is enduring and will never weaken with time. Thank You for giving me revelation of the amazing truth that You are "betrothed" (or committed) to me for eternity!

5:12 "His eyes are like doves beside streams of water, bathed in milk, and reposed in their setting" *[Bride speaking].*

Eyes speak of the Lord's vision—what He sees when He looks at us. The Lord's eyes are compared in this metaphor to dove's eyes. As mentioned before, doves have no peripheral vision; therefore, their eyes are focused straight ahead on the object of their attention. They are also known for their loyalty: when their mate dies, they will not seek another mate. *This metaphor portrays the Lord's eyes as singly focused on each one of us and assures us of His intense loyalty to us, His beloved bride.*

The metaphors "doves," "streams of water," and "milk" all point to the attribute of purity. In New Testament times, doves were sold in the temple for the Jewish rites of purification. Jesus admonished His disciples in Matthew 10:16 to be shrewd as serpents and "innocent" as doves. The Greek word translated "innocent" here is *akeraios* and means without any mixture of deceit; without any foreign material; or, we might say, "pure." Milk is white in color; white, of course, symbolizes purity. "Streams of water" represent the Holy Spirit in many places in the Scripture. Purity is obviously an attribute of the Holy Spirit, who appeared as a dove when He descended on Jesus after

His baptism. Taken together, these word pictures assure us that *the Lord sees us through eyes that are pure and without bias. He knows our hearts far better than we do and understands even the motives that underlie our actions. He sees both our virtues and our character flaws and sins and yet loves us as a father loves his child: with intense loyalty and unwavering commitment.*

> Lord, thank You that You see me through eyes that are pure and without bias. You see my heart, Lord, not just my actions. You know the cry of my heart is to love You with my whole heart, mind, soul, and strength and that desire to love You as You love me ravishes Your heart—it fills Your heart with great joy and delight!

5:13 "His cheeks are like a bed of balsam, banks of sweet-scented herbs; His lips are lilies dripping with liquid myrrh" *[Bride speaking].*

The bride compares the Lord's cheeks to a bed of balsam or spices. *Cheeks speak of the emotions* because what a person is feeling is usually reflected on their face. Many in the church throughout the centuries have presented a picture of a God without emotions, or if He is credited with emotions, anger or wrath are usually emphasized. However, the Scriptures tell us otherwise. Many Old Testament scriptures declare God's intense emotions; for example, Zephaniah 3:17: "The LORD your God is in your midst, a victorious warrior. *He will exult over you with joy*, He will be quiet [or renew you] in His love, He will rejoice over you with shouts of joy" (emphasis added). (The word *exult* means *to feel extreme happiness* or elation; to express great joy.) The prophet Hosea recorded the intense emotions of our God when he wrote through the Holy Spirit, "Therefore, behold, I will allure her [Israel] and bring her into the wilderness, and I will speak tenderly and to her heart. There I will give her her vineyards and make the Valley of Achor [troubling] to be for her a door of hope and expectation...And it shall be in that day, says the Lord, that you will call Me Ishi [my Husband], and you shall no more call Me Baali [my Baal or master]....And I will betroth you to Me forever; yes, I will betroth you to Me in righteousness and justice, in steadfast love, and in mercy. I will even betroth you to Me...in stability and in faithfulness, and you shall know (recognize, be acquainted with, appreciate, give heed to, and cherish) the Lord" (Hos. 2:14–16, 19–20, AMP).

In the New Testament, the writer to the Hebrews declares, "And He [Christ] is the radiance of His [God's] glory and the *exact representation of His nature...*" (Heb. 1:3, emphasis added). We see in the man Christ Jesus the fullness of the Father's emotions. The shortest verse in the Word of God reveals the tender emotions of our Father and our Lord when it records, "Jesus wept" (John 11:35). Nine times in the Gospels it is said that Jesus had compassion on a person or a crowd of people. The Greek word used in these verses is *splanchnizomai* and means to be moved as to one's inwards (or *splanchna*); to be moved with compassion; to yearn (be filled) with compassion (cf. Matt. 9:36, 14:14, 15:32, 20:34; Mark 1:41, 6:34, 8:2; Luke 7:13, 10:33). Matthew chapter eight gives the account of a leper who came to Jesus and bowed down to Him saying, "Lord, if You are willing, You can make me clean." The Wuest translation of the New Testament (which uses as many English words as are necessary to bring out the richness, force, and clarity of the Greek text) renders Jesus's response, "I am desiring it *from all my heart*. Be cleansed at once" (Matt. 8:2–3 WUEST, emphasis added).

It is also true that our Lord exhibited anger but only in His dealings with the religious leaders: those who claimed to know His Father but who gravely misrepresented Him to the people. He drove the money changers out of the temple, declaring, "It is written, 'My house shall be called a house of prayer,' but you have made it a den of thieves" (Matt. 21:12; Mark 11:15; John 2:14). As the Prophet (Deut. 18:15), Jesus could not tolerate the priests' blatant disregard for God's Word. Although the temple should have been a place of prayer, the priests allowed the money changers to set up tables in the court of the Gentiles. There the money changers exchanged Roman money for Jewish currency (at a liberal profit for themselves) since the priests taught that only Jewish currency was fit for worship. This was just one example that revealed how the priests invalidated the Word of

God for the sake of their tradition (Matt. 15:6–9). It must be emphasized that the Lord's anger is always *righteous* anger. His anger stems
from His hatred of sin because sin ultimately causes devastation in
the lives of the people that He loves.

"His cheeks are like a bed of balsam..."

The Hebrew word used for balsam in this verse is *bosem* and
means "*creating desire.*" This Hebrew word is only used twice in the
entire Word of God: here and in chapter 6, verse 2. *The bride is comparing the Lord's cheeks, which represent His emotions, to balsam—
more literally, to fragrant herbs that create desire in the heart of those
who are exposed to their fragrance. When we begin to understand the
depth of the Lord's emotions toward us, it creates a powerful desire
in our hearts to know Him in a deeper way.* Truly, no human love
can begin to compare with His sacrificial, unconditional, inexhaust-
ible love for us!

"...His lips are lilies dripping with liquid myrrh."

Lips symbolize spoken words in the Scripture (cf. Job 2:10; Ps.
51:15; Prov. 13:3; Matt. 15:8; Heb. 13:15; 1 Pet. 3:10). "Lily" is the Hebrew
word *shoshan* and probably refers to the white lily that grows wild in
Lebanon and other regions of northern Palestine. *The bride is comparing the Lord's words to white lilies, which signify righteousness
and purity.* The Lord's words are pure words as the Scripture declares
(Ps. 12:6; Prov. 30:5). Purity speaks of being without defilement or
contamination—unadulterated. Jesus prayed to the Father, "Sanctify
them in the truth; Your word is truth" (John 17:17). *Not only are the
words of our Lord pure, they are a vehicle to bring purity, or sanctification, to our hearts as we embrace them in faith and obedience.*
The bride adds that His words drip with liquid myrrh. Myrrh
speaks of the Cross and the call to die to "self" (our carnal nature).
*Therefore, lips dripping with "liquid myrrh" also speaks of the Lord's
life-giving reproof, which is always motivated by His love for us.*
There are numerous exhortations in His Word that encourage us to

embrace His loving reproof: "…Do not reject the discipline of the Lord, or loathe His reproof, for whom the Lord loves He reproves, even as a father, the son in whom he delights" (Prov. 3:11–12, quoted in Heb. 12:5–6). "Those whom I love, I reprove and discipline; therefore be zealous and repent" (Rev. 3:19). "…He disciplines us for our good, so that we may share His holiness" (Heb. 12:10). "Reprove a wise man and he will love you. Give instruction to a wise man and he will be still wiser…" (Prov. 9:8–9). "He whose ear listens to the life-giving reproof will dwell among the wise. He who neglects discipline despises himself, but he who listens to reproof acquires understanding" (Prov. 15:31–32).

The bride is extolling the value of the Lord's words which motivate us to righteousness. Even the Lord's reproof is motivated by His love for us and is a vehicle to purify our hearts as we embrace His words in faith and obedience.

> Lord, please open my heart to believe the depth of Your emotions for me as Your beloved child. Engrave on my heart the truth that Your heart is ravished—filled with great joy and delight—over me! You are the rare spice Bosem to me, and the revelation of Your emotions toward me are creating in my heart a desire to know You as my intimate Friend. Your words are pure and life-giving and are always motivated by Your love for me; they drip liquid myrrh, symbolizing Your life-giving reproof. Lord, help me embrace Your reproof and Your discipline so that I can share Your holiness.

5:14 "His hands are rods of gold set with beryl; His abdomen is carved ivory inlaid with sapphires" *[Bride speaking].*

Hands refer to works in this metaphor because from a human standpoint very little could be accomplished without the use of the hands. *Gold*, as stated earlier, *represents the divine nature or holiness* as the Book of Exodus makes clear. *A rod in Scripture can represent, among other things, the scepter of a king; hence, an emblem of power* (cf. Ps. 110:2; Rev. 2:27, 12:5, 19:15) *or an instrument of correction* (cf. 2 Sam. 7:14; Ps. 89:32; Prov. 22:15; Isa. 10:5). The bride is expressing her complete trust in the Lord's works, which are perfect. Moses said, "...Ascribe greatness to our God. He is the Rock, His work is perfect; for all His ways are justice, a God of truth and without injustice; righteous and upright is He" (Deut. 32:3–4, NKJV).

Hands that are rods of gold set with beryl speak of the Lord's work in our lives to bring forth holiness; this includes His use of the rod of correction when necessary. The reference to beryl, which was a stone in the high priest's breastplate, assures us that all of His works on our behalf, and especially His correction, are undergirded with intercession for us so that we come forth as gold refined in the fire. The bride is acknowledging that His lordship over our lives, even His discipline or rod of correction, is perfect and is always motivated by love for us just as a parent's discipline is motivated by love for their precious child.

Both beryl and sapphire were stones in the high priest's breastplate (Exod. 28:15–21). Beryl is a precious stone of great hardness, ranging in color from blue to pale yellow, and was the first stone in the fourth row of the high priest's breastplate (Exod. 28:20). Sapphire (now believed to be lapis lazuli, not what we know as sapphire) was the middle stone in the second row of the high priest's breastplate. Thus, both *beryl and sapphire refer to the Lord's role as our great High Priest* (cf. Hebrews chapters 2–10). Hebrews 2:17 in the Wuest Translation says, "...He might become a compassionate and faithful High Priest in things pertaining to God, with a view to offering that sacrifice for the sins of the people that would perfectly meet the demands of God's justice." This was, of course, the Lord's greatest "work" on our behalf, but in addition to that amazing act of love, He is right now seated at the right hand of the Father, constantly making intercession for us (cf. Rom. 8:34; Heb. 7:25).

"...His abdomen is carved ivory inlaid with sapphires."

The Hebrew word for "abdomen" in this verse is *meah* and means the intestines, the bowels, the abdomen, the inmost part, or the heart. The word translated "feelings" in Song 5:4 ("...my feelings were aroused for Him") is the same Hebrew word used here in Song 5:14 translated "abdomen." *It is associated with God's emotions, as in*

Isaiah 63:15 and Jeremiah 31:20: "Look down from heaven, and see from Your habitation, holy and glorious. Where are Your zeal and Your strength, the yearning of Your heart [*meah*] and Your mercies toward me? Are they restrained?" (Isa. 63:15, NKJV). "'Is Ephraim My dear son? Is he a delightful child? Indeed, as often as I have spoken against him, I certainly still remember him; therefore My heart [meah] yearns for him; I will surely have mercy on him,' declares the LORD" (Jer. 31:20).

Substituting the definition for *meah* (heart or feelings) for abdomen, what does it mean when the Holy Spirit says that the Lord's feelings for us are like carved ivory inlaid with sapphires? The Scripture gives us the interpretation for these metaphors. Ivory was rare and expensive in biblical times, and only the very rich could afford this luxury. King Solomon's throne at Jerusalem was made of ivory overlaid with gold (2 Chron. 9:17). The prophet Amos denounced the rich in Israel for their luxuries, including "houses of ivory" (3:15) and "beds of ivory" (6:4), while the poor were overlooked and exploited. The carved ivory of the wealthy was often inlaid with gold and precious stones. Thus, *ivory represents extravagance in this metaphor. The bride is extolling the extravagance of the Lord's emotions toward her, and by extension, toward His beloved bride.* Far from being restrained in His emotions, the Lord exults over His bride as the prophet Zephaniah declared. Webster's Dictionary defines exult: "to rejoice greatly, be jubilant; to leap up, leap with joy." Substituting the definition for exult, we could translate Zephaniah 3:17, "The Lord God is in your midst, a victorious warrior. He will rejoice greatly and leap for joy over you, He will be quiet (or 'renew you,' in some ancient versions) in His love, *He will rejoice over you with shouts of joy.*" This verse exposes the lie that our God is distant and unemotional, replacing it with the truth of the Lord's extravagant emotions toward His bride: He rejoices over us with shouts of joy!

> Lord, You are my Rock! Your work is perfect, and all of Your ways are just. You are a God of faithfulness and justice; You are righteous and upright (Deut. 32:3–4). Your ways are perfect, and Your lordship over

my life, even Your discipline, is motivated by Your love for me as a perfect Father. Lord, I ask You to pour out revelation of Your extravagant emotions for me, and open my heart to believe that You rejoice over me with shouts of joy!

5:15 "His legs are pillars of alabaster set on pedestals of pure gold; His appearance is like Lebanon choice as the cedars" *[Bride speaking].*

Legs enable us to walk—to move forward—to fulfill our purpose or destiny in this metaphor. Alabaster is rendered "marble" in most translations. It is strong, durable, and beautiful as it is capable of being polished to a high luster. It was used in Solomon's temple (cf. 1 Chron. 29:2) and was often used for the pillars of great buildings because of its strength. Therefore, *alabaster signifies strength and stability. Pedestals of pure gold refer to the feet, which in Scripture are used to designate actions,* as in Psalm 119:101, "I have restrained my feet from every evil way…" (cf. Ps. 119:105; Prov. 1:16, 6:18). *Gold,* as mentioned before, *represents the divine character or holiness.* Combining these metaphors, *the bride is expressing her complete confidence in the administration of the Lord's divine purposes and His sovereignty: the attribute by which He rules His entire creation.* Psalm 33:10–11 declares, "The LORD frustrates the plans of the nations and thwarts all their schemes. But the LORD's plans stand firm forever; his intentions can never be shaken" (NLT). David declared, "The LORD has established His throne in the heavens, and His sovereignty [or supreme authority] rules over all" (Ps. 103:19). A. W. Tozer aptly described the Lord's sovereignty in *The Knowledge of the Holy,* reminding us that no one can dissuade the Lord from His purposes, and nothing can turn Him aside from His plans. Because He is omniscient, there can be no unforeseen circumstances or accidents. Because He is sovereign, there can be no countermanded orders or breakdown in authority. Because He is omnipotent, He has all power to achieve His chosen ends.[8] Selah! (Pause and meditate on that!)

"…His appearance is like Lebanon choice as the cedars."

The New King James version renders this, "His countenance is like Lebanon, excellent as the cedars," substituting the word countenance for appearance. Mike Bickle teaches that *the countenance speaks of the impartation of God to His people.* Numbers 6:22–27 recounts the priestly blessing that the Lord gave to Moses and Aaron to speak over the sons of Israel: "Then the LORD spoke to Moses, saying, 'Speak to Aaron and to his sons, saying, "Thus you shall bless the sons of Israel. You shall say to them: The LORD bless you, and keep you; the LORD make His face shine on you, and be gracious to you; the LORD lift up His countenance on you, and give you peace." So they shall invoke My name on the sons of Israel, and I then will bless them.'" The New Living Translation renders this beautiful blessing, "May the LORD bless you and protect you. May the LORD smile on you and be gracious to you. May the LORD show you his favor and give you his peace" (Num. 6:24–26).

The psalmist wrote, "God be gracious to us and bless us, and cause His face to shine upon us" (Ps. 67:1). *The expression "cause His face to shine upon us" or "lift up His countenance on us" is not readily understood in today's vernacular. To the ancients it meant to show favor or to bless with good things.* Mike Bickle teaches that when the light of God's face shines on the human heart, He is imparting grace to the heart. The Father has infinite ability to impart to us the graces of godliness such as wisdom, purity, and passion for His Son.

The reference to Lebanon's cedars is a metaphor for excellence or something to be desired above all else. The cedars of Lebanon were magnificent evergreens often 120 feet high and 40 feet in girth. They were highly prized by the peoples of the Middle East for their superior wood, which was strong, resistant to decay, and fragrant. King Solomon contracted with Hiram king of Tyre for cedars from Lebanon to build the Jerusalem temple, as only the finest timber was fit for use in building the house of God (cf. 1 Kings 5:6–18). *The bride is extolling the excellence of the Lord's impartation to His people, which is to be desired above all else. As He "lifts up His countenance" upon us, He blesses us with His favor and imparts godly graces such as divine wisdom, purity, and passion for His Son.*

Lord, Your plans and divine purposes stand firm forever, and Your sovereignty rules over all. Because You are omniscient, there are no unforeseen circumstances; because You are omnipotent, You have all power to achieve Your divine purposes; because You are sovereign, You possess all power and authority, and no one can revoke Your orders. Sovereign Lord, I ask You to lift up Your countenance on me and cause Your face to shine on me with Your favor. Impart to my heart divine wisdom, purity, and passion for Your Son!

5:16 "His mouth is full of sweetness. And He is wholly desirable. This is my Beloved and this is my friend, O daughters of Jerusalem" *[Bride speaking].*

When the bride speaks of her Beloved's mouth as being full of sweetness, she is referring to the sweetness of her relationship with the Lord. *"His mouth" represents intimacy with her Beloved* as in Song 1:2, "May He kiss me with the kisses of His mouth!" A kiss is an expression of a personal and intimate relationship. The bride has tasted the sweetness of intimacy with the Lord; this has sustained her through her dark night of the soul and kept her from the enemy's trap of offense and bitterness toward God. She has just experienced the pain of rejection by those in spiritual authority over her and the removal of her place in ministry, and yet she speaks passionately to the daughters of Jerusalem of the surpassing joy of an intimate relationship with the Lord.

Intimacy with Jesus is the heart's cry of all who love Him, yet the challenge of our culture today is that we are bombarded on all sides with constant noise and distractions: television, video games, the Internet, social networking sites, and smart phones. Because we live with constant distraction, we find it hard to pray as Jesus directed: "But you, when you pray, go into your room, and when you have shut your door, pray to your Father who is in the secret place..." (Matt. 6:6, NKJV). The Lord admonished us to "shut the door"—in other words, shut out all the other distractions of our busy lives and devote time to talk with Him and listen for His voice to us. We cannot cultivate an intimate relationship with the Lord "on the run." We would not expect to sustain an intimate relationship with our spouse or best friend without devoting time to be alone with them, talking to them and listening to their heart. This principle is just as true in our relationship with the Lord! We cultivate intimacy with Jesus by setting aside undistracted time to pray (dialogue with Him) and by learning to fellowship with His Spirit—by talking to Him throughout our day, listening for His still small voice to our spirits, and paying attention to the impressions or the pictures He gives us.

> "...And He is wholly desirable. This is my Beloved and this is my friend, O daughters of Jerusalem."

The bride sums up her glowing description of her Beloved with the statement, "He is wholly desirable." In other words, everything about Him "creates desire" (Hebrew *bosem*) in her heart to know Him. *No one else can compare with this perfect God/Man, Christ Jesus, whose love for her far surpasses any human love.*

The bride emphasizes that He is both her Beloved and her *friend*. It is quite possible to love the Lord without being His friend. Friendship requires an investment of time and a desire to truly know the heart and mind of the other person. It involves dialogue, not just one-way communication. Mark Virkler writes in the introduction to *Dialogue with God*:

> When all the pieces were in place, I realized that I had received much more than I expected. I was looking for a voice; I found a Person. I was looking for guidance; I found a Shepherd. I was looking for the will of God; I found relationship with the Son of God.[9]

It is significant that John the Baptist, whom Jesus called the greatest man born of a woman, said of himself, "...the friend of the bridegroom, who *stands and hears him*, rejoices greatly because of the bridegroom's voice" (John 3:29, emphasis added). The friend of the bridegroom referenced in this verse is what we call the best man. He was usually the groom's closest friend, and his role was to serve the bridegroom in all matters related to the wedding. The Scripture tells us that our Father is preparing a bride for His Son (cf. Rev. 19:7–9). As friends of the Bridegroom, we serve Jesus by waiting on Him and listening for His voice: "...The friend who attends the bridegroom waits and listens for him..." (John 3:29, NIV). If we are not teaching the Lord's disciples to hear His voice, we are leading them to religion instead of a living relationship with the Son of God.

> Lord, help me learn to slow down the pace of my busy life to enter the secret place of prayer with You; please help me make time daily to shut out every distraction so that I can hear Your voice. Holy Spirit, reveal the Bridegroom to me. I want to be His friend who stands and hears His voice, serving Him as He calls His bride to the marriage supper of the Lamb.

Chapter 6

HOW THE LORD VIEWS IMMATURE YET SINCERE BELIEVERS

6:1 "Where has your Beloved gone, O most beautiful among women? Where has your Beloved turned, that we may seek Him with you?" *[Daughters of Jerusalem speaking]*.

THE DAUGHTERS OF Jerusalem are intrigued with this Man the bride has just described to them. They have been stirred to the depths of their hearts by her passionate description of His loveliness. The bride has just come through a heart-rending trial, and instead of being bitter toward the Lord, she is overflowing with love for Him. This defies all reason! Who is this Man that calls forth such unqualified devotion in her heart? She obviously knows Him in a way that they do not. No longer curious bystanders, they ask her where they can find Him. The daughters now want to seek Him alongside her.

The bride's life is being woven like a beautiful tapestry or embroidery in the Lord's hands; on the underside it appears random and disconnected and even unattractive, but on the outside it is harmonious and precious with its own unique beauty. Psalm 45:13–15 expresses this truth beautifully:

> The King's daughter is all glorious within; her clothing is interwoven with gold. She will be led to the King in embroidered work; the virgins, her companions who follow her, will be brought to You. They will be led forth with gladness and rejoicing; they will enter into the King's palace.

This psalm is rich in symbolism, highlighting both the inner beauty of the bride and her righteous acts. Clothing in the Scripture is a metaphor for the righteous acts of the saints (cf. Rev. 19:8). "Clothing interwoven with gold" speaks of righteousness produced by the Refiner's fire as the apostle Peter wrote: "... even though now for a little while, if necessary, you have been distressed by various trials, so that the proof of your faith, being more precious than gold which is perishable, even though tested by fire, may be found to result in praise and glory and honor at the revelation of Jesus Christ" (1 Pet. 1:6–7). The bride is "led to the King in embroidered work"; this represents the beautiful tapestry of her life which has been lovingly crafted by the hand of the Lord. The virgins or companions who follow her—the daughters of Jerusalem in this case—are those who have been drawn by the reflection of Jesus that they see in the bride's life. They "enter the King's palace" with joy as they come to know His saving grace through her witness.

> Lord, I want to trust You even in the most difficult and painful times of my life. Make me secure in knowing that the trials You allow in my life to refine me are motivated by Your love for me as a perfect Father. May my life be a witness to Your goodness and Your faithfulness so that others will want to know You in a deeper way.

6:2 "My Beloved has gone down to His garden, to the beds of balsam, to pasture His flock in the gardens and gather lilies" *[Bride speaking].*

In chapter 5, verse 6 of the Song, the bride is looking for her Beloved but can't find Him. In chapter 6, verse 1, after her heart-rending trial followed by her passionate description of His character and attributes, the daughters ask the bride where He has gone so that they can seek Him with her. It is significant that she now knows exactly where to find Him. He has been there with her in the garden of her heart the whole time throughout her "dark night of the soul." Although she lost the conscious sense of His presence, He never abandoned her. He carried her through the trial, covering her with His grace. This is reminiscent of the beautiful poem "Footprints in the Sand" by Carolyn Joyce Carty. In this poem the man sees two sets of footprints in the sand except at the times of trial and hardship in his life; during those times there was only one set of footprints. When he asked the Lord why He left him during those times of trial, the Lord replied, "My son, My precious child, I love you and I would never leave you. During your times of trial and suffering, when you see only one set of footprints, it was then that I carried you."

Even in our darkest times of pain and suffering, the Lord promised He would never leave us or forsake us (Heb. 13:5). The prophet Isaiah described the Lord's faithfulness to us with these words, "In all their suffering he also suffered, and he personally rescued them. In his love and mercy he redeemed them. He lifted them up and *carried them* through all the years" (Isa. 63:9, NLT, emphasis added).

The "beds of balsam" in the garden of her heart are highly significant. The term *balsam* is translated *spices* in many translations. Spices were highly valued in biblical times, much more than they are today, making it difficult for us to comprehend their meaning in the poetic language of the Song of Songs. As mentioned earlier, spices in ancient times were valuable and expensive and were considered a luxury among the Jewish people. They emitted a particular fragrance and were used to make incense, the holy anointing oil, cosmetics, perfume, and to prepare bodies for burial. The principal Hebrew word for spice, *besem*, refers to any aromatic vegetable compound such as myrrh, cinnamon, cassia, and so forth. However, *a rare spice, bosem, meaning "creating desire," was used by the Holy Spirit in only two places in the entire Scripture—in this verse and in Song 5:13 in reference to Jesus.*

In Song 5:13, bosem is used in reference to the revelation of Jesus's passionate emotions for us, which create desire in our hearts to know Him in a deeper way. *In this verse, bosem refers to the rare and precious spice of the bride's heart resulting from her intimate walk with the Lord. As she abides in Him, His very fragrance (symbolized by the spice "bosem") clings to her with a wonderful effect—it creates desire to know the Lord intimately in the hearts of those around her.*

"...to pasture His flock in the gardens and gather lilies."

In the first part of this verse, the bride tells the daughters that the Lord has gone down to His garden (singular) or the garden of her heart. In reality, He was there the whole time, carrying her through her dark night of the soul. In the latter part of the verse, the bride says the Lord has gone to pasture (or feed) His flock in the gardens (plural) or bodies of believers comprising His church. The Lord is a Shepherd who "feeds" His flock both individually and corporately.

The Lord is portrayed in the latter part of the verse as One who walks in the gardens (hearts) of His people, looking to "gather" the lilies of purity and righteousness. Lilies symbolize purity of heart—the very quality that allows us to "see" God (Matt. 5:8, also cf. Ps. 24:3–4). In his *Studies in the Sermon on the Mount*, D. Martyn Lloyd-Jones defined purity of heart as having an undivided love which regards God as our highest good and which is concerned only about loving Him. In other words, purity of heart comes from keeping the first commandment first in our lives: loving God with all our heart, mind, soul, and strength. This produces eyes of faith to "see" the Lord as David did, who wrote, "I have set the Lord continually before me; because He is at my right hand, I will not be shaken" (Ps. 16:8). Although the Lord sometimes gives vision to our spiritual eyes, David wrote of "seeing" in the sense of knowing the Lord, sensing He was near, and enjoying His presence. What a wonderful way to live! And this is what the Lord desires for all of us![1]

> Lord, I want to have a pure heart and an undivided love that regards You as my highest good. Help me keep the first commandment first in my life so that I will "see" You continually before me as David did—sensing You are near and enjoying Your presence. Then, as I abide in Your presence, cause Your beautiful fragrance "bosem" to cling to me so that it will create desire in the hearts of others to know You.

6:3 "I am my Beloved's and my Beloved is mine, He who pastures His flock among the lilies" *[Bride speaking]*.

In Song 2:16, the bride exclaimed, "My Beloved is mine, and I am His; He pastures His flock among the lilies." At this point in her journey, her first thought was of *her claim on the Lord;* His claim on her life was secondary. After her difficult trial in Song 5:6–7, she now makes the same exclamation but reverses the order. In the verse above, the bride acknowledges first *the Lord's claim on her life,* only afterward mentioning her own claim on Him. Further still in her journey, she loses sight of her claim altogether, exclaiming, "I am my Beloved's, and His desire is for me" (Song 7:10).

Once again the bride makes reference to the Lord pasturing His flock among the lilies. *"He pastures (or feeds) His flock among the lilies" refers to hearts that are pure or without guile (deceit). The Lord feeds His sheep in the place of purity and honesty. When our hearts are pure before Him, we can hear His voice with much less distortion.* By contrast, if we hold an idol in our heart, something we have placed before the Lord, we will be unable to hear His voice clearly and may even hear the voice of our own soul.

> Lord, I acknowledge Your claim on my life. I am not in this for what You can do for me but because I love You! My life is no longer my own; it is Yours to use as You please. Please purify my heart, Lord. Give me a heart like Nathanael—one that is pure and without guile—so that I can hear Your voice more clearly.

6:4 "You are as beautiful as Tirzah, My darling, as lovely as Jerusalem, as awesome as an army with banners" *[Bridegroom speaking].*

The bride has been dialoguing with the daughters of Jerusalem who asked her where to find her Beloved so that they could seek Him with her. She has finally come to understand by faith and the revelation of the Holy Spirit that the Lord never left her—He was with her throughout her dark night of the soul in the garden of her heart. She answers the daughter's question, "Where has Your Beloved gone?" by telling them that He feeds His sheep—both individually and corporately—"among the lilies" or wherever there are pure hearts. She then exclaims, *"I am my Beloved's and my Beloved is mine!" Amplifying her statement, we might say, "My heart is fully the Lord's, and my life is His to use as He pleases. Far greater than that, He has given His heart to me and bound Himself to me by covenant through His own precious blood."*

Suddenly Jesus interrupts her dialogue with the daughters of Jerusalem and breaks His silence. He has not spoken to her since Song 5:2 when He revealed Himself to her as the Jesus of Gethsemane. He has watched her grow in faith and love through the most difficult trial of her life, and His heart overflows with love for the one who has captured His heart. He exclaims, "You are beautiful to me!" comparing her beauty to Tirzah, to Jerusalem, and to an army with banners. Each of these metaphors has deep significance and reveals to us how the Lord sees us, His precious bride.

"You are as beautiful as Tirzah, My darling…"

Tirzah was the most beautiful city in the northern kingdom of Israel and became its capital under King Jeroboam. *The name Tirzah means benevolent. The Lord is praising the bride's inner beauty expressed in benevolence—kindness and generosity in providing help to others, especially the poor.*

"…as lovely as Jerusalem…"

Jerusalem is often referred to in the Scriptures as "the holy city" because it was the site of the temple: the earthly dwelling place for the Shekinah glory of God (cf. Isa. 48:2, 52:1; Neh. 11:1, 18; Matt. 4:5, 27:53; Rev. 11:2). First Kings 14:21 tells us it is the city where God chose to put His name. The psalmist Asaph called it "the perfection of beauty" (Ps. 50:2). Speaking through the prophet Isaiah, God named Jerusalem *Hephzibah*, meaning "My delight is in her" (Isa. 62:4). *In this metaphor, the Lord compares the bride's beauty to Jerusalem, representing holiness of heart.* King David's song of thanksgiving (sung after he brought the ark of the covenant to the tabernacle at Jerusalem) exhorts the people to "Worship the LORD in the beauty of holiness!" (1 Chron. 16:29, NKJV). *The Lord sees the bride arrayed in the beauty of holiness and calls her Hephzibah, exclaiming, "My delight is in you!"*

"…as awesome as an army with banners."

An army with banners symbolizes a victorious army. In ancient times, warring armies displayed a banner with their king's insignia during battle. When an army was defeated, their banner was stripped from them and they were marched in procession through the streets of the conquering king's city in chains behind their defeated king. The conquering king led the procession, proudly displaying his banner as he led the victory march through the city. *In this metaphor the Lord is commending the bride's victory over her own soul in the twofold test she endured in Song 5:6–7. Instead of becoming bitter and accusing God when she was rejected by those in spiritual authority over her, she chose humility.* She chose to believe that the Lord was using the Saul type leaders in her life for her good, knowing that He causes *all* things to work together for good to those who love Him (Rom. 8:28). *The bride chose to cooperate with the Holy Spirit in her trial, allowing Him to conform her to the image of her Beloved, Jesus. This humility of heart, this victory over her own soul, is very precious to the Lord.*

> Lord, open my heart to believe I am beautiful in Your eyes; that You see my heart and my willing spirit and Your heart is ravished (filled with great joy and delight) over me! Impart to me the grace of benevolence, Lord, that I would be kind and generous in providing help to others, especially the poor. I ask that You would help me walk before You with holiness of heart, having victory over my soul as I learn to abide in You. Clothe me with Your humility, Lord, so that even when others sin against me, I will know that You are allowing it for my good to make me more like You.

6:5 "Turn your eyes away from Me, for they have confused [or overcome] Me; your hair is like a flock of goats that have descended from Gilead" *[Bridegroom speaking]*.

Both the King James Version and New King James Version translate this, "Turn your eyes away from me, for they have *overcome* me" (emphasis added). The Lord is speaking to the bride using the language of love poetry, expressing the depth of emotion He feels because of her steadfast love and trust in Him throughout her "dark night of the soul." Instead of accusing Him and turning away from Him in anger, she remained faithful to Him, choosing to believe in His supreme goodness and faithfulness to her. *The Lord speaks as the Lover of her soul, exclaiming that she has deeply moved His heart by her loyalty and love for Him even when it appeared He had abandoned her.* The Lord longs for those who love Him, not for what He does for them, but for who He is! This selfless love overwhelms the heart of our great King!

There are relatively few on the earth that long to *know the Lord* as He truly is—that yearn to know His heart, His emotions, and His thoughts. Rather than being satisfied with knowledge *about* God, which is religion, they hunger for relationship (or *friendship* with Him) even as Abraham, Enoch, David, Paul, and John longed to know Him as their friend. This is what "overcomes" (overwhelms with emotion or conquers) the heart of Jesus!

> "...your hair is like a flock of goats that have descended from Gilead."

The Lord spoke these words of endearment to her previously in Song 4:1. As noted earlier, hair in the Scripture is associated with God-given strength as in the life of Samson (cf. Judges chapters 13–16) as well as with the Nazirite vow. The Lord compares her hair to a flock of goats who have descended the mountain after feeding at the famous pastures of Mount Gilead. The goats of that region were renowned for their shiny black hair due to the superior pastures found on the mountain. *The Lord speaks of the bride's hair as being beautiful and shiny, which symbolizes the dedication of her heart to Him and her desire to minister to others with the strength that He provides, not her own strength. Her desire is to abide in Him: to be yoked with Him in service so that she serves alongside Him, depending on His strength and the life of His Spirit flowing through her as she ministers to others.*

> Lord, I want to know Your heart, Your emotions, Your thoughts, and Your ways. I want to be Your friend even as Abraham, Enoch, David, Paul, and John were Your friends. Teach me to "wait upon You": to share my heart with You and then listen for Your words of life to me. Make my heart sensitive to Your promptings and impressions and the still small voice of the Holy Spirit. Help me remain in that posture of heart throughout the day, Lord, as I learn to abide in You.

6:6 "Your teeth are like a flock of ewes which have come up from their washing, all of which bear twins, and not one among them has lost her young" *[Bridegroom speaking].*

The Lord spoke these words of praise to the bride previously in Song 4:2. As mentioned before, *teeth symbolize the ability to chew meat or spiritually—to teach the meat of God's Word.* The Lord is praising the bride for her ability to both assimilate and to teach the meat of God's Word to those she disciples. In contrast, Paul wrote to the carnal believers at Corinth that they were not yet able to receive the meat of God's Word or what he called solid food: "And I, brethren, could not speak to you as to spiritual men, but as to men of flesh, as to infants in Christ. I gave you milk to drink, not solid food; for you were not yet able to receive it. Indeed, even now you are not yet able, for you are still fleshly..." (1 Cor. 3:1–3).

The phrase "come up from their washing" speaks of the bride's desire to be continually washed with the water of the Word. She understands that it is one thing to teach God's Word but another to walk in it. The beloved apostle John wrote, "I have no greater joy than this, to hear of my children walking in truth" (3 John 1:4). The bride desires not only to teach the truth, she desires to *be true*. In other words, she desires her life to be an expression of the truth of the gospel. Art Katz wrote that when Jesus said, "I am the Truth," He was implying that *truth is more than a sum of right answers. It is not something to have at all but something, first and above all else, to be.*

Paul wrote to the Ephesian church that the Lord would sanctify us, cleansing us "by the washing of water with the word" (Eph. 5:26). Hebrews 4:12 reminds us, "For the word of God is living and active and sharper than any two-edged sword, and piercing as far as the division of soul and spirit, of both joints and marrow, and able to judge the thoughts and intentions of the heart." Paul admonished Timothy, "All Scripture is inspired by God and profitable for teaching, for reproof, for correction, for training in righteousness" (2 Tim. 3:16). He wrote to the Corinthians, "For if we would judge ourselves, we would not be judged [by the Lord]. But when we are judged, we are chastened [or disciplined] by the Lord, that we may not be condemned with the world" (1 Cor. 11:31–32, NKJV). *We "judge ourselves" by allowing the Word of God to wash us, showing us where we have been defiled by sin or sinful attitudes so that we can repent and ask for the Lord's forgiveness, thereby keeping a clear conscience (or pure heart) before Him.*

The Lord compares the bride's teeth to a flock of ewes (or female sheep). It is unusual for sheep to bear twins, yet the Lord compares her teeth to sheep that have not only carried their young full term, they have borne twins. *This speaks of her reproductive ability, i.e., her ability to draw others into the kingdom and to disciple them so that they are able to receive the meat of God's Word.*

"And not one of them has lost her young" is a metaphor for the bride's constant vigilance for those under her care and for her intercession on their behalf. The apostle Paul spoke of this vigilance and motherly concern for the churches under his care when he wrote, "But we proved to be gentle among you, as a nursing mother tenderly cares for her own children" (1 Thess. 2:7). He wrote to the church at Corinth, "Then, besides all of this, I have the daily burden of my concern for all the churches. Who is weak without my feeling that weakness? Who is led astray, and I do not burn with anger?" (2 Cor.

11:28–29, NLT). This maternal concern for those she disciples is a reflection of the Lord's own heart for His children and brings Him great joy.

> Lord, I ask You to sanctify me: daily cleansing my heart by the washing of Your Word. Help me to judge myself as Your Word reveals sin or sinful attitudes so that I can repent and receive Your forgiveness, thereby keeping a pure heart before You. Help me nourish those You give me to disciple with the meat of Your Word when they are able to receive it, Lord. And give me the heart of a spiritual parent so that I will be vigilant and faithful in prayer on their behalf.

6:7 "Your temples are like a slice of a pomegranate behind your veil" *[Bridegroom speaking].*

The Lord spoke these words of praise to the bride previously in Song 4:3. The temples are the area between the eyes and the hairline. They represent the thought life since this is where the organ of thought—the brain—is located. As mentioned before, Jewish tradition teaches that the pomegranate is a symbol for righteousness. The veil was a symbol for modesty and submission in many ancient cultures. Therefore, combining these metaphors, *the Lord is commending the bride for submitting her thought life to the Word of God so that she can walk in His righteous ways.*

Paul wrote that we are to bring every thought captive to the obedience of Christ (2 Cor. 10:5), knowing that every sin we commit originates in the mind including sinful attitudes such as pride, jealousy, covetousness, etc. These sinful attitudes grieve the Holy Spirit just as much as the overt sins such as lying, stealing, drunkenness, and sexual sins. The key to walking in the Spirit is to set our mind on the things of the Spirit, as Paul wrote to the church at Rome: "…But those who are habitually dominated by the Spirit put their minds on the things of the Spirit" (Rom. 8:5, WUEST).

> Lord, wash me daily with the water of Your Word and show me areas of my life that need to be brought into submission to it. I want to "walk in

the Spirit" by fellowshipping with Him throughout my day and setting my mind on the things that please Him.

6:8–9 "There are sixty queens and eighty concubines, and maidens without number; but My dove, My perfect one, is unique: she is her mother's only daughter; she is the pure child of the one who bore her..." *[Bridegroom speaking]*.

Queens, concubines, and maidens in this verse are a metaphor for the court of heaven, which includes levels of angelic beings. Just as the court of an earthly king had levels of attendants—with the queens or wives the highest in rank, followed by concubines, and then maidens—the court in heaven has levels of angelic beings. We know that there are cherubim, also called "living beings," around the throne of God (cf. Ezek. chapter 1 and 10:15). There are seraphim surrounding the throne who continually proclaim His holiness (cf. Isa. 6:2–3). The Book of Daniel refers to the angel Michael as one of the "chief princes" (Dan. 10:13) and as "the great prince who stands guard over the sons of your [Daniel's] people" (Dan. 12:1). He is depicted as a very high ranking warrior angel and the angel specifically assigned to protect Israel.

Jesus is the commander of the angelic hosts of heaven and is called the "Lord of Hosts" many places in the Scripture (cf. Ps. 24:10; Isa. 10:16, 51:15; Jer. 50:34; Zech. 4:6; Mal. 1:14, etc.). The Hebrew word for "hosts" is *tsaba* and means a mass (of persons, especially for war), an army, the host of heaven, etc. The basic meaning is service done for a superior, usually military service. Just as an earthly army must have levels of authority in order to accomplish its goals, we can infer that there are levels of angelic beings under the authority of the Lord of Hosts (or Commander of the Angelic Armies), Jesus.

"...but My dove, My perfect one, is unique..."

The Lord once again calls the bride "My dove": a reference to her loyalty and devotion and the single focus of the eyes of her heart on Him alone. His second term of endearment is "My perfect one." The

Hebrew word for "perfect one" is *tam* and means complete, whole, upright, pious, innocent, sincere, undefiled, or having integrity. *She is perfect in the sense that her heart is wholly devoted to Him, and she is learning to walk in His righteous ways as she progressively comes to abide in Him.* Finally, the Lord commends her as being "unique." *The literal translation for unique is "one," meaning the only one who has His attention or the gaze of His heart.* It is difficult for us as finite beings to understand how the Lord can focus the eyes of His heart on each one of us, as individuals, when there are so many people in the world. It is helpful to remember that while we are limited, He is unlimited; while we are created, He is uncreated; while we occupy space and time, He does not. *Our God is a Spirit and is omnipresent (present in all places at the same time); therefore, He can hold each one of us in view concurrently as if we were the "only one."*

"...she is her mother's only daughter..."

Although many commentators believe the word "mother" here symbolizes the church, I believe it symbolizes God, who created man in His own image and who Scripture portrays as having both masculine and feminine qualities (cf. Ps. 91:4; Isa. 66:10–13, 46:3–4, etc.). The Father purposed before the creation that His Son would have a bride. Because He is omniscient (possessing all knowledge), He knew that His children would choose the path of independence and rebellion against Him, but He had a plan from the beginning to redeem them and restore them to relationship with Himself. That plan in the heart of God from the very beginning cost Him more than we can understand. It required the excruciating torture and death of His Son on the cross. Jesus is called "the Lamb slain *from the foundation of the world*" by the Holy Spirit in the Book of Revelation (Rev. 13:8). *The only proof we need of the staggering and amazing love the Father has for us is the Cross.*

William P. Young does a wonderful job portraying the value God places on us as His children in *The Shack*:

[Papa speaking to Mack] "You have such a small view of what it means to be human. You and this Creation are incredible, whether you understand that or not. You are wonderful beyond imagination. Just because you make horrendous and destructive choices does not mean you deserve less respect for what you inherently are—the pinnacle of my Creation and the center of My affection."[2]

Being created in God's image, we are truly the pinnacle of His Creation. He did not die to redeem fallen angels but those He created to live in fellowship with Himself. This is what is symbolized by the metaphor, "she is her mother's only daughter."

"...she is the pure child of the one who bore her..."

The Hebrew word for "pure" here is *bar,* and one of its meanings is "chosen." *This phrase could have been translated, "she is the chosen child of the one who bore her." We are His chosen ones; the ones He loved enough to die for!*

Lord, open my heart to believe that because You are omnipresent, You see me as "unique": the only one who has the gaze of Your heart. Give me revelation of my incredible value as Your child; the one You loved enough to die for. And make me secure in knowing that I am the pinnacle of Your creation and the center of Your affection—Your chosen one.

6:9–10 "... The maidens saw her and called her blessed, the queens and concubines also, and they praised her, saying, 'Who is this that grows like the dawn, as beautiful as the full moon, as pure as the sun, as awesome as an army with banners?'** *[Bridegroom speaking].*

The word translated "maidens" is literally "daughters" in this verse. The Lord is quoting the daughters of Jerusalem who, along with the angelic host, are watching His bride grow in her ability to abide in Him and walk in His righteous ways. They praise the bride, saying: "Who is this that grows like the dawn...?" Proverbs reveals the meaning of this metaphor: "But the path of the righteous is like the light of dawn, that shines brighter and brighter until the full day" (Prov. 4:18). *The daughters are praising the bride for her progressive sanctification and growth in righteousness as she is learning to abide in her Beloved, Jesus.*

"…as beautiful as the full moon…"

The moon does not produce light as the sun does; it simply reflects the light of the sun. *"As beautiful as the full moon" is a metaphor describing the glory the bride is adorned with as she abides in the Lord. She reflects His glory as the moon reflects the light of the sun.* Paul described this beautifully in his second letter to the church at Corinth: "But we all, with unveiled face, beholding as in a mirror the glory of the Lord, are being transformed into the same image from glory to glory, just as from the Lord, the Spirit" (2 Cor. 3:18).

Paul uses specific wording in this verse to highlight truth that is often missed in a casual reading. The first significant phrase is "unveiled face." In verse 13, Paul references a veil that Moses wore over his face to cover (or "hide") the glory that made his face shine when he went in to speak with the Lord. Because the children of Israel were afraid to look at Moses when his face shone, whenever he left the Lord's presence he put a veil over his face, but when he went in to speak with the Lord he removed the veil. *Paul is using the term "veil" as a metaphor for something that hides the true reality of what is underneath it. When he speaks of "unveiled faces" in verse 18, he is referring to veils of deception in our hearts—the things we "hide" behind whether false beliefs about God or a false image that belies who we really are.*

Jesus said to truly worship the Father we must worship in spirit and in truth. "In truth" refers both to the truth of who we really are, our masks removed, and to the truth of who He really is, not the god we have created in our own image. A. W. Tozer wrote:

> Among the sins to which the human heart is prone, hardly any
> other is more hateful to God than idolatry, for idolatry is at

bottom a libel on His character. The idolatrous heart assumes God is other than He is—in itself a monstrous sin—and substitutes for the true God *one made after its own likeness*. ... Almost every heresy that has afflicted the church through the years has arisen from believing about God things that are not true, or from overemphasizing certain true things so as to obscure other things equally true. ... We can hold a correct view of truth only by daring to believe everything God has said about Himself.[3]

The second significant word in this passage is "mirror." Unlike today's mirrors, a mirror in New Testament times gave an imperfect reflection of the person using it. Mirrors of that day were usually made of highly polished brass or bronze and consequently gave a dim and distorted reflection. Although our ability to behold the Lord is also imperfect, as we seek to know Him and to see Him as He truly is (our own hearts laid bare before Him) the Holy Spirit allows us to glimpse His glory. The Greek word for "glory" is *doxa* and means not the outward glorious appearance, attracting attention to the person or thing itself, but *that glory shown from within reflecting in the appearance* which attracts attention. The Lord's glory is so powerful that to even catch a glimpse of it is to be changed by it in our inner man. We are transformed into His image with ever-increasing glory by the Spirit so that our lives become a witness of the risen Lord.

"...as pure as the sun..."

The Hebrew word for "pure" is *bar*, which is derived from the word *barar* meaning to cleanse or purify. *The daughters are commending the bride for her purity of heart.* The bride's response to her twofold test (losing both the sense of the Lord's presence and her covering for ministry) exemplifies 1 Peter 1:7, "so that the proof of your faith ... even though tested by fire, may be found to result in praise and glory and honor at the revelation of Jesus Christ." It is noteworthy that the Greek word for "tested" here is *dokimazo* and means to prove or *bring forth the good in us. Every test we go through is for our good: to bring forth the good in us, to strengthen our faith, to purify our hearts, and to draw us closer to the Lord.*

"...as awesome as an army with banners?"

The Lord is speaking in this verse, repeating the daughters' praise. As stated before, an army with banners was a victorious army. *The daughters are praising the bride for the victory she has over her own soul and over the demonic powers that tempted her to accuse God when she was tested.*

> Lord, show me the veils that lie over my heart: both false beliefs about You and the masks that hide who I really am to others. Help me remove those veils so I can see You as You truly are and behold Your glory. I thank You that as I behold Your glory, it will change me on the inside. Your very own glory will begin to reflect in my appearance, drawing the lost toward You.

6:11 "I went down to the orchard of nut trees to see the blossoms of the valley, to see whether the vine had budded or the pomegranates had bloomed" *[Bride speaking].*

In Song 2:10–15, the Lord called the maiden to come with Him to the vineyards where the vines were in blossom. He informed her that the time had arrived for *pruning.* ("The vines" was not in the original text but was added by translators.) Although the Lord called her to go with Him to the vineyards (the place of service in His body), His emphasis was on pruning the vineyard (singular) of her heart. As she worked with Him in His vineyards, He used relationships and situations that she encountered to reveal sinful attitudes, hidden motives, and judgments in her heart. Then as she repented of these sinful attitudes and motives, the Holy Spirit purified her heart and conformed her more to the image of her Beloved.

In the passage before us, the bride says she went down to the orchard of nut trees with its vines and pomegranate trees to see if there were buds on the vines or blossoms on the trees. *This orchard of nut trees with its vines and pomegranate trees is referring to the corporate body of Christ. The budding vines and trees in blossom refer to different bodies of believers in various stages of maturity as symbolized by buds and blossoms with no mention of fruit.* Because the bride is abiding in the Lord, she is able to see these bodies of believers through His eyes and is not offended by the areas where they are lacking. She demonstrates the servant heart of her Lord, seeking only to work alongside Him in His vineyards, yoked to Him, as He tends His maturing vines.

> Lord, give me a servant's heart and enable me to see Your people through Your eyes. Enable me to look beyond the things that would offend the flesh and to see with spiritual eyes the beautiful vineyards You will produce by Your loving cultivation. Lead me to the specific vineyards where You want me to serve, and help me remain yoked to You, working alongside You as You tend Your maturing vines.

6:12 "Before I was aware, my soul set me over the chariots of my noble people" *[Bride speaking].*

The Revised Standard Version translates this verse, *"Before I was aware, my fancy set me in a chariot beside my prince."* After the Lord's vindication of the bride in Song 6:4–9 and the expression of His deep love for her and praise for the virtues He sees developing in her character, *she is surprised by a desire to leave the comfort of what is familiar to be with Him serving the immature in His body. Almost without her notice, she finds herself seated beside "the Prince," Jesus, in a swift chariot: the fastest form of travel at that time. She now desires to go with Him, yoked with Him in service, wherever He might lead.*

> Lord, please enlarge my heart to believe the deep truths contained in Your Song that reveal how You see me and what You feel about me personally. But also reveal to me how You see Your beloved bride, the body of Christ. Enable me to see Your people through Your eyes as beloved children in different stages of maturity. Give me a servant's heart so that I will be willing to serve them alongside You wherever You might lead.

6:13 "Come back, come back, O Shulammite; come back, come back, that we may gaze at you! *[Daughters of Jerusalem speaking]*. Why should you gaze at the Shulammite, *[Bride speaking]* as at the dance of the two companies?" *[Daughters of Jerusalem speaking]*.

The King James Version renders this, "Return, return, O Shulamite; return, return, that we may look upon thee. What will ye see in the Shulamite? As it were the company of two armies." The punctuation in the KJV makes it easier to see why I believe the speakers in this verse are both the daughters of Jerusalem and the bride. (It is important to note that the original Hebrew text did not contain punctuation; the punctuation was added later by translators.) The daughters are crying out to the bride to return to them. They are distressed that she is leaving them to serve another body of believers. In their immaturity they are still self-focused, thinking of themselves instead of considering others in the body of Christ.

The daughters refer to the bride in this verse as "Shulammite"; this is the only time the title is given to her in the Song. Shulammite means daughter of peace and is the feminine form of Solomon. *The daughters' use of this title implies that they now recognize the maiden as the King's bride. Her life demonstrates that she is now "one spirit with Him"* (1 Cor. 6:17), *fulfilling the great mystery Paul spoke of regarding Christ and the church* (Eph. 5:31–32).

Earlier in the Song (6:1) the daughters expressed their desire to seek the Lord with the bride and asked her where He had gone. She replied that He had gone down to His gardens to pasture His flock (or care for His sheep). Yet at this point in their journey, the immature daughters were not ready to leave the comfort of the familiar to be with the Lord where He was serving. They wanted the bride to continue as their teacher and mentor. They had not yet learned to fellowship with the Holy Spirit, who is the Teacher. Jesus Himself told us, "But the Helper, the Holy Spirit, whom the Father will send in My name, *He will teach you all things, and bring to your remembrance all that I said to you*" (John 14:26, emphasis added). Watchman Nee described the biblical role of the Holy Spirit in his book *The Normal Christian Life*:

> We have learned in China that, when leading a soul to Christ, we must be very thorough, for there is no certainty when he will again have the help of other Christians. We always seek to make it clear to a new believer that, when he has asked the Lord to forgive his sins and to come into his life, his heart has become the *residence of a living Person*. The Holy Spirit is now within him, to open to him the scriptures that he may find Christ there, to direct his prayer, to govern his life, and to reproduce in him the character of the Lord.[4]

> "...Why should you gaze at the Shulammite..." [Bride speaking].

Concerning this verse, J. Hudson Taylor wrote that the bride cannot understand why any attention would be paid to her. She is just a servant of the King—the One whose beauty and glory is beyond description. Even as Moses was unconscious that His face shone with divine glory after he had been in the Lord's presence, so it is with the bride. She is unaware that the Lord's glory is now reflected in her appearance.[5]

> "...as at the dance of the two companies?" [Daughters of Jerusalem speaking].

The latter part of this verse is ambiguous and has been understood by commentators in several different ways. Some believe this statement is spoken by the bride; others believe it is spoken by the Bridegroom; still others believe it was spoken by the watchmen (or church leaders) of Song 5:7. The meaning of this statement can be interpreted in multiple ways depending on who is speaking.

It is my opinion that the daughters of Jerusalem are speaking here, answering the bride's question as to what they see when they gaze at her. It is important to note that their response according to the literal Hebrew translation is "as the dance of two camps (or *Mahanaim*)."[5]

Mahanaim literally means "two camps or two companies." In order to understand the symbolism of this statement, it is helpful to read Genesis chapters 32 and 33, which give the account of Jacob's reunion with his estranged brother Esau. Genesis 32:1–2 tells us, "Now as Jacob went on his way, the angels of God met him. Jacob said when he saw them, 'This is God's camp [or company].' So he named that place Mahanaim." As mentioned previously, Mahanaim means two camps or two companies. Jacob saw both the spiritual and the physical companies at this campsite. *When he saw the angels*, he said, "This is God's company"; in other words, the "spiritual company" or host of angels. The second "company" at this camp was the "physical company": Jacob, his two wives, his two maids, his eleven children, and numerous servants.

The daughters' reference to the dance of the two companies symbolizes both the physical and the spiritual evidence of the bride's walk with the Lord. They see not only the physical evidence of her life in God, revealed in good works, they also see the spiritual evidence displayed in her reliance on the Holy Spirit for His wisdom, His fruit, and His gifts. Just as the Bridegroom, Jesus, lived His earthly life as a perfect Man, dependent upon the Holy Spirit, so the bride is learning to live her life as one crucified with Christ, allowing Him to live His life through her as she depends on His Spirit. She is learning to be "supernaturally natural," moving seamlessly between what we often term the secular and the sacred.

> Lord, please open the eyes of my heart to see what You made available to me at the Cross—that because of Your sacrifice for me, my heart has become the holy of holies where You dwell by Your Spirit. Open my heart to understand that He is not some watered down version of You; He is Your very Spirit: fully equal to You and to the Father. Give me a spirit of revelation to know the depths of this incredible Treasure that I carry in my heart in the Person of the Holy Spirit! Transform what has been mental assent into living faith in my heart, Lord! Teach me to fellowship with Your Spirit—sharing my life with Him, talking to Him throughout my day, and listening for His still small voice to me.

Make me sensitive to His promptings and impressions, and help me to be quick to obey them. Teach me to submit to His discipline so that He can conform me to Your image. Help me learn to depend on Him to overcome my selfish nature, trusting Him to replace the reactions of my "old man" with His fruit. And cause me to zealously desire and to pray for His gifts to be manifest in my life so that others will experience Your love and Your power in a tangible way and be drawn to You.

Chapter 7

SEEING OTHERS THROUGH THE LORD'S EYES

7:1 "How beautiful are your feet in sandals, O prince's daughter! The curves of your hips are like jewels, the work of the hands of an artist" *[Daughters of Jerusalem speaking].*

THE DAUGHTERS OF Jerusalem continue their answer to the bride's question, "Why should you gaze at the Shulammite?" They exclaim, "How beautiful are your feet in sandals, O prince's daughter!" *The bride's feet in sandals symbolize her commitment to spread the good news, or "gospel of the kingdom," to those her life touches.* Paul made reference to this in his letter to the church at Rome (quoting the prophet Isaiah), "For 'Whoever will call upon the name of the Lord will be saved.' How then shall they call upon Him in whom they have not believed? How will they believe in Him whom they have not heard? And how will they hear without a preacher? How will they preach unless they are sent? Just as it is written, *'How beautiful are the feet of those who bring good news of good things!'"* (Rom. 10:13–15; verse 15 is quoting Isa. 52:7).

Even more than her words, the bride's life is a letter for all to read—a demonstration of the "good news." Paul wrote to the church at Corinth, "The only letter of recommendation we need is you yourselves. Your lives are a letter written in our hearts; everyone can read it and recognize our good work among you. Clearly, you are a letter from Christ showing the result of our ministry among you. This 'letter' is written not with pen and ink, but with the Spirit of the living God. It is carved not on tablets of stone, but on human hearts" (2 Cor. 3:2–3, NLT).

155

"...The curves of your hips are like jewels, the work of the hands of an artist."

The King James Version translates this, "...the joints of thy thighs are like jewels, the work of a cunning workman." This is the most literal translation as the Hebrew word for "curves" is *kaph* and means the curved or hollow part of the hand, etc. Obviously, the curved or hollow part of the bone of the thigh would be where the joint connects it to another bone.

Genesis 32 provides the meaning of this metaphor: "Then Jacob was left alone [at the camp Mahanaim], and a man [angel] wrestled with him until daybreak. And when he saw that he had not prevailed against him, he touched the socket of his thigh; so the socket of Jacob's thigh was dislocated while he wrestled with him. Then he said, 'Let me go, for the dawn is breaking.' But he said, 'I will not let you go unless you bless me.' So he said to him, 'What is your name?' And he said, 'Jacob.' He said, 'Your name shall no longer be Jacob, but Israel; for you have striven with God and with men and have prevailed'" (Gen. 32:24–28). The prophet Hosea tells us that this "angel" was actually the preincarnate Christ: "In the womb he [Jacob] took his brother by the heel, and in his maturity he contended with God. Yes, he wrestled with the angel and prevailed; He wept and sought His favor. He found Him at Bethel and there He spoke with us, even the LORD, the God of hosts; the LORD is His name" (Hos. 12:3–5).

The *Keil & Delitzsch Commentary on the Old Testament* gives profound revelation regarding this interaction, which I will shorten and paraphrase for the sake of time and intent. Jacob had stolen Esau's birthright by cunning and deceit, causing him to flee from his brother's wrath and the land of promise. Later he desired to return to the land of Canaan and receive the inheritance promised him in his father's blessing. He sent word to Esau through messengers that he was returning, to which Esau responded by riding out to meet him with four hundred men. This filled Jacob with fear, and he prayed for the Lord to deliver him from Esau's hand (Gen. 32:9–12). To save him from the hand of his brother, the Lord first met him as an enemy to show him that his real opponent was God Himself and that he must first overcome God before he could hope to overcome his brother. Jacob wrestled with the Lord, who appeared to him in the form of an angel and touched the socket of his thigh to dislocate it, symbolizing the futility of "fighting against flesh and blood" (Eph. 6:12). However, by no means did Jacob relent; he wept and sought the Lord's favor (as Hosea tells us) by the power of faith and prayer and would not let Him go until He blessed him. By this interaction, Jacob entered into a new season in his life. As the sign of this, the Lord gave him a new name, Israel, which means "he who strives with God."

It is important to note that a name in biblical times was chosen for a specific reason, unlike our culture today. For example, Adam named his wife "Eve" because she was the mother of all the living. Eve means "living" or "life" (cf. Gen. 3:20). A name might also represent something significant about the person or the circumstances surrounding their birth (cf. Gen. 29 and 30 regarding the birth of Jacob's children). *Often a name represented the essential quality or nature of a person. This aspect is most clearly demonstrated by the many names of God that He used to reveal His character to His people under the old covenant (for example, Jehovah Rapha, which means "the Lord our healer," or Jehovah Tsidkenu, which means "the Lord our righteousness").* Often when God changed someone's name, their new name represented their prophetic destiny. God promised Abram that He would make a great nation of him when he left Haran (cf. Gen. 12:2). When He confirmed the promise to Abraham twenty-four years later, He changed Abram's name (which means "exalted father") to Abraham (meaning "father of a multitude"). God changed Sarai's name to Sarah, which means "princess," saying, "...kings of peoples will come from her" (cf. Gen. 17:16). Although God's promise was impossible in the natural (Abraham was one hundred years old and Sarah was ninety), He opened Sarah's womb and gave her a child. This child Isaac became the father of Jacob; Jacob became the father of the twelve tribes of Israel or the Jewish nation. Thus, Abraham fulfilled his prophetic destiny and became the "father of a multitude."

By changing Jacob's name (which means "one who supplants")

to Israel, meaning "he who strives with God," the Lord confirmed the nature of Jacob's new relationship with Him as one who strives with God in faith and prayer. *"The joints of thy thighs are like jewels, the work of a cunning workman..."* (KJV) *symbolizes the work of the Holy Spirit, the master Workman, who has taught the bride (through trials, i.e., striking the joint of her thigh) to strive with the Father in faith and prayer. This sacrificial intercession is more beautiful to the Father than the most stunning jewels would be to the human eye. The bride does not wrestle with flesh and blood but instead strives with the Holy Spirit in prayer; the Spirit then releases the angels to move* "spiritual forces of wickedness in the heavenly places" (cf. Eph. 6:12).

> Lord, I want my life be a "living letter" for all to read, written not with pen and ink but with the power of Your Spirit in a transformed life. May my life demonstrate the "good news"—the gospel of Your kingdom—more than my words. Teach me to strive with You in faith and prayer, releasing Your angels to move spiritual forces of wickedness in the heavenly places. Help me to lay down my life for others in sacrificial intercession, which is more beautiful than the most stunning jewels in Your eyes.

7:2 "Your navel is like a round goblet which never lacks mixed wine; your belly is like a heap of wheat fenced about with lilies" *[Daughters of Jerusalem speaking].*

In order to understand the symbolism of this verse, it is helpful to look at each of the metaphors individually. The navel is the visible scar on the body caused when the umbilical cord is removed from a newborn baby; thus, the navel symbolizes the ability to receive nourishment. Wine in the Scripture often symbolizes the Holy Spirit (cf. Acts 2:1–13; Matt. 9:17, etc.). Mixing wine with water ("mixed wine") was a Hellenistic practice common in Palestine before New Testament times. Water symbolizes both the Word of God (cf. Eph. 5:26, Heb. 10:22) and the Holy Spirit in many places in Scripture (cf. John 4:14, 7:38–39; Isa. 44:3, etc.). Therefore, "mixed wine" symbolizes both the written Word of God (Greek *logos*) and the present tense word of the Spirit (Greek *rhema*). For a comparison of the Greek words logos and rhema, see Mark 7:10–13, which uses "logos" to refer to the written Scriptures and Ephesians 6:17 where "rhema" refers not to the whole Bible, but the individual scripture that the Spirit brings to our remembrance for use in time of need. Combining these metaphors, *the daughters are praising the bride for her ability to receive the nourishment of both the written Word of God (Greek "logos") and the "rhema" (spoken) word of the Spirit.*

"…your belly is like a heap of wheat fenced about with lilies."

Jesus said in John 7:38, "He that believeth on me, as the scripture hath said, out of his belly shall flow rivers of living water" (KJV). Wheat refers to those who come to saving faith in the parables of Jesus (cf. Matt. 3:12, 13:24–30; Luke 3:17; John 12:24). Lilies are white and represent purity. The reference to the bride's belly as large like a "heap of wheat" implies that she is pregnant and ready to give birth. Combining these metaphors, *the Holy Spirit is describing the bride as one who is pregnant with the harvest. Rivers of living water flow from her "belly" or spirit, drawing the lost toward the Savior. These rivers of living water include both the fruit and the gifts of the Holy Spirit and not only attract unbelievers, they establish the believers that she disciples in purity and holiness.*

Lord, open my mind to understand the Scriptures (Luke 24:45) so that I can receive the nourishment of Your written Word. Open my spiritual ears to listen as a disciple (Isa. 50:4) so that I can receive the nourishment of Your "rhema" word—the voice of Your Spirit. I want to hear Your word behind me saying, "This is the way to walk" before I turn to the right or to the left (Isa. 30:20–21). Cause Your Spirit to flow from my spirit as a river of living water to draw the lost to You and to establish in purity and holiness those You give me to disciple.

7:3 "Your two breasts are like two fawns, twins of a gazelle" *[Daughters of Jerusalem speaking]*.

The daughters are repeating the Lord's commendation of the bride in chapter 4, verse 5. As mentioned earlier, *the breast symbolizes the ability to spiritually feed and nurture others and to help new believers establish a firm foundation for their faith.*

The gazelle is a small, swift antelope. The Dorcas gazelle is found in hot and barren areas of Syria and Palestine. This species is especially swift and has been clocked at speeds of forty-five miles per hour for six or seven miles. *Metaphorically, the gazelle speaks of both divine strength and endurance in the bride's ministry to young believers.* Children can be taxing and demanding (whether natural or spiritual children). However, the bride is not trying to carry the burden of ministry in her own strength—she is relying on the Lord and is yoked to Him.

The metaphor "twins of a gazelle" symbolizes an enlarged capacity to nurture young believers. The gazelle would normally have only one offspring; thus, twins in this metaphor represent a "double portion" (cf. 2 Kings 2:9). I believe "twins" also represents the gems of truth contained in both the old and new covenants or what the Holy Spirit calls the "eternal covenant" (see comments on Song 4:5). *The daughters are praising the bride for her ability to nurture young believers, establishing their foundation on both the old and new covenants—or full counsel of Scripture. The bride is yoked to the Lord, depending on His strength and endurance, and allowing Him to carry the burden of ministry.*

> Lord, please give me Your divine strength and endurance to nurture younger believers as I remain yoked to You, allowing You to carry the burden of ministry. I ask for a double portion of the spirit of wisdom and revelation in the knowledge of You so that I can help young believers build a firm foundation for their faith.

7:4 "Your neck is like a tower of ivory, your eyes like the pools in Heshbon by the gate of Bath-rabbim; your nose is like the

tower of Lebanon, which faces toward Damascus" *[Daughters of Jerusalem speaking]*.

The Lord compared the bride's neck to the tower of David in chapter 4, verse 4. He was commending her resolute will, which is conformed to His will, and her authority in the spirit as one who knows how to use the shield of faith and the weapons of our warfare. Here the daughters of Jerusalem compare the bride's neck to a tower of ivory. As mentioned earlier, *the neck symbolizes the will and ivory symbolizes extravagance.* Ivory was a luxury in biblical times that only the very rich could afford. *The daughters are praising the bride's extravagant devotion to the Lord as one whose will is set to do His will, no matter what the cost.*

> "...your eyes like the pools in Heshbon by the gate of Bath-rabbim..."

The eyes speak of spiritual sight (seeing from the Lord's perspective) or our ability to receive revelation. The pools in Heshbon by the gate of Bath-rabbim were fish pools, so named because they were very clear, allowing the fish to be seen swimming below the surface. Jesus said when our eyes are "clear" (Greek *haplous*—of single focus, pure, without duplicity) our whole body will be full of "light" (Greek *phos*— the light of the sun, which is never kindled and never quenched). Jesus is the Sun of Righteousness spoken of in Malachi 4:2 (also cf. Matt. 6:22–23; Luke 11:34–36). In other words, when our eyes are in single focus on Jesus and His kingdom, our whole body will be full of His light and we will be enabled to see from His perspective.

The eyes are said to be the gateway or window to the soul because what we allow our eyes to focus on has either a positive or a negative impact on our soul. Art Katz wisely wrote:

> A lust is any desire that has not its origin from above, which is to say, God Himself is not the Author of it.... There is even a way in which we "legitimize" desire and lust, but it will captivate the soul. We become familiar to seeing it, and to others approving it, or using it, or wearing it, until by gradations,

there is a way in which the world has an increasing influence upon our life and *the dulling of our spirits*. To live soberly is also to live with a careful eye about what you allow yourself, that would have an injurious effect upon your spirit.[1]

The daughters are commending the bride for having "clear" eyes, which results in the ability to see from the Lord's perspective. She has learned to guard her heart with all diligence, for from the heart flow the springs of life (or the life-giving ministry of the Holy Spirit) (Prov. 4:23).

"...your nose is like the tower of Lebanon, which faces toward Damascus."

Watchman Nee explains that the nose speaks of discernment:

This is a kind of spiritual intuition that enables a person to identify the things that are of God. It is not by reason or logic, but by a spontaneous and inwardly accurate feeling, which enables a person to *discern spiritual matters*.[2]

The tower of Lebanon is a reference to a lofty structure built in the wall of the city of Lebanon and used for the purpose of protection or attack. Watchmen were positioned in these towers to warn of approaching enemies. These elevated structures were usually positioned at a gate or a corner in the wall (cf. 2 Chron. 14:7, 26:9). This tower is said to face toward Damascus, the capital of Syria, which was Israel's greatest enemy. *The bride's nose compared to the tower of Lebanon symbolizes her spiritual discernment: the ability to clearly recognize what is of God and what is of the enemy.*

The Scriptures speak of two kinds of discernment: the first is a general discernment that comes from obedience to the Word of God. Hebrews 5:14 tells us that those who digest the meat (or solid food) of God's Word and practice it train their senses to discern good and evil. The second is the spiritual gift of discernment, or discerning of spirits, i.e., the ability to discern the spiritual origin of a message or act (1 Cor. 12:10). Both kinds of discernment are vitally important because they enable us to "see" and understand the enemy's schemes and strategies against us (cf. 2 Cor. 2:11). *The daughters are praising the bride for her spiritual discernment that enables her to recognize the schemes of the enemy—both in her own life and in the lives of those she disciples.*

> Lord, I want to be Your bond-servant: one whose will is set to do Your will, no matter what the cost. I ask You to give me clear eyes in single focus on You and Your kingdom, enabling me to see from Your perspective. I ask You to help me live soberly, turning away from things that would dull my spirit. I ask You to help me walk in radical obedience to Your Word so that my senses will be trained to discern good and evil. And I ask for the spiritual gift of discernment so that I can recognize the enemy's strategies in my life and in the lives of those I disciple.

7:5 **"Your head crowns you like Carmel, and the flowing locks of your head are like purple threads; the King is captivated by your tresses"** *[Daughters of Jerusalem speaking].*

Mt. Carmel is an impressive promontory that crowns the Carmel range of mountains extending from the hill country of Samaria to the Mediterranean Sea. It is famous as the place where Elijah killed the 450 prophets of Baal after humiliating them before the Israelites in a contest to prove who was the one true God. In this metaphor Mt. Carmel is associated with the bride's head or, more specifically, her mind. Truly, the mind is our battleground. James wrote, "But each one is tempted when he is carried away and enticed by his own lust. Then when lust is conceived [or the thought in our mind is entertained and influences our will], it gives birth to sin..." (James 1:14–15). Paul wrote to the church at Rome, "Those who are dominated by the sinful nature *think* about sinful things, but those who are controlled by the Holy Spirit *think* about the things that please the Spirit. So letting your sinful nature control your mind leads to death. But letting the Spirit control your mind leads to life and peace" (Rom. 8:5–6, NLT, emphasis added). Paul wrote, "For the weapons of our warfare are not carnal but mighty in God for pulling down strongholds, casting down arguments and every high thing that exalts itself against the knowledge of God, bringing every thought into captivity to the obedience of Christ..." (2 Cor. 10:4–5, NKJV). *"Your head crowns you like Carmel" is a metaphor for the bride's thought life; the Holy Spirit controls her thoughts, taking them captive to make them obedient to the one true God, Jesus Christ.*

> "...and the flowing locks of your head are like purple threads;
> the King is captivated by your tresses."

Hair, as mentioned earlier, is associated with God-given strength as in the life of Samson and with the Nazirite vow, symbolizing consecration to the Lord. The word Nazirite means "separated" or, more specifically, "one who is separated unto the Lord." One of the requirements of the Nazirite vow was that "no razor shall pass over his head" (Num. 6:5). First Kings 6:7 gives us insight into the reason for this requirement: "And the temple, when it was being built, was built with stone finished at the quarry, so that no hammer or chisel or any iron tool was heard in the temple while it was being built" (NKJV). The iron used to make both a razor and the tools to finish the stone for the temple were offensive to God because *iron represents man's effort or man's strength apart from reliance on God.*

The color purple is also significant in this verse. Purple dye was very costly in biblical times because it was difficult to obtain. The shell of a marine mollusk had to be broken and a small gland in the neck of the mollusk removed and crushed. The crushed gland gave out a milklike fluid that turned purple or scarlet upon contact with the air. Because of its extreme costliness, only royalty or the very wealthy wore robes of purple. *The daughter's reference to the bride's hair as purple threads symbolizes the costly consecration of her life to the King of kings and her dependence on Him (through the indwelling Spirit) rather than dependence on her own strength and resources. The King, Jesus, is captivated by the consecration of her heart, which is summed up in Paul's words: "I have been crucified with Christ; and it is no longer I who live, but Christ lives in me; and the life which I now live in the flesh I live by faith in the Son of God, who loved me and [delivered] Himself up for me" (Gal. 2:20).*

Lord, please help me set my mind on the things that please Your Spirit. I want to take every thought captive that would influence me toward sin—especially thoughts leading to wrong attitudes like superiority and pride. Help me replace those sinful thoughts with Your truth. Enable me to live a life of consecration to You, and teach me to abide in You—depending on Your strength and resources instead of my own.

7:6 "How beautiful and how delightful you are, My love, with all your charms!" *[Bridegroom speaking].*

Up to this point, the daughters of Jerusalem have been answering the bride's question of Song 6:13, describing what they see when they gaze at her. (Compare Song 7:5 to this verse. The daughters exclaim in Song 7:5, "…the King is captivated by your tresses." In the verse before us, Jesus Himself is speaking: "…My love, with all your charms!") But now the Bridegroom interjects, affirming her with His words of life. She is beautiful in His eyes as He has described in great detail earlier in the Song, but more than that, she is delightful to Him! The word "delight" means *to give great joy or pleasure.* Selah! (Pause and think about that!) *The Lord, the King of Kings and Creator of the universes, says that we bring great joy and pleasure to His heart!* What an amazing and powerful truth! The Lord reaffirms this truth in Psalm 16:3: "As for the saints who are in the earth, they are the majestic ones in whom is *all My delight*" (emphasis added). Just as an earthly father delights in his children, our heavenly Father delights in us! *The knowledge of this one incredible truth, given by the revelation of the Holy Spirit, will bring freedom from every chain the enemy uses to try to bind us and to keep us from fulfilling our God-given destiny.* It is the *revelation* of this truth that will heal the broken areas of our hearts and change us in our inner man so that we become more like our Bridegroom.

Precious Lord, I ask You for revelation of the incredible truth that You delight in me and that I bring great joy to Your heart! Engrave this truth on my heart until it becomes part of my spiritual DNA and changes me on the inside. Apply it as a healing balm to heal every broken place in my heart so that I will become all that You created me to be.

7:7 "Your stature is like a palm tree, and your breasts are like its clusters" *[Bridegroom speaking].*

The word "stature" refers to a certain level of attainment, in this verse referring to spiritual attainment. The palm tree in Scripture is a symbol for victory and is associated with vigorous growth and success as in Psalm 92. Verses 12–15 of this psalm in the Amplified Bible describe stature like a palm tree:

> The [uncompromisingly] righteous shall flourish like the palm tree [be long-lived, stately, upright, useful and fruitful]; they shall grow like a cedar in Lebanon [majestic, stable, durable, and incorruptible]. Planted in the house of the Lord, they shall flourish in the courts of our God. [Growing in grace] they shall still bring forth fruit in old age; they shall be full of sap [of spiritual vitality] and [rich in the] verdure [of trust, love, and contentment]. [They are living memorials] to show that the Lord is upright and faithful to His promises; He is my Rock, and there is no unrighteousness in Him.

This portion of the psalm describes the Lord's praise for the bride perfectly. Combining these metaphors, *the Lord is commending the bride for her spiritual maturity: she is walking in His righteousness, stability, and fruitfulness. Her life is a living memorial to show that He is upright and faithful to His promises.*

Breasts like the clusters of a palm tree refer to the bride's ability to nurture young believers. The palm tree indigenous to Palestine is the date palm, which from June through September yields generous clusters of brown, red, yellow, or mahogany dates. Dates are considered an almost ideal food as they provide a wide range of essential nutrients. *Thus, the Lord is commending the bride for her ability to nurture young believers with a "balanced diet"—both the meat of the Word and the wine of His Spirit. The bride teaches these young believers that their hearts are now the residence of a living Person who will reveal Jesus to them in the Scriptures, direct their prayer, govern their lives, and reproduce in them the Lord's character as they learn to fellowship with His Spirit.*

> Lord, help me nurture the younger believers that You assign to me with a balanced diet—the meat of Your Word and the wine of Your Spirit. Help me come to know You in an intimate way as I fellowship with Your Spirit so that I can pass on to them what I know by experience, not theory.

7:8 "I said, 'I will climb the palm tree, I will take hold of its fruit stalks.' Oh, may your breasts be like clusters of the vine, and the fragrance of your breath like apples" *[Bridegroom speaking].*

"I will climb the palm tree, I will take hold of its fruit stalks," is a picture of the Holy Spirit, the Spirit of our Bridegroom, who is dedicated to "taking hold" of our theology—our understanding of God ("fruit stalks" in this metaphor)—as the Spirit of Truth. He opens our minds to understand the Scriptures (Luke 24:45) *as we acknowledge Him as the Teacher* (cf. 1 John 2:27 where the Greek word used for "anointing" is only found in this verse and means a communication and reception of the Holy Spirit). The Lord promised us that the Holy Spirit would teach us all things (John 14:26) and guide us into all the truth (John 16:13). When the Holy Spirit takes hold of our theology and gives us revelation of God as He truly is, it changes us in our "inner man." We are able to behold His glory and are transformed more and more into His image as we behold Him (2 Cor. 3:18).

"...Oh, may your breasts be like clusters of the vine..."

Breasts symbolize the ability to nurture others. Clusters of the vine (or grapes) symbolize the fruit of abiding in the True Vine, Jesus. The Lord is expressing His desire that the bride would nurture others from the overflow of her relationship with Him as she abides in Him, receiving His direction and "words of life" (John 6:68). The longing of the Father's heart is that His children would receive their life (Greek *zoe*: "life as God has it")—and all that sustains them—from Him as a branch abiding in the Vine (cf. John 6:32–33). This is a positional truth the moment we are born again, but it must become an experiential truth that is evident to others by the witness of our lives. Jesus said, "Remain in me, and I will remain in you. For a branch cannot produce fruit if it is severed from the vine, and *you cannot be fruitful unless you remain in me* (John 15:4, NLT).

Paul wrote to the church at Colossae, "Since *you have been raised to new life in Christ*, set your sights on the realities of heaven, where Christ sits in the place of honor at God's right hand.... For you died to this life, and your real life is hidden with Christ in God. And when *Christ, who is your life [zoe]*, is revealed to the whole world, you will share in all his glory (Col. 3:1–4, NLT, emphasis added). *The Lord longs for us to move beyond knowing Him only as our Savior and Lord to knowing Him as our Life.*

Paul wrote to the church at Rome, "Therefore we have been buried with Him through baptism into death, so that as Christ was *raised from the dead* through the glory of the Father, so we too might walk in newness of life [*resurrection life*]. For if we have become united with Him in the likeness of His death, certainly we shall also be in the likeness of His resurrection" (Rom. 6:4–5, emphasis added). Paul is saying in these verses that the way to walk in the resurrection life of Christ (as a branch abiding in the Vine) is to first *identify with Christ in His death* ("become united with Him in the likeness of His death"). In other words, even as *Jesus humbled Himself by becoming obedient to the point of death*, even death on the cross (Phil. 2:8), we become obedient to the Holy Spirit, allowing Him to crucify our "self" life. The last half of the verse promises that as we do this, *we will be united with Christ in the likeness (or resemblance) of His resurrection life (a life of victory over the sinful nature and one where we experience and demonstrate His power)! We allow the Holy Spirit to crucify our self life, to reduce it to nothing, so that Jesus can be everything—this is the "way of the cross" and the process by which Christ becomes our Life.*

"...and the fragrance of your breath like apples."

Earlier in the Song, the bride exclaimed, "Like an apple tree among the trees of the forest, so is my Beloved among the young men. In His shade I took great delight and sat down, and His fruit was sweet to my taste" (Song 2:3). *"Breath" in Scripture is from the same Hebrew word as "spirit" in many places in the Scripture; apples symbolize the fruit of Christ in Song 2:3; therefore, "the fragrance of your breath like apples" refers to the fragrance of Christ that clings to the bride's spirit through her fellowship with the Holy Spirit.* Paul wrote to the Corinthian church:

> But thank God! He has made us his captives and continues to lead us along in Christ's triumphal procession. Now he uses us to spread the knowledge of Christ everywhere, like a sweet perfume. Our lives are a Christ-like fragrance rising up to God. But this fragrance is perceived differently by those who are being saved and by those who are perishing. To those who are perishing, we are a dreadful smell of death and doom. But to those who are being saved, we are a life-giving perfume…
>
> —2 CORINTHIANS 2:14–16, NLT

> Lord, I ask that Your Spirit would take hold of my theology as the Spirit of Truth, bringing correction where I have been presumptuous with Your Word. I ask that He would open my mind to understand the Scriptures as I acknowledge Him as my Teacher. Help me cooperate with Him as He crucifies my "self life" so that I can walk in Your resurrection life. And help me abide in You, the True Vine, so that Your fragrance—bosem—will create desire in the hearts of others to know You, enabling me to "spread the knowledge of Christ everywhere, like a sweet perfume."

7:9 "And your mouth like the best wine *[Bridegroom speaking]*! It goes down smoothly for my Beloved, flowing gently through the lips of those who fall asleep" *[Bride speaking]*.

The bride's mouth is a metaphor for her intimacy with the Lord as in Song 1:2, "May He kiss me with the kisses of His mouth!" Because wine often symbolizes the Holy Spirit in Scripture (cf. Acts 2:4–13;

Eph. 5:18), *the Bridegroom's reference to her "mouth like the best wine" speaks of the bride's intimacy with Him through her fellowship with His Spirit.* Paul prayed that this intimate relationship with the Lord would be the experience of each one of us as we fellowship with the Holy Spirit: "The grace of the Lord Jesus Christ, and the love of God, and the *companionship and intimate conversation with the Holy Spirit* be with you all" (my expanded translation of 2 Cor. 13:14 using the definitions for fellowship and communion).

> "…It goes down smoothly for my Beloved, flowing gently through the lips of those who fall asleep" [Bride speaking].

"It (referring to the wine of the Holy Spirit) goes down smoothly for (or "for the sake of") my Beloved" speaks of the bride's instant obedience to the Holy Spirit's leadership. She has become the Lord's bond-servant. The Greek word for "bond-servant" is *doulos* and means one who is in a permanent relation of servitude to another, his (or her) will altogether consumed in the will of the other. *The bride's instant obedience to the Holy Spirit is for the sake of her Beloved, Jesus, and is the result of her deep love for Him.*

"Those who fall asleep" is a metaphor for carnal Christians as Romans 13:11–14 makes clear:

> And do this, knowing the time, that now *it is high time to awake out of sleep*; for now our salvation is nearer than when we first believed. The night is far spent, the day is at hand. Therefore let us cast off the works of darkness, and let us put on the armor of light. Let us walk properly, as in the day, not in revelry and drunkenness, not in lewdness and lust, not in strife and envy. But put on the Lord Jesus Christ, and make no provision for the flesh, to fulfill its lusts.
>
> —NKJV, EMPHASIS ADDED

First Thessalonians 5:5–6 gives a similar exhortation:

You are all sons of light and sons of the day. We are not of the night nor of darkness. Therefore *let us not sleep, as others do, but let us watch and be sober.*

—NKJV, EMPHASIS ADDED

Therefore, "flowing gently through the lips of those who fall asleep" refers to the witness of the bride's life, evidenced by her obedience to the Holy Spirit's leadership, which has a deep effect on carnal believers (those who do not maintain a sober watchfulness in their walk with the Lord). As they observe the bride's intimacy with the Lord and the joy of walking in fellowship with Him, a longing in their own hearts is awakened to know Him in a deeper way.

> Lord, the deepest desire of my heart is to know You intimately as I learn to fellowship with Your Spirit. Holy Spirit, I ask You to reveal Yourself to me as a Person—the third person of the Trinity—fully equal to Jesus and the Father. I want to know Your personality, Your thoughts, and Your emotions. Teach me to talk to You throughout my day and to listen for Your voice to me; make me sensitive to Your promptings and impressions. Help me exchange my fleshly thoughts, emotions, and reactions for Your thoughts, Your emotions, and Your reactions. Help me learn to depend on You for Your wisdom, Your fruit, and Your gifts. And teach me to appropriate by faith all that the Father has made available to me through You.

7:10 "I am my Beloved's, and His desire is for me" *[Bride speaking]*.

Notice the progression in the bride's perspective from the earlier days of her walk with the Lord. In Song 2:16 she says, "My Beloved is mine, and I am His..." Her first thought is of herself; she confesses that He belongs to her and His sacrifice was because of love *for her*; only secondarily does she acknowledge that she belongs to Him. In Song 6:3, after the testing of Song 5:2–7, the order is reversed. She now says, "I am my Beloved's and my Beloved is mine." At this point in her journey her first thought is of Him, and she acknowledges first His claim on her life.

We see further progression in the verse before us: "I am my Beloved's, and His desire is for me." Now the emphasis is completely on the Lord. She acknowledges again His ownership of her life but more than that, His *desire* is for her! The word "desire" in this verse is the Hebrew *tshuwqah* and means stretching out after, a yearning, or a longing. (Selah—pause and think about that! The God of the universes longs, even yearns, for us! The Hebrew word pictures Him stretching out to us in order to draw us to Himself!)

The bride has come to understand in an ever-increasing way that she is the apple of His eye, that she is precious in His sight, and that He delights in her (cf. Deut. 32:10; Ps. 17:8; Zech. 2:8; Isa. 43:4; Ps. 16:3; Prov. 11:20, 12:22). She is secure in the knowledge that *her Beloved loves her to the same degree that the Father loves Him* (John 15:9)! It is this revelation that has freed her from her fear and the love of self so that her heart is now His without reservation. As a result, in the next verse she asks Him to go to the fields and vineyards with her, yoked in partnership, to serve those that He loves.

> Lord, I am Yours and Your desire is for me! Your Word says that You long for me; the Hebrew word even pictures You stretching Yourself out with yearning to draw me to Yourself! Thank You for opening my heart to believe that I am the apple of Your eye, that I am precious in Your sight, and that You delight in me! You love me as much as the Father loves You! Thank You for engraving these truths on my heart by the revelation of Your Spirit.

7:11 "Come, my Beloved, let us go out into the country, let us spend the night in the villages" *[Bride speaking].*

The literal translation of this verse is, "Come, my Beloved, let us go out into the field…" *In the parable of the tares, Jesus explained that the field is the world* (Matt. 13:38). *In this verse, the bride is asking the Lord for the privilege of serving with Him in His field: the world.* It is noteworthy that the bride initiates this request, not the Lord as in the earlier verses of the Song. Four times in verses 11–12 she says, "let us." Contrast this with Song 5:2–3, "…'Open to Me, My sister,

My darling...I have taken off my dress, how can I put it on again? I have washed my feet, how can I dirty them again?'"; Song 6:2, "My Beloved has gone down to His garden...," and Song 6:11, "I went down to the orchard..." The bride speaks of herself or of the Lord in these earlier passages but does not acknowledge their union as she does in Song 7:11–12.

"...let us spend the night in the villages."

The latter part of this verse suggests that the bride has adopted the sojourning nature of the Lord. When a scribe came to Jesus and declared that he would follow the Lord wherever He went, Jesus replied, "...The foxes have holes and the birds of the air have nests, but the Son of Man has nowhere to lay His head" (Matt. 8:20). *The bride's statement in this verse demonstrates that she is now willing to move from one place to another, following the Lord as He seeks lost and wounded sheep.* Her statement also suggests a shift in ministry focus. Whereas in the earlier verses of the Song, her focus was exclusively on the vineyards, or bodies of believers, she now turns her attention to the lost as well. She understands that while the Lord concentrated His attention on the disciples (or "early church") before His crucifixion (cf. Matt. 15:24), His *purpose* was to train them before sending them out to carry the good news—or gospel of the kingdom—to His field: the world (cf. Matt. 24:14; Luke 24:45–47). This was God's plan for His people all along (cf. Isa. 49:5–6). The maiden demonstrates in this verse and the one which follows that she now has the Lord's heart for both the lost—the world that He loves—and for His bride, the church.

> Lord, please give me Your heart for Your field: the world that You love. Give me Your sojourning nature that seeks after the lost and wounded lambs, and help me remain yoked to You as You tend Your sheep.

7:12 "Let us rise early and go to the vineyards; let us see whether the vine has budded and its blossoms have opened,

and whether the pomegranates have bloomed. There I will give You my love" *[Bride speaking].*

The bride's focus in the previous verse was on the lost (the Lord's field: the world). In this verse, she turns her attention to His vineyards (or bodies of believers). At the beginning of her journey, she learned by experience the folly of serving in the vineyards at the expense of her own vineyard (Song 1:6 "…My mother's sons were angry with me; they made me caretaker of the vineyards, but I have not taken care of my own vineyard.") In her immaturity, she could not maintain her intimacy with the Lord while meeting the demands of ministry. As demonstrated by the verse before us, the bride has now matured in her ability to abide in the Lord so that she is able to balance *being drawn* in an intimate relationship with the Lord and *running together* with Him in ministry. This was her prayer of Song 1:4, "Draw me after you and let us run together!…"

> "…let us see whether the vine has budded and its blossoms have opened, and whether the pomegranates have bloomed…"

This reference to the vines and pomegranates is reminiscent of Song 6:11, "I went down to the orchard of nut trees to see the blossoms of the valley, to see whether the vine had budded or the pomegranates had bloomed." In the verse just referenced the bride says, "I went down…" while in this verse and the previous verse she no longer uses the pronoun "I" but "us," referring to her union with the Lord. Yoked with Him, she now goes where He leads and ministers with the strength that He provides, not her own strength.

The different bodies of believers in this verse, represented by vines and pomegranates, are somewhat immature as suggested by buds and blossoms with no mention of fruit. The maturing bride is no longer concerned with serving only those from her particular "stream" in the body of Christ; the most immature believer from any stream is now a candidate for discipleship if they exhibit signs of life and the hope of fruit-bearing. She now sees all believers as Jesus's inheritance from the Father, equally loved by Him and worthy of her service.

"...There I will give You my love."

The bride is now able to maintain an intimate relationship with Jesus while serving with Him in His gardens and vineyards. *She demonstrates her love for Him as she feeds His sheep* (cf. John 21:15–17).

> Lord, please help me balance being drawn in an intimate relationship with You and running with You in service. Help me put the first commandment first—loving You with my whole heart, mind, soul, and strength—which will enable me to fulfill the second great commandment: loving others as myself. As I minister to You first, fill my heart with Your rivers of living water so they will flow out of my heart to those I serve.

7:13 "**The mandrakes have given forth fragrance; and over our doors are all choice fruits, both new and old, which I have saved up for You, my Beloved**" *[Bride speaking].*

The mandrake was commonly known as the "love-apple." It grew throughout Palestine in deserted fields and had white or purple flowers. The fleshly forked root made it resemble a human form; thus, it became associated with fertility or reproductive ability. The only other mention of this fruit in the Bible is Genesis 30:14–16. In this account, Leah's son Reuben found mandrakes in the field and presented them to his mother. Rachel (who was barren) was convinced that they could cure her infertility, so she struck a bargain with Leah to obtain the mandrakes. *"The mandrakes have given forth fragrance" refers to the reproductive ability of the bride. As she works in the gardens and vineyards yoked to Jesus, His fragrance ("bosem") clings to her. It is this fragrance of Christ emanating from her life that "creates desire" in the hearts of others to know Him.* As Paul said, we manifest the sweet aroma of the knowledge of Christ in every place (2 Cor. 2:14).

The phrase "over our doors" refers to the lintel, which was a horizontal piece of wood or stone spanning the door of Hebrew homes. Before the Israelites' exodus from Egypt, the blood of the sacrificed Passover lamb was sprinkled on the lintel and doorposts of the Israelites' homes as a sign. When the destroying angel saw the blood, he passed over their homes but killed all the firstborn of the Egyptians (Exod. 12:23–32). This blood applied to the lintel was, of course, a type of the blood of Jesus—the true Passover Lamb. Jesus Himself calls it "My blood of *the* covenant" (Matt. 26:28; Mark 14:24, emphasis added). The Holy Spirit called it the *eternal* covenant in the letter to the Hebrews: "Now the God of peace, who brought up from the dead the great Shepherd of the sheep through the blood of the *eternal covenant*, even Jesus our Lord" (Heb. 13:20, emphasis added).

The bride has become a "disciple of the kingdom" in fulfillment of Jesus's words in Matthew 13:52, "Therefore every scribe who has become a disciple of the kingdom of heaven is like a head of a household, who brings forth out of his treasure things new and old." *These "things new and old" are the choice fruits of the new and old covenants, or eternal covenant, as the writer of Hebrews calls it. As the bride sits at the Lord's feet, being taught by Him* (John 14:26), *He reveals His covenant to her.* Psalm 25:14 says, "The secret of the LORD is for those who fear Him [meaning to revere Him—to show Him deep respect, love, and awe], and He will make them know His covenant." *The bride ministers first to the Lord, "waiting upon Him" or sitting at His feet to be taught by Him. He reveals His covenant to her (giving her choice fruits to nourish others) because of her deep love and respect for Him.* Then, as she works with Him in His vineyards, she freely offers these choice fruits to nourish those that He loves. Thus it may be said that she has saved up choice fruits for (or for the sake of) her Beloved.

> Lord, cause Your fragrance—bosem—to cling to me as I spend time in Your presence. I want to manifest Your sweet aroma wherever I go, creating desire in the hearts of others to know You. Help me become a disciple of the kingdom with revelation from the Holy Spirit regarding Your covenant with us. Enable me to offer choice fruits of both the old and new covenants, or "eternal covenant," to nourish those You love and to help them grow in godliness.

Chapter 8

THE PLACE OF ABIDING: LEANING ON OUR BELOVED

8:1 "Oh that You were like a brother to me who nursed at my mother's breasts. If I found You outdoors, I would kiss You; no one would despise me, either" *[Bride speaking].*

THE EASTERN BACKGROUND of the Song sheds light on this somewhat ambiguous verse. In the eastern tradition, brothers and sisters from the same mother would be permitted to kiss one another in public without drawing attention to themselves or causing offense, whereas a husband and wife would not do this. It is in this sense that the bride longs for Jesus to be as a brother to her so that she might lavish her love on Him in public, not only in private. Her statement also suggests that she has not yet overcome the "fear of man" since she speaks of being "despised" by others.

The fear of man is often one of the last vestiges of the flesh to be revealed to us by the Holy Spirit. The Lord once told me that we can either walk in the fear of man or the fear of the Lord, but we cannot walk in both simultaneously. He said to the degree that we choose to protect and defend our reputations in the eyes of men, we forfeit the fear of the Lord. When we choose intimacy with the Lord there must be a commitment to stop protecting "self" but, instead, to allow Him to be our Defender. King David is a wonderful example of this. Second Samuel chapter 6 tells of the ark of the covenant being brought up from the house of Obed-Edom to the city of Jerusalem. David and the people were rejoicing before the Lord with shouts of joy, trumpet blasts, and dancing. Verses 14–22 record, "And David danced before the LORD with all his might, wearing a priestly garment...But as the ark of the LORD entered the city of David, Michal, the daughter of Saul, looked down from her window. When she saw King David leaping and dancing before the LORD, she was filled with contempt for him.... When David returned home to bless his own family, Michal, the daughter of Saul, came out to meet him. She said in disgust, 'How distinguished the king of Israel looked today, shamelessly exposing himself to the servant girls like any vulgar person might do!" David retorted to Michal, 'I was dancing before the LORD, who chose me above your father and all his family! He appointed me as the leader of Israel, the people of the LORD, so I celebrate before the LORD. Yes, and I am willing to look even more foolish than this, even to be humiliated in my own eyes!'" (NLT). (Selah! Pause a moment and think about David's heart posture before the Lord!) Contrast this with the heart posture of the believing rulers of the Jews in Jesus's day: "...many even of the rulers believed in Him [Jesus], but because of the Pharisees they were not confessing Him, for fear that they would be put out of the synagogue; for they loved the approval of men rather than the approval of God" (John 12:42–43). *The bride is asking the Lord to deliver her from the fear of man in this verse. She is asking Him to give her an undivided heart— one that is fully His.*

> Lord, I echo the bride's prayer in this verse and ask You to deliver me from the fear of man. Please help me remove this veil over my heart, and enable me to lay down the need to protect my heart and my reputation. I choose to allow You to be my Defender, Lord. I ask You to give me an undivided heart—one that is fully Yours.

8:2 "I would lead You and bring You into the house of my mother, who used to instruct me; I would give You spiced wine to drink from the juice of my pomegranates" *[Bride speaking].*

This verse is a continuation of the bride's prayer in the preceding verse where she expressed her longing to show her love for the Lord freely—not only in the secret place of her devotional time with Him, but before others (being "God conscious," not "self conscious"). She asked Him to release her from the fear of man or, we could say, "the desire for the approval of men." "I would lead you and bring you into the house of my mother, who used to instruct me" refers to the body of believers who first instructed her in the things of God. The bride desires to share the deep things of God that He has imparted to her with those who were her spiritual fathers and mothers. She now wants the Lord's approval, not man's, and is even willing to risk rejection for His sake. Jesus said that a prophet is honored everywhere except in his own hometown and among his own family (Matt. 13:57). Often those closest to us, especially those who taught us at the beginning of our journey, are the most resistant to receiving from us. *The bride's prayer is that she would be freed from the fear of man, even willing to risk rejection, if her service to those who first instructed her in the things of God would bring glory and honor to the Lord.*

> "...I would give You spiced wine to drink from the juice of my pomegranates."

Spiced wine was often served to honored guests in ancient times. The addition of spices enhanced the flavor of the wine but also added to its cost. *The bride desires to serve Jesus with her best, regardless of personal cost.* Her heart cries, with the apostle Paul, "...everything else is worthless when compared with the infinite value of knowing Christ Jesus my Lord. For his sake I have discarded everything else, counting it all as garbage, so that I could gain Christ and become one with him..." (Phil. 3:8–9, NLT).

As mentioned earlier, wine symbolizes the Holy Spirit many places in Scripture, and pomegranates symbolize righteousness according to Jewish tradition. Although we never "arrive" at righteousness as a permanent state, we are clothed with the Lord's righteousness through faith in Him as we learn to depend on His indwelling Spirit. We are severed from our old life and grafted into the True Vine, Jesus. As F. J. Huegel wrote:

The branch which, contrary to nature, is grafted into a tree of another species must die to the old life. It must send its roots into a new trunk, and so it receives a new life.[1]

Combining these metaphors, *the bride declares that the spiced or costly wine she desires to serve to the Lord is a sacrificial life of dependence on the Holy Spirit. She no longer strives to be righteous according to external rules but fellowships with the Holy Spirit, depending on Him for His fruit, and is thereby clothed with the Lord's righteousness.*

> Lord, help me choose to walk in the fear of the Lord even if it means risking rejection. Help me live a sacrificial life of dependence on Your Spirit, and clothe me with Your righteousness. I want to give You my best, Lord, regardless of the cost. Truly, everything else is worthless when compared with the infinite value of knowing You!

8:3 "Let His left hand be under my head and His right hand embrace me" *[Bride speaking].*

The bride made this statement earlier in the Song; however, the context of her statement was very different. In chapter 2, verse 6, she was learning to enter the Sabbath rest of the believer and was enjoying the fruit of the revelation of His Word and the joy of the Spirit in the banquet house or "house of wine." She was enjoying what many have called the "honeymoon stage" in the life of a new believer, being hidden and protected from the assaults of the enemy while the Lord established intimacy in their relationship.

The context of her statement in this verse is altogether different than in Song 2:6. She has matured in her relationship with the Lord through seasons of pruning, painful separation, and rejection by church leaders in answer to her prayer for not only the warm south winds of refreshing in His presence, but also the cold north winds or trials that conform us to His image. The Lord has encouraged and validated her with words of love and affirmation, restoring her wounded soul (Ps. 23:3), so that a shift has occurred in the deepest part of her being. She now seeks to live for His approval rather than the approval of men (cf. John 12:42–43).

As mentioned earlier, the Hebrew word for "embrace" literally means to enfold or envelop. *The bride is asking for the tender embrace of the Lord—to be enveloped by His presence as she meets with Him in the secret place. She is expressing her desire to walk in intimate relationship with Him above everything else in her life. She has learned to put the first commandment first: to love Him with her whole heart, mind, soul, and strength. Out of this place of intimacy and abiding all of her activity now flows, and she is empowered to fulfill the second great commandment—to love others as herself.*

> Lord, let Your left hand be under my head and Your right hand embrace me. Envelop me in Your presence as I meet with You in the secret place. Help me keep the first commandment in first place in my life—loving You with my whole heart, mind, soul, and strength, so that I can fulfill the second great commandment—loving others as myself.

8:4 "I want you to swear, O daughters of Jerusalem, do not arouse or awaken My love until she pleases" *[Bridegroom speaking].*

This is the third time the Lord has charged the daughters of Jerusalem not to disturb the bride while she rests in His embrace. In the first instance (Song 2:7), the bride was learning to enjoy the Sabbath rest of a believer. The Lord was protecting her from distractions and the assaults of the enemy until He could establish a firm foundation in her relationship with Him. In the second instance (Song 3:5), she had just recovered the sense of His presence after a time of perceived separation. She was holding Him tightly, relieved to recover the intimacy with Him that she could no longer live without. In the verse before us, the bride has grown through a time of severe testing that revealed the true motives of her heart. Her response to the trial proved her devotion was to the Lord Himself, not to a church or even to her "ministry." Instead of being offended at the Lord for allowing the trial, she responded with the heart of David, who went into the temple to worship after his child by Bathsheba died (cf. 2 Sam. 11:1–12:23). Whereas before this point in her journey the Lord had to woo her to come with Him to serve in the vineyards, she now asks Him to be given the privilege of serving with Him. The Lord's charge to the daughters of Jerusalem in each case is the same: He tells them to swear that they will not disturb the bride while she is resting in His embrace.

Because the daughters of Jerusalem have not learned to encounter the Lord in the secret place, their focus is usually on activity. They are reminiscent of Martha, the sister of Mary, who was distracted by her preparations for the dinner she was serving. Luke records that Martha had gone to great effort to prepare a meal for Jesus and His disciples while her sister Mary sat at the Lord's feet listening to His words. Martha resented being left not only to prepare the meal, but to do all the serving as well, so she asked the Lord to tell Mary to help her. The Lord responded, "Martha, Martha, you are worried and bothered about so many things; but only *one thing is necessary*, for Mary has chosen the good part, which shall not be taken away from her" (Luke 10:41–42, emphasis added). (Selah! Pause and think about the implications of this encounter. Martha was doing a very noble thing—she was working hard to serve Jesus by preparing a nutritious meal for Him and His disciples. I am certain the Lord appreciated her hard work on His behalf. Yet He tells her, in essence, that He would rather she spend time with Him than serve Him. Our Lord defined an intimate relationship with Him as the *one necessary thing* in life, superseding even our service for Him!)

The bride has chosen the "one necessary thing," which we could paraphrase as "putting the first commandment first"—loving God with her whole heart, mind, soul, and strength. *When the first commandment is in first place in our life, the living waters of the Holy Spirit flow unhindered from our hearts. Far from hindering service to the Lord, keeping the first commandment first in our lives enriches our service to the Lord. As Jesus said, "It is the Spirit who gives life; the flesh profits nothing..." (John 6:63). Only that which is born of the Spirit in the secret place of the Lord's presence is able to impart the life of God to those we serve.*

> Lord, help me choose the "one necessary thing" in life—an intimate, present-tense relationship with You. Don't let me be ignorant of the enemy's schemes to distract me, even with seemingly "good" things. Help me put the first commandment first in my life, so Your rivers of living water will flow freely from my heart to those I serve.

8:5 "Who is this coming up from the wilderness leaning on her Beloved *[Daughters of Jerusalem speaking]*? Beneath the apple tree I awakened you; there your mother was in labor with you, there she was in labor and gave you birth" *[Bridegroom speaking]*.

This question posed by the daughters of Jerusalem has the sense of wonder and admiration. They know the bride well but have never seen her as she appears now. What do they see in her appearance that is so arresting? *The bride is now reflecting the Lord's glory as she comes up from the wilderness, leaning on her Beloved.*

The wilderness represents the seasons of trial and testing we must all walk through in our time as strangers and pilgrims on the earth. Paul reminded us that great benefit results from these trials: "For momentary, light affliction is producing for us an eternal weight of glory far beyond all comparison" (2 Cor. 4:17). This momentary, light affliction serves to drive us into deeper intimacy with the Lord with an amazing result: "And we all, who with unveiled faces contemplate the Lord's glory, are being transformed into his image with ever-increasing glory, which comes from the Lord, who is the Spirit" (2 Cor. 3:18, NIV). Note again the phrase, "who with *unveiled faces* contemplate the Lord's glory." As mentioned earlier, a veil is something that hides the reality lying beneath it. When we hide from God or others (i.e., "wear a mask" or put forth a false persona) we are walking in darkness, not light. Light exposes and lays bare. Only by becoming transparent with the Lord and others do we walk in the light as He is in the light. The wilderness "trials" that we walk through with the Lord serve a valuable purpose in our lives: they remove the veils from our faces. In other words, they cause deep pockets of unperceived pride, ambition, anger, etc., to rise to the surface of our hearts. These sinful attitudes serve as a veil over the eyes of our hearts (cf. Eph. 1:18, ASV) just as a bridal veil distorts the view of a bride until it is removed. When we repent of our sinful attitudes, the Holy Spirit removes these "veils" from our hearts, enabling our spiritual eyes to see the Lord more clearly. Then, as He teaches us to "behold the Lord" (i.e., to hold the Lord in view with our spiritual eyes; Ps. 16:8), we begin to reflect the Lord's glory in our lives.

Equally important is the fact that the bride is now *leaning on her Beloved*. She has learned by experience the crucial lesson that apart from Him she can do nothing. As the Lord taught us, "Abide in Me, and I in you. As the branch cannot bear fruit of itself unless it abides in the vine, so neither can you unless you abide in Me. I am the vine, you are the branches; he who abides in Me and I in him, he bears much fruit, for apart from Me you can do nothing" (John 15:4–5). She is now leaning on her Beloved or, we could say, abiding in the Vine: drawing on His life to sustain her even as a natural branch draws the life-giving sap from the vine.

> "...Beneath the apple tree I awakened you; there your mother was in labor with you, there she was in labor and gave you birth" [Bridegroom speaking].

The bride spoke of the Bridegroom as resembling an apple tree in Song 2:3, "Like an apple tree among the trees of the forest, so is my Beloved among the young men. In His shade I took great delight and sat down, and His fruit was sweet to my taste." She acknowledged His shade, or spiritual covering, over her life and the spiritual nourishment He provided as she learned to hear His voice and rest in His presence.

In the verse before us, the Lord reminds the bride that *He awakened her heart "beneath the apple tree," freeing her from the snare of religion and establishing intimacy in their relationship.* Those who were spiritual parents to her during this pivotal time in her development are referred to as "your mother" and symbolize those who covered her in prayer and discipled her. The apostle Paul spoke of himself as a spiritual father to those in the church at Galatia, declaring, "My little children, for whom I labor in birth again until Christ is formed in you" (Gal. 4:19, NKJV). The example of Paul's life demonstrates that "giving birth" as a spiritual parent is a continuous process of laboring in prayer until Christ is formed in the character of those we disciple.

> Lord, help me remove the veils that distort my ability to see You as You truly are. I want to behold Your glory so that I can be transformed into Your image. Give me an "eternal perspective" so that I will view the wilderness seasons and trials of my life as momentary light afflictions that are producing in me a glory that far outweighs the pain of my trials and will last forever. Help me emerge from my wilderness seasons leaning more and more on You until I put no confidence in my flesh. And teach me to labor in prayer with You until Your character is formed in the lives of those You give me to disciple.

8:6 "Put Me like a seal over your heart, like a seal on your arm. For love is as strong as death, jealousy is as severe as Sheol; its flashes are flashes of fire, the very flame of the LORD" *[Bridegroom speaking].*

The New International Version translates this verse: "Place me like a seal over your heart, like a seal on your arm; for love is as strong as death, its jealousy unyielding as the grave. It burns like blazing fire, like a mighty flame."

In the ancient world a seal was an implement for imprinting an impression on clay or wax. Seals were used to affix the ancient equivalent of written signatures to documents or to secure commodities such as wine or olive oil from tampering. God is often portrayed in the Scripture as "sealing" those who are His own. Paul wrote to the church at Ephesus, "Do not grieve the Holy Spirit of God, by whom you were sealed for the day of redemption," and to the church at Corinth, "Now He who establishes us with you in Christ and anointed us is God, who also sealed us and gave us the Spirit in our hearts as a pledge" (Eph. 4:30; 2 Cor. 1:21–22). The Greek word for "seal" in these verses means to stamp (with a signet or private mark) for security or preservation. The Greek word for "pledge," in reference to the Holy Spirit, means part of the purchase money or property given in advance as security for the rest. God "seals" us and marks us as His own by the Holy Spirit when we are born again and then gives us His Spirit in our hearts as a pledge, i.e., something given as assurance of what is to come.

However, in the verse before us Jesus is inviting the bride to set Him like a seal of fiery, all-consuming love over her heart. In this case, it is not God sealing our hearts but the Lord asking us to initiate the transaction and to set Him as a seal on our hearts. *The purpose of this fiery seal of love is the removal of anything that would hinder us from being whole-hearted (from loving Him with our whole heart, mind, soul, and strength).*

The Bridegroom asks His bride to set Him as a seal not only on her heart, but also on her arm. The arm symbolizes strength or power in Scripture (cf. Exod. 6:6; Deut. 4:34, 11:2, 26:8; 2 Kings 17:36, etc.). The Lord wants us to rely not on our natural strength or ability, but on His strength and ability as we serve yoked to Him. When we understand this by the revelation of the Spirit, His statement in Matthew 11:29–30 becomes clear: "Take My yoke upon you…for My yoke is easy and My burden is light." *When we are yoked to Him, we don't attempt to do things that He has not called us to do, and we are enabled to do the things He has called us to do because we have full access to His unlimited strength and power!*

"…For love is as strong as death, jealousy is as severe as Sheol…"

Again, the NIV translation renders this: "For love is as strong as death, its jealousy unyielding as the grave." Death is considered unyielding, or uncompromising, because it is the one constant in life that we cannot control—no one escapes death. The word translated jealousy can also be translated "ardent zeal" or "passion." Using this substitution, the Lord is saying, *"For My love for you is as strong and as certain as death; My passionate love for you, like death, is unyielding and invincible."*

As Mike Bickle says, *we set the Lord as a seal on our hearts by asking Him to reveal Himself to us as the God of all-consuming love.* In practical terms, this means learning to "fellowship" with His Spirit: coming to know Him as a Person; talking to Him; listening for His still small voice; paying attention to His promptings, His impressions, and His conviction; and acknowledging Him as Boss (being quick to obey Him). As we do this, the Holy Spirit purifies our hearts by the fire of His love, showing us hidden motives, sinful attitudes, and judgments that must be repented of so that He can blow them away with His breath. This is precisely the way gold was purified in ancient times: the gold was heated to a very high temperature, which caused the dross or impurities to rise to the surface. The smith then blew the dross from the molten surface with a bellows, leaving a surface that was unmarred which reflected the image of the smith. *God, the Holy Spirit, wants us to invite Him to be the Smith in our hearts, sealing them with His fiery love so that the impurities can rise to the surface and be blown away, leaving lives that more perfectly reflect the Lord's image.*

> "...For love is as strong as death...its flashes are flashes of fire,
> the very flame of the LORD."

First John 4:8 tells us, "...God is love." But Hebrews 12:29 also reminds us that "...our God is a consuming fire." A. W. Tozer explains that God's attributes are not isolated traits of His character but facets of His unitary being; therefore, no attribute of God is in conflict with another. His justice must be present in His mercy and His love present in His judgment.[2]

One of the facets of God's love is that it is jealous (passionate) and relentless, eventually consuming anything that tries to suppress or to supplant it. Revelation 19:12 tells us that our Lord's eyes are like flames of fire. If the eyes are the window to the soul and allow us to glimpse the very heart of a person, the Lord's eyes, which are described like flames of fire in this verse, reveal the fiery, passionate, purifying love in His heart that burns for His bride.

> Lord, I set You as a seal on my heart and ask You to reveal Yourself to me as the God of all-consuming love. I ask Your Spirit to purify my heart with the fire of Your love, revealing my hidden motives, sinful attitudes, and judgments so that I can repent of them, allowing You to blow the dross away with Your breath. I also set You as a seal upon my arm and ask You to help me do only what You give me to do, relying on Your strength and ability to do it as I remain yoked to You.

8:7 "**Many waters cannot quench love, nor will rivers overflow it; if a man were to give all the riches of his house for love, it would be utterly despised**" *[Bridegroom speaking].*

Under normal circumstances, water will extinguish fire. But the fire of our Bridegroom's love is so strong that *nothing* can extinguish it. His love is the most powerful thing in the universe. *The fire of His love led Him to the cross, where He willingly laid down His life for our sakes.*

The author of Hebrews tells us that *for the joy set before Him* Jesus endured the cross, despising its shame (Heb. 12:2). I once asked the Lord what "the joy set before Him" referred to in this verse. His reply was brief: "You!" He went on to say that the joy set before Him referred to all of those who would choose to accept His sacrifice, but that He would have endured the cross even if I were the only one who benefited from it. *Jesus would have gone to the cross even if each one of us, individually and personally, were the only one who benefited from His sacrifice!*

> "...if a man were to give all the riches of his house for love, it
> would be utterly despised."

In order to illustrate this verse, Mike Bickle tells a story of a very wealthy couple whose son becomes ill. The couple must sell all that they have in order to pay their son's medical bills. When someone praises them for the sacrifice they made for their son, they are stunned. The loving parents reply that they gladly gave up all of their material possessions in order to save the life of their beloved son. They gave all the riches of their house for love and it was utterly despised, because their love for their son saw no cost as too great. This is, of course, a picture of our Lord's love for us demonstrated at the Cross. *He gave everything for us, enduring the torture of the Cross and despising its shame, because His love for each one of us saw no cost as too great.*

> Lord, thank You that Your love for me is the most powerful thing in the universe and nothing can extinguish it! Open my heart to believe that I was the joy set before You when You endured the torture of the cross, and that You would have endured its torment even if I were the only one who benefited from Your sacrifice. Please give me that same love for You in return, Lord. I ask You to fulfill John 17:26 in my life—cause me to love You with the same love that the Father has for You.

8:8 "We have a little sister, and she has no breasts; what shall we do for our sister on the day when she is spoken for?" *[Bride speaking].*

The bride's conscious union with the Bridegroom is revealed in her statement: "*We* have a little sister," instead of "*I* have a little sister." She is running with Him in partnership now even as she originally prayed in Song 1:4, "Draw me after you and let us run together..."

The little sister is said to have no breasts, symbolizing she is now part of Christ's family but is still young and immature. Breasts speak of the ability to nurture others. The little sister is still in the process of establishing a firm foundation for her faith. She is not yet ready to nurture those younger in the faith or to be a "caretaker of the vineyards" (Song 1:6). She is taking care of her own vineyard, establishing her relationship with the Lord as first priority. She has been well taught by the bride and will not make the mistake of putting the cart before the horse. She knows that the only foundation for her faith that will stand the storms of life is to build upon the Rock (Matt. 7:24–27; Ps. 144:1), establishing an intimate relationship with the Lord and learning to hear the still small voice of the Holy Spirit. She must come to know Him as Teacher (John 14:26; 1 John 2:27), Counselor (Isa. 9:6), Helper (John 14:16, 26, 15:26, 16:7), and Boss (John 14:23).

> "... what shall we do for our sister on the day when she is spoken for?"

"The day she is spoken for" in Middle Eastern culture refers to the day a young girl's father agrees to give her hand in marriage to a suitor. From this day forward, she is officially betrothed (or engaged) to the young man. *In the verse before us, the day the sister is spoken for symbolizes the day she is born again or, we could say, the day she is "betrothed" to the Lord Jesus.*

It is important to note that a betrothal (or engagement) in biblical times is not what we think of as an engagement in our Western culture. According to rabbinical law, a betrothal was equivalent to an actual marriage and could only be dissolved by a formal divorce. This is why Matthew records that Joseph, who was engaged to Mary, wanted to "divorce" her quietly when he found out that she was pregnant (Matt. 1:19, NIV).

A betrothal according to Jewish tradition prescribed that the bridegroom would travel from his father's house to the home of his prospective bride; he would then negotiate with her father to determine the price (*mohar*) that he would pay to purchase his bride. Once the purchase price was paid, the marriage covenant was established, and the young man and woman were regarded as husband and wife. From that moment on, the bride was declared to be consecrated (or set apart) exclusively for her bridegroom. They would then drink from a cup of wine over which a betrothal benediction had been pronounced. After the marriage covenant had been established, the groom would return to his father's house. He would remain separate from his bride for a period of twelve months while he prepared living accommodations for them in his father's house. At the end of the period of separation, the groom would go to gather his bride. They would then return to the groom's father's house where the wedding guests had already assembled. The wedding party would then lead the bride and groom to the bridal chamber (*huppa*) where they would consummate the marriage that had been covenanted earlier. The day the bride and groom were betrothed they entered into a marriage covenant but the consummation of the marriage took place twelve months after the betrothal. In the same way, we are betrothed to the Lord Jesus the day we are born again, but the consummation of our marriage covenant with Him will occur when we are united with Him forever at the marriage supper of the Lamb (cf. Rev. 19:7–9). (Selah! Pause and think about how each stage in the Jewish betrothal/marriage mentioned above symbolizes a New Testament reality that is fulfilled in Jesus! Our God is a Poet who loves to use symbolism to reveal truth to His children.)

The bride is now abiding in the Lord. She no longer makes her own plans and then asks the Lord to bless them; she asks for His direction and guidance regarding how they can best serve this young believer to bring her forth to maturity.

> Lord, teach me to run with You in partnership, yoked with You, seeking Your guidance and direction—instead of making my own plans and then asking You to bless them. Show me how to work with You to bring to maturity those You have given me to disciple. And help me establish them on the only true foundation for their faith—an intimate relationship with You.

8:9 "If she is a wall, we will build on her a battlement of silver; but if she is a door, we will barricade her with planks of cedar" *[Bridegroom speaking].*

Here the Bridegroom answers the bride's question to Him regarding how they can help this young believer mature. What is done for her, however, will depend on where she is in relation to Him. If she is a wall, built upon the rock (the firm foundation of an intimate relationship with Him), strong and stable, they will build on that foundation a "battlement of silver." A battlement was a rampart built around the top edge of a castle with regular gaps for firing arrows or guns. Silver speaks of redemption (1 Pet. 1:18–19); the word *redeem* means to buy back or recover. Combining these two word pictures, *a battlement of silver refers to intercession, or spiritual warfare, to recover what the enemy has stolen.* If this young believer has a firm foundation for her faith, the Lord and His bride will teach her about intercession to recover what the enemy has stolen both in her own life and in the lives of others.

"…but if she is a door, we shall barricade her with planks of cedar."

James aptly described the type of believer mentioned in this verse:

> If any of you lacks wisdom, you should ask God, who gives generously to all without finding fault, and it will be given to you. But when you ask, you must believe and not doubt, because the one who doubts is like a wave of the sea, blown and tossed by the wind. That person should not expect to receive anything from the Lord. Such a person is double-minded and unstable in all they do.
>
> —JAMES 1:5–8, NIV

The young believer referred to in this verse as a door is not able to walk in victory when she encounters trials, because she does not yet have a firm foundation in her relationship with the Lord—she is double-minded and unstable. Jesus also described this immature believer in the parable of the sower. He explained that the seed which fell upon the rocky places represents the one who hears the gospel, but because he has no firm root for his faith, when affliction or persecution come because of the Word, "he sees in it that of which he disapproves and which hinders him from acknowledging its authority" (cf. Matt. 13:3–9, 18–23; quotation from Matt. 13:21, WUEST).

The Bridegroom advises that an immature believer should be "barricaded with planks of cedar." A barricade is a barrier to impede the advance of an enemy. As mentioned earlier, "cedar" is the Hebrew word *erez*, which is from an old Arabic root meaning firmly rooted strong tree. Combining these metaphors, *the Lord is saying that if the young believer is a door, unstable and easily moved to and fro, she will need to be surrounded with barriers (or intercession) to impede the advance of the enemy in her life until she can become firmly rooted in her faith. Planks of cedar in this verse speak of teaching and discipleship that will enable the little sister to establish strong roots, i.e., the firm foundation of an intimate relationship with the Lord.*

> Lord, help me seek Your heart and Your wisdom as I disciple those You've entrusted to me. Show me how to work with You to bring them forth to maturity. Give me the heart of a spiritual parent who will labor with You in intercession until Your character is formed in them.

8:10 "I was a wall, and my breasts were like towers; then I became in His eyes as one who finds peace" *[Bride speaking].*

As the bride has progressed in her relationship with the Lord, He has instilled in her a confidence and security in the knowledge of *who she is in Him.* She has discovered the purpose (or "good works") that God planned for her to walk in (Eph. 2:10) and has grown in her ability to invest the gifts that He has given her. *As a result of this confidence, she exclaims in poetic language, "I was a wall, built on the firm foundation of relationship with Him; I became a spiritual mother to young believers, both nurturing them and protecting them through intercession* (the reference to towers)." At first glance, this statement might seem arrogant but, in fact, the opposite is true. Her statement actually reflects true humility. As the Lord told Rick Joyner, *true humility is agreement with the truth.*[3] She is simply agreeing with the truth of how the Bridegroom sees her. When we are able to see ourselves as the Lord does, by the revelation of the Holy Spirit, we become a force to be reckoned with in the spiritual realm. Demons will flee from a righteous man or woman, confident in the knowledge of who they are in the Lord's eyes, who will boldly exercise their authority in Him (cf. John 14:30, Luke 10:19; see also Mark 13:34, NKJV).

"...then I became in His eyes as one who finds peace."

The King James Version renders this, "...then was I in His eyes as one that found favor." The Hebrew word translated peace (or favor) in this verse is *shalom*; this word occurs 237 times in the Bible. *The principal meaning of shalom is completion and fulfillment; it is the desirable state of wholeness in which relationships are restored.* King David wrote, "For it is You who blesses the righteous man, O LORD, You surround him with favor as a shield" (Ps. 5:12). *The bride has learned to clothe herself with the Lord's righteousness, and His favor now surrounds her as a shield.* As J. Hudson Taylor wrote, Naphtali's blessing is hers: she is "rich in favor and full of the LORD's blessings" (Deut. 33:23, NLT).

> Lord, make me a wall—built on the firm foundation of an intimate relationship with You—so that I can be a spiritual parent to young believers. Help me both nurture them and protect them through intercession on their behalf. Enable me to walk in true humility, which is simply agreement with the truth of how You see me. Give me confidence in the knowledge of who I am as Your child, so I can boldly exercise the authority You gave me, pushing back the kingdom of darkness. And surround me with Your favor so that my life will be evidence of Your goodness and will attract the lost to You.

8:11 "Solomon had a vineyard at Baal-hamon; He entrusted the vineyard to caretakers. Each one was to bring a thousand shekels of silver for its fruit" *[Bride speaking].*

As noted earlier, King Solomon is a type of Jesus. Isaiah 5:1–7 reveals that the Lord's vineyard is a metaphor for His people: "Let me sing now for my well-beloved a song of my beloved concerning His vineyard....For the vineyard of the LORD of hosts is the house of Israel..." (Isa. 5:1, 7). Baal-hamon was the site of one of King Solomon's vineyards, although its exact location is unknown. The name Baal-hamon is rich with symbolism: Baal was a common term for husband, owner, master, or lord. Hamon literally means multitude. Combining the two terms, the name means "lord of multitudes."

Our Bridegroom has a vineyard, the church (or corporate body of Christ), which He has entrusted to caretakers. The parable of the landowner in Matthew 21:33–43 is helpful in interpreting this verse. The caretakers in this account were literally tenant farmers who were expected to pay the landowner part of the proceeds (in this case, one thousand shekels of silver) as rent at the proper seasons. Mike Bickle notes, "The 'thousand' is a complete number which speaks of fullness or the full measure that God requires according to what was entrusted to each person."[4] The parable of the talents recorded in Matthew 25:14–30 teaches that we will receive eternal rewards based on our faithfulness with what God has entrusted to us according to our ability. *The point is not how much we produce but whether we are faithful with what we have been given according to our ability.* The slave that gained two more bags of silver (or talents) received the same commendation from the Lord as the slave that gained five more bags of silver. Only the slave that did not invest what he had been given, or produce more with it ("more" denoting fruit for the kingdom of God), was rebuked by the Lord (Matt. 25:24–30). *Each individual believer is expected to use what God has entrusted to them to produce fruit for His kingdom as a caretaker of His vineyard. The thousand shekels of silver are a metaphor for the full measure that God requires from each person according to what He entrusted them with.*

Our Bridegroom said, "You did not choose Me but I chose you, and appointed you *that you would go and bear fruit…*" (John 15:16, emphasis added). "Maintain a living communion with Me, and I with you. Just as the branch is unable to be bearing fruit from itself as a source unless it remains in a living union with the vine, so neither you, unless you maintain a living communion with Me. As for Myself, I am the vine. As for you, you are the branches. *He who maintains a living communion with me and I with him, this one is bearing much fruit, because apart from Me you are not able to be doing anything*" (John 15:4–5, WUEST, emphasis added).

> Lord, help me be a good steward of all that You have entrusted to me. I want to yield a crop for Your kingdom that is not only the full measure of what You require from me according to my ability, but one hundred times what was sown in my heart. Help me maintain a living

communion with You—fellowshipping with Your Spirit—as I care for
Your vineyard, knowing that apart from You I can do nothing.

8:12 "My very own vineyard is at my disposal; the thousand
shekels are for You, Solomon, and two hundred are for those
who take care of its fruit" *[Bride speaking].*

*The phrase "at my disposal" means "available to use as I wish." In
other words, the bride understands that she has the freedom to use the
gifts and abilities the Lord has entrusted to her as she chooses—for her
own gain or for the sake of His kingdom. Yet she is also aware that
she will be required to give an account of her stewardship to the Lord.
This stewardship is the fruit produced for His kingdom based solely
on what He has entrusted to her according to her ability. The bride is
confident that she has given the Lord the "thousand shekels of silver,"
or full measure of her stewardship, according to her God-given ability.*

"…and two hundred are for those who take care of its fruit."

*"Those who take care of its fruit" are those who labored with her in
team ministry to produce fruit for the kingdom of God in the vineyard
(or ministry) assigned to her. The bride acknowledges that they will have
a portion with her when she receives her eternal rewards, knowing she
was only able to fulfill her stewardship as she worked alongside them
ministering as a team. The two hundred shekels of silver symbolize the
portion of reward her coworkers will receive for their work with her in
the ministry, or vineyard, that God assigned to her.* Paul wrote to the
church at Philippi that while he appreciated their financial gifts to
him on many occasions, he desired even more than their gifts that
fruit would abound to their *eternal account* (Phil. 4:17, KJV).

The apostle Paul also had much to say on the topic of team
ministry:

But we have all been baptized into one body by one Spirit….If
the whole body were an eye, how would you hear? Or if your
whole body were an ear, how would you smell anything? But
our bodies have many parts, and God has put each part just

where He wants it.... All of you together are Christ's body, and each of you is a part of it. Here are some of the parts God has appointed for the church: first are apostles, second are prophets, third are teachers, then those who do miracles, those who have the gift of healing, those who can help others, those who have the gift of leadership, those who speak in unknown languages.

—1 Corinthians 12:13–28, nlt

Paul continued this topic in his letter to the Ephesians:

He makes the whole body fit together perfectly. As each part does its own special work, it helps the other parts grow, so that the whole body is healthy and growing and full of love.

—Ephesians 4:16, nlt

The implication is that when the whole body is *not* doing its own special work, or when parts of the body are being excluded, the body of Christ will not be healthy and growing and full of love. What's more, we will miss the "big picture" from God's perspective, which can only be understood in team ministry with each part of the body contributing its unique perspective.

Lord, enable me to give You the "thousand shekels of silver"—the full measure of my stewardship according to my God-given ability. Teach me about the importance of team ministry, and open my heart to understand that though we differ in the gifts that You have given us, we need each other to see the whole picture from Your perspective.

8:13 "O You who sit in the gardens, my companions are listening for Your voice—let me hear it!" *[Bride speaking].*

Some read this as the words of the Bridegroom to the bride, but I see it as the words of the bride spoken to her Bridegroom. *"O you who sit in the gardens" is the Lord Jesus who not only dwells in the garden (or heart) of the bride, but in the gardens (or hearts) of all of His people. "My companions are listening for Your voice" refers to the disciples that she has trained to abide in Him (or maintain a living communion with Him) who are listening for His voice.*

I believe the most magnificent benediction Paul penned to the churches under his care closes his second letter to the Corinthian church: "The grace of the Lord Jesus Christ, and the love of God, and the *fellowship of the Holy Spirit*, be with you all" (2 Cor. 13:14, emphasis added). As noted earlier, the Greek word for "fellowship" is *koinonea* and means communion or fellowship. Webster's New World Dictionary defines fellowship as companionship or mutual sharing; communion is defined as intimate relationship or intimate conversation. Substituting these definitions in Paul's benediction, it would read: "The grace of the Lord Jesus Christ, and the love of God, and *the companionship, mutual sharing, and intimate relationship with the Holy Spirit* be with you all." The apostle Paul continually experienced this kind of fellowship with the Holy Spirit and prayed that we would experience it as well!

The prophet Isaiah, who lived approximately seven hundred years before the birth of Christ, prophesied of this living communion with the Lord: "The LORD God has given me the tongue of disciples, that I may know how to sustain the weary one with a word. He awakens Me morning by morning, *He awakens My ear to listen as a disciple. The Lord God has opened my ear*; and I was not disobedient, nor did I turn back" (Isa. 50:4–5, emphasis added). Although Isaiah was speaking of the Messiah in the context of this verse, our Messiah temporarily laid aside his divine nature (Phil. 2:5–8) and lived His earthly life as a man dependent on the Holy Spirit in order to model God's original intent for our lives. Jesus did what He saw His Father doing and spoke what the Father gave Him to speak through His dependence on (or fellowship with) the Holy Spirit.

The bride has faithfully fulfilled her stewardship in the Lord's vineyard by training His followers to hear His voice and to maintain a living communion with Him, yet her heart's cry is that she would continually hear His voice as well. She prayed at the beginning of her journey, "May he kiss me with the kisses of his mouth!" (Song 1:2). She asked for an intimate relationship with the Lord, and He graciously granted her request, orchestrating the many trials and experiences of her life to that end. Through this process the Lord "awakened her ear to listen as a disciple" and taught her to fellowship with His Spirit.

Jeanne Guyon described this intimacy in union with the Lord, or "kiss" that the bride requested at the beginning of her journey, as a deep and abiding union with Christ that continues in the midst of any circumstance, as opposed to feeling the sense of His presence for a few moments or hours. She wrote of this union with God as a spiritual marriage.[5] Paul affirmed this idea in his letter to the church at Ephesus, "'For this reason a man shall leave his father and mother and shall be joined to his wife, and the two shall become one flesh.' This mystery is great; but I am speaking with reference to Christ and the church" (Eph. 5:31–32). He wrote to the church at Corinth, "…the one who joins himself to the Lord is one spirit with Him" (1 Cor. 6:17). The bride is now experiencing this deep and abiding union with Christ, yet she understands that she must continually guard their relationship and listen daily for the Lord's voice. Even as the manna spoiled if it was not eaten on the day it was collected, our union with the Lord is a present tense relationship that can be lost through neglect (cf. Exod. 16:12–21).

> Lord, help me train those You entrust to me to hear Your voice and to maintain a living communion with You. But never let me lose sight of my own need to daily sit at Your feet, listening for Your words of life. I want to experience the spiritual marriage that Jeanne Guyon wrote of—that deep and abiding union with You that continues through any circumstance.

8:14 "Hurry, my Beloved, and be like a gazelle or a young stag on the mountains of spices" [Bride speaking].

In Song 2:8–9 the bride heard her Beloved coming in search of her, climbing on the mountains and leaping on the hills like a gazelle or young stag. He was fervently seeking her! *At the end of this most beautiful of songs, she is fervently seeking Him, crying out in intercession for His return.*

David prayed, "Let my prayer be set before You as incense..." (Ps. 141:2, NKJV). *As spices were used to make the incense burned in the tabernacle and the temple as part of the Israelites' worship, so the mountains of spices represent the prayers of the saints that ascend as a memorial before God:* "Another angel came and stood at the altar, holding a golden censer; and much incense was given to him, so that he might add it to the prayers of all the saints on the golden altar which was before the throne. And the smoke of the incense, with the prayers of the saints, went up before God out of the angel's hand" (Rev. 8:3–4).

At the close of this age, the Lord's corporate bride will be "looking for the blessed hope and the appearing of the glory of our great God and Savior, Christ Jesus" (Titus 2:13). She will cry out in intercession with Paul, "Maranatha!" ("O Lord come!") (1 Cor. 16:22). Then our glorious Bridegroom will "...present to Himself the church in all her glory, having no spot or wrinkle or any such thing..." but a bride that is holy and blameless (Eph. 5:27). We will "...rejoice and be glad and give glory to Him, for the marriage of the Lamb has come and His bride has made herself ready" (Rev. 19:7).

This most beautiful of songs ends with a prayer for the return of the Bridegroom just as the canon of Scripture ends with a prayer for His return: "He who testifies to these things says, 'Yes, I am coming quickly.' Amen. Come, Lord Jesus!" (Rev. 22:20).

> Precious Lord, please engrave the truths of the Song on our hearts as we turn these verses into a prayer dialogue with You. Open our spiritual eyes to behold Your glory through our meditation on this beautiful Song, and transform us into Your image with ever-increasing glory by Your Spirit. We long for Your return, Lord. The Spirit and the bride say, "Come, Lord Jesus!"

NOTES

CHAPTER 1:
ESTABLISHING THE FOUNDATION OF INTIMACY

1. Jeanne Guyon, *Song of the Bride* (Auburn, ME: The Seedsowers Christian Books Publishing House, 1990), 1–2.
2. J. Hudson Taylor, *Union and Communion* (Minneapolis, MN: Bethany House Publishers, 2000), 22.
3. Mark and Patti Virkler, *Dialogue with God* (Alachua, FL: Bridge-Logos Publishers, 1986).
4. Alex Ness, *Pattern for Living* (Pefferlaw, Ontario: n.d.), 234.
5. Taylor, *Union*, 27.
6. Norman Grubb, *Rees Howells: Intercessor* (Fort Washington, PA: Christian Literature Crusade, 1952).
7. Taylor, *Union*, 29.

CHAPTER 2:
HIS BANNER OVER US IS LOVE

1. Taylor, *Union*, 32.
2. Watchman Nee, *The Song of Songs: The Divine Romance Between God and Man* (Anaheim, CA: Living Stream Ministry, 1993), 27.
3. Guyon, *Song*, 27–28.
4. Taylor, *Union*, 40–41.

CHAPTER 3:
SETTING OUR EYES ON THE ETERNAL THINGS

1. Rick Joyner, *The Harvest* (Pineville, NC: MorningStar Publications, Inc., 1989), 140.

CHAPTER 4:
THE LORD'S RAVISHED HEART FOR HIS BRIDE

1. A. W. Tozer, *The Knowledge of the Holy* (New York: HarperSanFrancisco, 1961), 20.
2. O. Palmer Robertson, *The Christ of the Covenants* (Phillipsburg, NJ: Presbyterian and Reformed Publishing Co., 1980), 28–29, 41.
3. Derek Prince, *Blessing or Curse* (Tarrytown, NY: Chosen Books, 1990), 40.
4. L. E. Maxwell, *Born Crucified* (Chicago, IL: Moody Press, 1945), 50.

5. Mike Bickle, "Song of Songs Study Notes, Session 12," www.fotb
.com.
6. Ibid.
7. Ibid.
8. Nee, *The Release of the Spirit* (Indianapolis, IN: Sure Foundation
Publishers, 1965), 10.
9. Ibid., 11.
10. Ibid., 12.
11. Ibid., 13.
12. Ibid., 14–15.

CHAPTER 5:
UNVEILING THE MAGNIFICENCE OF CHRIST JESUS

1. Nee, *Divine Romance*, 80–81.
2. Art Katz, *True Fellowship* (Laporte, MN: Burning Bush Press,
2003), 144.
3. Michael Molinos, *The Spiritual Guide* (Sargent, GA: Seedsowers
Christian Books Publishing House, 1982), 72.
4. Nee, *Divine Romance*, 82.
5. *Vine's Expository Dictionary of Old and New Testament Words*
(Iowa Falls, IA: Fleming H. Revell Company, 1981), 55–56.
6. Tozer, *Knowledge*, vii, 3–4.
7. Ibid., 80.
8. Ibid., 111–112.
9. Virkler, *Dialogue*.

CHAPTER 6:
HOW THE LORD VIEWS IMMATURE YET SINCERE BELIEVERS

1. D. Martyn Lloyd-Jones, *Studies in the Sermon on the Mount*
(Grand Rapids, MI: Wm. B. Eerdmans Publishing Company, 1997), 112.
2. William P. Young, *The Shack* (Newbury Park, CA: Windblown
Media, 2007), 193.
3. Tozer, *Knowledge*, 3, 79–80.
4. Watchman Nee, *The Normal Christian Life* (Ft. Washington, PA:
Christian Literature Crusade, 1963), 133–134.
5. Taylor, *Union*.
6. The Interlinear Bible, Hebrew/Greek/English, http://biblehub
.com/interlinear/songs/6-13.htm.

CHAPTER 7:
SEEING OTHERS THROUGH THE LORD'S EYES

1. Art Katz, *Apostolic Foundations* (Laporte, MN: Burning Bush Press, 1999), 117–118.
2. Nee, *Divine Romance*, 106.
3. Taylor, *Union*, 74.

CHAPTER 8:
THE PLACE OF ABIDING: LEANING ON OUR BELOVED

1. F. J. Huegel, *Bone of His Bone* (Sargent, GA: The Seedsowers, 1997), 21.
2. Tozer, *Knowledge*, 80.
3. Rick Joyner, *The Final Quest* (Charlotte, NC: MorningStar Publications, 1996).
4. Mike Bickle, "Studies in the Song of Solomon: Progression of Holy Passion, Session 24, 2007), 6.
5. Guyon, *Song*.

ABOUT THE AUTHOR

STACIE SHIVELY HOLDS an Associate in Theology degree from Grace Training Center in Kansas City, Missouri. She was first introduced to the Song of Solomon as an allegory portraying both the Lord's extravagant love for His bride and the believer's progression in developing an intimate relationship with Jesus through a class taught by Mike Bickle (at that time a pastor and president of Grace Training Center). Students were challenged to go deep in their study of the Song and turn it into a prayer dialogue with Jesus. The devotional commentary you hold in your hands is the result of that challenge. Stacie's passion is to see the hearts of believers unlocked to believe God's extravagant love for them. She lives in Powell, Ohio with her husband, Randy, and their two dogs.

CONTACT THE AUTHOR

E-mail: staciebernardshively@icloud.com